Praise for *Digital Vortex*

"To compete in the digital era, companies need to change their operating models every 18-24 months. For big companies, that pace of change can seem impossible, but their very survival depends on it. *Digital Vortex* offers the practical strategies and frameworks these companies need to increase agility so they can evolve their operating models continuously, and unlock entrepreneurship in their business."
– **Kevin Bandy**, Chief Digital Officer, Cisco

"Digital disruption is real, is happening now, and is fundamentally changing the way organizations will compete in decades to come. There has never been a time of greater promise, or greater peril. Those that don't transform now will quickly face mass extinction. The team at the Global Center for Digital Business Transformation are out in front of this mega-trend, and *Digital Vortex* is a must-read for those who are ready to lead the way."
– **Doug Connor**, Global Vice President for Digital Transformation, SAP

"*Digital Vortex* provides a comprehensive yet practical blueprint for any organization that aspires to build the foundational capabilities that will enable a resilient digital future."
– **Luis Hernández Echávez**, Executive Vice President, CEMEX

"'Digital' is more than technology; it's a way of life, and we all need to be prepared to participate. From value vampires to value vacancies, there's a new world of business strategy that needs to be mastered. *Digital Vortex* demystifies this next new frontier and provides ample guidance for the digitally unprepared."
– **Bill Fischer**, co-author, *The Idea Hunter: How to Find the Best Ideas and Make Them Happen*, co-creator, DeepDive™ innovation methodology

"By addressing the challenges to the incumbent from many perspectives – culturally, technologically, and strategically – *Digital Vortex* tackles all of the issues my company is dealing with in understanding the opportunities and threats inherent in the fast-changing environment fueled by new digital technologies. The case studies and 'self-reflection' questions are invaluable in enabling us to relate to those who have been successful in this transition and gives us an urgent incentive to change."
– **Jonathan Grover**, Senior Vice President,
Global Information Technology, Ferring Pharmaceuticals

"This book provides good guidance for all incumbents struggling with their role in a digital world. We're all looking at the new market players and trying to learn as much as possible, but introducing the 'Lean Startup' approach in a traditional company is just not an option. This book does not tell you what your strategy should be, but gives you a solid structure to build your own digital transformation."
– **Agnieszka Kühn**, Global Head of Digital Transformation, Daimler Financial Services

"If you're in senior management and still trying to crystallize how digital technologies are going to impact your business, read this book. It unravels the issues and helps you to set a clear path for the future."
– **Guy Laurence**, President and Chief Executive Officer, Rogers Communications

"There is a huge amount of hype around digital and digital transformation. *Digital Vortex* cuts through this hype to provide a clear roadmap for organizations to understand how to leverage digital opportunities and neutralize threats. It is a must-read for any executive facing digital disruption."
– **Steve Lee**, Chief Information Officer, Singapore Changi Airport

"A great and inspiring book presenting a holistic view on digital transformation and disruption."
– **Helga Maier**, Director of Digital Business, Swarovski

"I hear it all the time from our customers and partners: companies need to move faster. This book is so valuable because it shows how companies can put technology at the core of their strategy to move faster – in the right direction. *Digital Vortex* will help executives anticipate where their markets are headed, to make great decisions, and to execute with speed and purpose."
– **Thierry Maupilé**, Vice President of Strategic Partnerships, Cisco

"Practical and insightful, with a superb storyline and compelling logic, *Digital Vortex* goes to the heart of what established firms need to do to stay ahead as the digital economy eclipses the traditional. A must-read for managers in any industry."
– **Maury Peiperl**, author, *Managing Change* and Dean, Cranfield School of Management

"Name an industry, and odds are it's being disrupted by competitors deploying digital technology. *Digital Vortex* is a research-based look at this phenomenon, as well as a savvy guide to how your company can gain the nimbleness required in this new environment."
— **Daniel H. Pink**, author, *Drive* and *To Sell Is Human*

"As a shoe retailer with stores around all of Europe, we experience digital disruption every day through the changing behavior of our customers and potential customers. It is no longer a matter of if we should engage and focus more on integrating digital as part of our core business but rather how to do it. It is business-critical for all aspects of our value chain. Reading *Digital Vortex* has given us the inspiration and the tools on how to initiate this – and most importantly to prioritize digital transformation with the highest attention from top management."
— **Per Reimer**, Chief Executive Officer, KRM (ECCO shoes)

"In *Digital Vortex*, the author team from Cisco and IMD provides outstanding insight into how digital disruption threatens established companies. Critically, they offer the in-depth, actionable advice leaders need to deal with the inexorable wheel of technological innovation. A must-read for every executive concerned about company survival."
— **Michael Watkins**, author, *The First 90 Days: Proven Strategies for Getting Up to Speed Faster and Smarter*

"*Digital Vortex* takes an immensely broad and complicated topic – digital disruption – and masterfully distills it in a practical and applicable way. If you want to understand disruptive competitors, and what they mean for your company, read this book. Once you do, your business will never be the same – and that is just what's required to thrive in today's digital world."
— **J.B. Wood**, President and Chief Executive Officer, Technology Services Industry Association, and co-author, *B4B: How Technology and Big Data Are Reinventing the Customer-Supplier Relationship*

DIGITAL VORTEX

How Today's Market Leaders Can Beat
Disruptive Competitors at Their Own Game

Jeff Loucks, James Macaulay, Andy Noronha and Michael Wade

Digital Vortex:

How Today's Market Leaders Can Beat Disruptive Competitors at Their Own Game

Jeff Loucks, James Macaulay, Andy Noronha and Michael Wade

Copyright © 2016 IMD - International Institute for Management Development

Ch. de Bellerive 23, P.O. Box 915, CH-1001 Lausanne, Switzerland

ISBN-10: 1-945010-01-0

ISBN-13: 978-1-945010-01-9

To my sons, Dominic and Malcolm, who are growing up in
the Digital Vortex, with all its challenges and opportunities. – J.L.

To the memory of Jim Macaulay – a great business mind,
an even better father. – J.M.

To my children, Alessandra and Mateus.
Never stop daring, discovering, and disrupting! – A.N.

To Heidi, for your patience, support, and love …
and for putting up with yet another academic indulgence. – M.W.

Contents

Foreword

Over my 20 years as CEO of Cisco, one of the most important lessons I learned was that you must have the courage to disrupt yourself. This means anticipating and capturing market transitions ahead of peers, often requiring leaders to make bold moves and step outside of their comfort zone. I like to think of these transitions as opportunities, rather than challenges. I believe this mindset enables leaders to transform themselves, their businesses and, ultimately, the future of technology.

We are now in the midst of one of the biggest technology transitions ever – the Digital Age – where digitization will have five to 10 times the impact of the Internet to date. According to Cisco's analysis, there were 15 billion devices connected to the Internet in 2015, and by 2020 this will grow to more than 50 billion. This unprecedented level of connectivity will create trillions of dollars in opportunity, and leaders who embrace it now will be poised to harness the full value of digital transformation moving forward. If they don't, four out of 10 leading firms will be displaced in the next five years due to digital disruption.

At Cisco we anticipated this shift and, in partnership with the International Institute for Management Development (IMD), formed the Global Center for Digital Business Transformation (the "DBT Center" for short), a five-year commitment. Through this innovative joint initiative, we created a first-of-its-kind global research hub where corporate and academic leaders can come together at the forefront of digitization to explore and address the biggest issues facing customers, business and society in today's hyper-connected world.

We chose IMD, the pre-eminent leader in executive education, as our partner because they shared our belief that a new model and a sustained effort were required to help our customers collectively understand and succeed in the Digital Age. Over the first year of our partnership, Cisco employees worked alongside faculty and researchers from IMD to investigate digital disruption, engage with companies to define what disruption means for them, and identify ways to overcome challenges created by this environment.

As a result, I am proud to introduce you to *Digital Vortex: How Today's Market Leaders Can Beat Disruptive Competitors at Their Own Game*, which illustrates today's competitive landscape – what the authors call the "Digital Vortex" – as a series of digital-driven market transitions that together are driving exponential change in business.

Digital Vortex documents how disruptors construct their business to create market change, and delivers what organizations need most—cutting-edge research, prescriptive insights, and the "next practices" that mature organizations and institutions can use to go on offense and become disruptors themselves. This is something at the top of every CEO and statesman's agenda. The dynamics of the "Digital Vortex" will require organizations and governments to acquire a new level of agility that will allow them to not only change what they do, but to adapt often. This book sets out a practical roadmap for how to do this – how to disrupt, rather than be disrupted.

No matter the industry, location, or market share, leaders are facing a tipping point which I invite everyone to embrace. This book and the research and tools contained in it present an opportunity for leaders to take advantage of this critical moment in the history of technology, in which all businesses are impacted and can learn how to pull ahead and lead.

John T. Chambers
Executive Chairman
Cisco Systems, Inc.

Introduction

The four authors of this book – Jeff Loucks, James Macaulay, Andy Noronha, and Michael Wade – came to the subject of digital transformation from very different starting points. Three of us were part of an internal research group at Cisco, the Silicon Valley-based global networking leader. The fourth was a professor at IMD, a Swiss-based business school focused largely on executive education. Between 2012 and 2014, we all noticed a large upswing in interest in digital topics from our key stakeholders. At Cisco, this interest led to a study on the convergence of technology mega-trends, the potential value of which was assessed at $19 trillion over 10 years.[1] Digital technologies were growing and advancing quickly, and Cisco was at the epicenter of this.

A majority of IMD's 9,000 annual visiting executives were interested in digital, but were mostly happy to take a "wait and see" attitude. Some even expressed a healthy skepticism. Digital itself was poorly defined, and they found it hard to relate to highly touted examples of internet giants such as Google, Amazon, and Facebook, which seemed more relevant for products that could be turned into ones and zeroes than to industries that mined, made, or moved things. The applicability of digital to their own mostly legacy businesses, and the timeline for incorporating digital business models, were unclear. Many of them also felt a sense of *déjà vu*. They had lived through the bursting of the internet bubble in 2000, and had seen multiple subsequent waves of technology-fueled hyperbole.

As time went on, another word was added to the digital lexicon: disruption. Airbnb and Uber get a lot of press (perhaps too much), but their emergence was a watershed event because digital business models were now threatening industries that had been decidedly physical – this wasn't the newspaper business. Neither hotel firms nor taxi companies had appeared ripe for this type of disruption, nor were they ready for it. These industries were utterly blindsided. Suddenly, startups targeting other more hidebound sectors began attracting media attention and venture funding. Market change was accelerating across the board.

By the time 2015 rolled around, executives were asking both IMD and Cisco whether startups could use digital technologies and business models to disrupt *their* industry or company. Curiosity turned to urgency, and the nature of the questions changed: "How are these disruptors attacking established businesses so successfully and quickly?" "Could they attack my business, too?" "How can I use these digital business models to compete more effectively?" Digital was no longer something of abstract, academic interest. It had become personal.

In response, Cisco and IMD jointly established The Global Center for Digital Business Transformation (DBT Center) in mid-2015. This Center brought together two complementary perspectives on digital transformation: IMD, which came to it from the business and management side, and Cisco, which came to it from the technology side. Together, these two perspectives created a unique and powerful research lens through which to examine digital disruption. The DBT Center brought the four of us authors together as research collaborators.

Initially, we didn't have very good answers to the questions these executives were asking us. After conducting a search of the academic and consulting literatures, we realized that no one else had these answers either. There was no shortage of books and white papers purporting to show how companies could use digital to transform themselves, but most of the recommendations were very technical, fell squarely in the realm of traditional change management, or amounted to marketing collateral. While it may be important for companies to "drive transformation from the top down" and to "change the culture," these generic prescriptions were of limited practical value for organizations staring digital disruption in the face. They cast little light on the nature of the threat digital disruptors pose to established companies, or on the strategies companies must follow to combat these threats.

Through workshops, learning events, training programs, and research projects, we and our team have tried hard to stay very close to practice. We have eschewed the ivory tower, and built up a knowledge base from hundreds of conversations with digital and non-digital executives across industries and geographies. To be clear, this is not a book about Cisco, but capitalizes on the company's unique position as a leading enabler of digital change with enterprises all over the world to ground and grow our learnings.

The insights we present in this book are the output of DBT Center research and events, including:

- A quantitative survey of 941 senior business leaders from established companies located around the world
- Dozens of in-depth interviews with founders and senior executives from startups and disruptive firms
- Analysis of the business models of more than 100 digital disruptors to understand how they work, and the value they create for end customers

4

- Workshops and events with hundreds of senior executives from market incumbents discussing their challenges around digital disruption and their opportunities to use digital to transform their own businesses

From this research, we have distilled lessons about how disruption occurs, the strategies required to deal with it, and the capabilities that organizations must develop to bring these strategies to fruition. While it is fun to study entrepreneurial startups, we wrote this book with established companies in mind – those who want to know how to thrive amid digital disruption. We are well aware that many – if not most – of the startups we profile in this book may not succeed in the long run. Such is the fate of the startup. We have included them not because we believe they themselves will necessarily topple today's market leaders or because they are deserving of any special reverence. In fact, we are not exalting startups at all. Rather, the most significant disruptions these startups (and a few keen incumbents) have introduced can be dissected, studied, and applied to large, traditional companies. At various spots in this book, we make the point that it is the disruption that matters, not the disruptor. Thus it is the digital disruptions these firms *represent* that are likely to be longer-lasting, and the true source of competitive change, serving as both threats and opportunities for incumbents.

Definitions

"Digital" has the dubious distinction of being one of the most commonly used business terms today, and also one of the least well defined. Through our research, we have crystallized several digital concepts that will guide us throughout the book.

> **Digital:** We define digital as the convergence of multiple technology innovations enabled by connectivity. Naturally, these innovations evolve over time, but the most relevant technology innovations today include big data and analytics; cloud computing and other platform technologies; mobility solutions and location-based services; social media and other collaborative applications; connected devices and the Internet of Things (IoT); artificial intelligence and machine learning; and virtual reality. For us, digital must have a foundation in one or more of these technologies, and the key is connectivity.

Digital Disruption: We define digital disruption as the effect of digital technologies and business models on a company's current value proposition and resulting market position. Although digital disruption need not be negative, it's often cast in this light. As we will see throughout this book, however, digital disruption can illuminate opportunities as well as threats.*

Digital Business Transformation: We define digital business transformation as organizational change through the use of digital technologies and business models to improve performance. First, the objective of digital business transformation is to improve business performance. Second, digital business transformation is based on a digital foundation. Organizations are continually transforming, but to qualify as a digital business transformation, one or more digital technologies must exert a significant influence. Third, digital business transformation requires organizational change – change that includes processes, people, and strategy. In sum, digital business transformation involves much more than technology.

This is not a book that is, strictly speaking, about "transformation" – at least not in the classic sense of the word. It serves as the capstone of the first year of the DBT Center partnership between IMD and Cisco, and presents the primary lessons we have gleaned to date. Over the course of the next four years of the partnership, we will delve deeply into many transformation-oriented subjects and the organizational change roadmap for companies. Instead, this book should be viewed as a manual for incumbents to harness digital disruption and compete effectively with startups and non-traditional rivals.

The Structure of This Book

In this book, we explain how digital disruption works, how innovators create digital disruption, and the strategies that are required for

---

* It should be noted we are not interested in distinguishing between types of innovation (e.g., the constructs of "sustaining" vs. "disruptive" innovation put forth by Clayton Christensen). For us, disruption is the effect on competition. Anything that causes significant and rapid change in the competitive landscape is therefore "disruptive." Quite simply, if digital technologies and business models are used to create this effect, then digital disruption is occurring. We then seek to understand those business models and the capabilities of firms that create digital disruption, and extract learnings from them that can be applied to the context of a market incumbent.

incumbents to navigate in this environment. We focus on transformation (i.e., "organizational change") in the guise of increasing the overall agility of the company, surfacing the people, process, and technology enablers that separate digital disruptors from incumbents.

This book has been divided into two sections. Section 1 makes sense of digital disruption through an image – which we call the "Digital Vortex" – and explains its effects on competition across industries. Here, we explore the mechanics of disruption by identifying the types of customer value and the business models that underpin it. We also propose strategies and approaches that executives can take to respond to this disruption. Throughout, leaders from large market incumbents will learn how to beat disruptors at their own game.

In Chapter 1, we reveal the serious and imminent threat digital disruption poses to all industries, based on an extensive body of original research and analysis, and we explain the workings of the Digital Vortex, which provides the conceptual framework for the book. Digital disruption is real, and we believe its effects on those who fail to act appropriately will be severe and swift. Companies can use the analogy of a vortex to understand the nature of disruption and the rules that govern it. This analogy helps you make sense of disruption – and how and why you will be affected.

Chapter 2 explores the specific business models digital disruptors use to deliver value for customers, and why established companies have trouble competing when disruptors enter their markets. We describe how digital disruptors create three types of value – cost value, experience value, and platform value – delivered through 15 distinct business models. The most successful disruptors use what we call "combinatorial disruption" to blend these business models to create offerings that are often less expensive and better than what market incumbents can provide. These business models provide the building blocks for incumbents' own forays into creating disruption.

In Chapter 3, we show how the nature of competition has fundamentally changed in the Digital Vortex – as have the players. We introduce the term "value vampire," which is a nightmarish form of disruptor for established companies. The signature effect of value vampires is their permanent reduction of the size of the markets they attack. These attacks leave incumbents scrambling to replace revenue shortfalls and profit margins – if they survive at all. We also explore the positive side of digital disruption – the ability for established companies to use digital business models themselves to capture new opportunities. We call these "value vacancies" because in the Digital Vortex, competitive advantages are far from permanent.

In Chapter 4, we see that as value vampires and other disruptors attack core businesses, companies must turn their greatest weaknesses into strengths. They must understand the critical difference between disrupting a market and occupying – or winning – it. We introduce four generic response strategies. Two (Harvest and Retreat) are defensive, and two (Disrupt and Occupy) are offensive. These strategies will help you understand what it takes to compete in the disruptive environment of the Digital Vortex.

In Section 2, we examine how you can respond to disruption by building a foundation of agility. Agility, we believe, is the single most important weapon in the arsenal of organizations competing in an increasingly digital world. Sustained success in the Digital Vortex is impossible without robust agility.

While each company and industry may need to develop agility in specific ways, the core concepts and capabilities remain the same. When you possess strong agility, you can adjust quickly to changing market conditions and anticipate these changes to your advantage. You will be able to sense how a disruptor can attack your core market, and how you can proactively deliver a more compelling value proposition to your customers. You will learn to detect the appearance of a tough digital disruptor or an opportunity in an adjacent market. Survival in the Digital Vortex requires transformation, and transformation requires agility.

In Chapter 5, we introduce "digital business agility," the capability companies must develop in order to use digital business models to create new forms of value. Digital business agility consists of three distinct components that reinforce one another: hyperawareness, informed decision-making, and fast execution. We define these concepts and show why you must have a combination of all three to compete effectively in the Digital Vortex.

In Chapters 6-8, we elaborate on each of the three components of digital business agility, and we provide examples of how companies – both established firms and startups – are developing them. We highlight the "next practices" and new technologies to consider as you build your own hyperawareness, informed decision-making, and fast execution capabilities. Together, the components of digital business agility allow you to become aware of threats and opportunities, to make good decisions consistently, and to execute at the speed required to thrive amid digital disruption. We can consider the operational changes required to develop digital business agility as a type of internal "digital disruption" in the service of achieving superior capabilities.

The conclusion of the book focuses on applying the research findings and ideas to your organization. It features exercises that you can use to determine how vulnerable you are to digital disruption, and the steps you can take to fight back and go on the offensive. This book is about understanding how disruptors operate, and learning how to compete in what can be a frightening and volatile new world. Ultimately, you will need to make your own determination about the exact forms that hyperawareness, informed decision-making, and fast execution must take within your organization. To conclude, we provide you with models to follow as you embark on your transformation journey, and our perspective on the big questions that will preoccupy leaders in the years ahead as they come to grips with the reality of competing in the Digital Vortex.

SECTION 1

Chapter 1: Disruption in the Digital Vortex

The difference between digital disruption and traditional competitive dynamics boils down to two main factors: the velocity of change and the stakes involved. Digital disruptors innovate rapidly, and they use their innovations to gain market share and scale far faster than competitors who cling to predominantly physical business models. They are especially dangerous because they grow enormous user bases seemingly overnight, and are agile enough to exploit business models that threaten incumbents, often in multiple markets.

A striking example of digital disruption can be found in the telecommunications industry. In 2009, WhatsApp started attacking the $100 billion global text messaging market[1] by offering a free alternative to pricey SMS messages. The company soon moved on to allowing users to make free mobile voice calls. The strengths of WhatsApp's platform of 800 million users attracted Facebook, which purchased the company for $22 billion in 2014.[2] Facebook, through WhatsApp and its other brands, isn't looking to disrupt only the telecommunications industry. After introducing peer-to-peer (P2P) payments via Facebook Messenger, the company is now poised to extend this service to WhatsApp's users. Facebook is also testing a business model that would help it challenge Google's domination of the mobile advertising market by charging businesses for the ability to contact its users directly. All this disruption comes from a single innovative platform with the seemingly simple function of letting consumers send "free" messages to each other via smartphones.

In a way, the potential success or failure of these ventures is beside the point.* Inevitably, some strategies bear fruit; others do not. However, there's no question that the stakes are incredibly high – not only for Facebook's potential revenue, but also for the many companies facing disruption. Between 2012 and 2018, WhatsApp and other over-the-top

---

* Tellingly, WhatsApp itself is now being disrupted by a new slate of companies with lofty ambitions and deep pockets. Apple's iMessage platform and WeChat, from Chinese internet giant Tencent, are already taking big shares of global messaging and voice traffic.

(OTT) services are projected to drain global telecommunications companies of $386 billion in revenue from mobile voice calling alone.[3] How many telecommunications service providers will be able to withstand such a decline in their core businesses?

Digital disruption is not an issue just for firms in high-technology sectors. As we will demonstrate in this book, digital disruption's impact is felt across many industries, including in what are generally thought of as more traditional markets. For example, the high-end fashion sector, which has been slow to embrace digital change in the past, has been disrupted by both digitally savvy incumbents, such as Burberry, and by new entrants including Net-A-Porter and Gilt (now part of Saks Fifth Avenue). We are also seeing disruption across many business-to-business (B2B) markets, including agri-business, commercial banking, energy, insurance, manufacturing, pharmaceuticals, professional services, real estate, supply chain and logistics, and more.

When facing the specter of disruption, companies must first understand the nature of the competitive change it represents – the technologies and business models that will be most disruptive – before determining how to respond. To gain a clearer picture of how digital disruption is affecting markets worldwide, the DBT Center surveyed 941 business leaders across 12 industries and 13 countries. The responses, presented throughout this book, reveal that digital disruption has thrown many industries into a state of flux and that the rate of change is accelerating.

Disruptive Dynamics

The number of digital disruptors that have amassed millions of users (and billions of dollars in value) has grown tremendously during the past three years. A case in point: In venture-capital-speak, a "unicorn" is a startup with a valuation of at least $1 billion. So named because, historically, they are very rare animals, unicorns are becoming fixtures of the competitive scene as venture funding seeks disruptive companies with the potential to become the next Alibaba (the Chinese e-commerce portal that raised $25 billion in capital in 2014, the largest IPO in history).[4] According to researchers CB Insights, by mid-2016 there were more than 150 unicorns,[5] 14 with valuations exceeding $10 billion. Two of these unicorns (Uber and Chinese smartphone maker Xiaomi) were alone worth nearly $100 billion.[6]

The results of our survey uncovered several troubling findings about the potential for disruption among incumbents, as well as their readiness to adapt. As Figure 1 illustrates, surveyed executives believed that roughly four

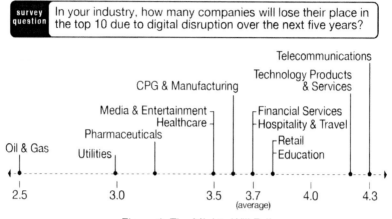

Figure 1: The Mighty Will Fall
Source: Global Center for Digital Business Transformation, 2015

of the top ten incumbents (in terms of market share) on average would be displaced by digital disruption in the following five years. The number of displaced incumbents ranges from a high of 4.3 out of 10 for the telecommunications industry to a low of 2.5 for the oil and gas industry. The threat extends beyond the "mere" displacement of big companies to encompass the very survival of entire industries. Executives in the industries we studied believed digital disruption has significantly increased the risk of being put out of business altogether (see Figure 2).

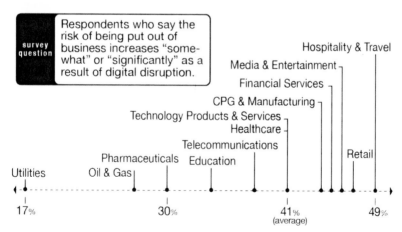

Figure 2: Existential Crisis
Source: Global Center for Digital Business Transformation, 2015

Despite the potentially dire consequences, 45 percent of the surveyed companies dismissed digital disruption as unworthy of board-level attention (see Figure 3). This level of indifference extended even to industries such as hospitality and travel and telecommunications, sectors rocked by disruption for more than a decade.

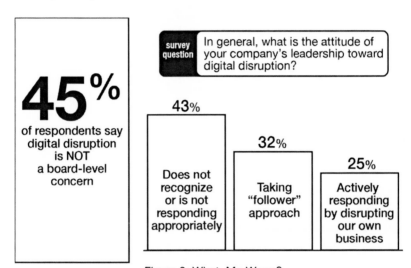

Figure 3: What, Me Worry?
Source: Global Center for Digital Business Transformation, 2015

This blithe inattention in the executive ranks was matched by inadequate strategies for coping with digital disruption. About 43 percent of companies either did not acknowledge the risk of digital disruption or had not addressed it sufficiently (again, see Figure 3). Nearly a third were taking a "wait and see" approach in the hope of emulating successful competitors. The velocity and high stakes of digital disruption, however, make it unlikely that 32 percent of companies will succeed in taking a "fast-follower" approach. Only 25 percent described their approach to digital disruption as proactive – i.e., an approach that demonstrated their willingness to disrupt *themselves* to compete.

A Digital Vortex

Given the speed, chaos, and complexity of digital disruption, it can be difficult to identify patterns or trends, much less an effective course of action. Even so, a fundamental understanding of how digital disruption works is vital if companies are to devise effective strategies to counter (or exploit) it.

The image of a vortex helps us conceptualize the way digital disruption impacts firms and industries. A vortex exerts a rotational force that draws everything nearby into its center. There are many examples of vortices in nature, including whirlpools and the wake of an aircraft. Although vortices are complex, they have three main features relevant to digital disruption:

1. A vortex pulls objects relentlessly toward its center, and as objects approach the center, their velocity increases exponentially.[*]
2. Vortices are highly chaotic. For example, an object on the periphery of a vortex one moment can be drawn directly into the center the next, while others take a much longer, circuitous route. In other words, objects don't follow uniform or predictable paths from the outside to the center.
3. Objects within a vortex frequently collide, or break apart and recombine, as they converge toward the center.

The Digital Vortex is the inevitable movement of industries toward a "digital center" in which business models, offerings, and value chains are digitized to the maximum extent. The force of the vortex separates physical and digital sources, yielding "components" that can be readily combined to create new disruptions and blur the lines between industries.

We began to conceive of digital disruption as a vortex while using survey data to determine which industries were at greatest risk of digital disruption within the next five years. We asked executives in each of the 12 industries we studied to estimate the likelihood of disruption based on four variables (see Appendix A, "Digital Vortex Methodology").[†]

Their responses were translated into a ranking that predicts the extent of digital disruption by industry. The industries poised for greatest

---

[*] This is true for a particular type of vortex, known as an "irrotational" vortex. Other forms of vortices possess different characteristics. For an overview of how vortices work, see Wikipedia contributors, "Vortex," *Wikipedia, The Free Encyclopedia*, accessed April 5, 2016, en.wikipedia.org/w/index.php?title=Vortex&oldid=706651597

[†] The DBT Center is not alone in pointing to profound and accelerating levels of disruption, particularly in those industries we consider closest to the middle of the Digital Vortex. Recent analysis from Citi found that digital disruption in the music sales, video rental, travel booking, and newspaper industries "resulted on average in a 44% share-shift from physical to digital business models over a 10-year period. Further, digital disruption accelerates over time – market share shifts gradually (~1.6%/year) until an inflection point around year 4 when traditional share declines rapidly accelerate to >6% per year." See "Digital Disruption: How Fintech Is Forcing Banking to a Tipping Point," *Citi Global Perspectives & Solutions*, March 2016, ir.citi.com/D%2F5GCKN6uoSvhbvCmUDS05SYsRaDvAykPjb5subGr7f1JMe8w2oX1bqpFm 6RdjSRSpGzSaXhyXY%3D

disruption are those in which the most digitization is occurring. Those on the periphery are less vulnerable to disruption, and may enjoy greater insularity. However, *all* industries – including those that have been more stable in recent years – will witness competitive upheaval as a result of digital disruption.

As seen in Figure 4, the industry that will experience the most digital disruption between now and 2020 is technology products and services. This sector is unique because it supplies the technological foundations of all disruptions, and its proximity to the center reflects the extent of ongoing digital disruption. By contrast, pharmaceuticals will experience the least digital disruption. However, even this industry is vulnerable to digital disruption. Technology-fueled innovations such as personalized medicine, gene sequencing, and cost arbitrage through digital marketplaces are putting pressure on pharmaceutical companies around the world.

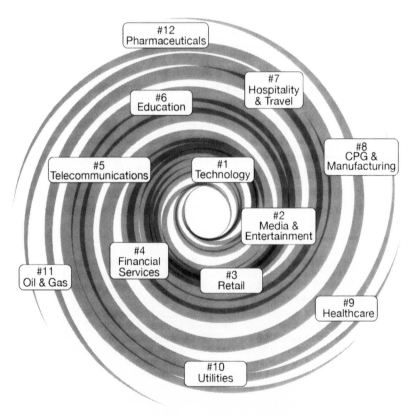

Figure 4: Digital Disruption by Industry
Source: Global Center for Digital Business Transformation, 2015

The center of the Digital Vortex symbolizes a "new normal" – one characterized by rapid and constant change as industries become increasingly digital. Note: An industry's position relative to the center of the Digital Vortex reflects the state of competition that firms in that industry will face, not the strength of their digital capabilities. Moreover, the center does not represent an end state in which markets stabilize around new competitive leadership for an extended period. Finally, proximity to the center doesn't imply that an industry (or company) is headed "down the drain."

Ripple Effects: The Autonomous Car

Let's consider an example of a digital innovation that can affect multiple industries at once. The automotive industry sits near the outer edge of the Digital Vortex, within the manufacturing sector. Compared, for example, with financial services and telecommunications that are situated close to the vortex's center, the automotive industry occupies a position of at least relative safety. However, consider the industry's prospects in light of the emergence of a key market disruption: autonomous cars. Recent forecasts project there will be 10 million self-driving vehicles by 2020,[7] with up to 15 percent of new cars sold being autonomous by 2030.[8] Indeed, semi-autonomous cars are already on the streets, driving themselves on highways and parking themselves. Google, Apple, and others are actively developing autonomous vehicles, and Tesla already offers many autonomous features in its range of electric cars. Let's assume then that autonomous cars enter the mainstream of automobile use.

Which industries will be disrupted in a world where the roads are increasingly populated by autonomous cars? There are some obvious answers. Clearly, the automobile manufacturing sector itself will be affected. Extensive ride-sharing will almost certainly accompany a rise in autonomous cars, which will mean that fewer vehicles need to be produced, and that fewer people will need (or want) to own a car. The automotive repair industry will also be affected because autonomous cars will experience fewer accidents. It is no secret that most car accidents can be attributed to human error. McKinsey estimates autonomous vehicles could result in a 90 percent decrease in automobile crashes.[9] Public transportation is also an obvious area of impact. Autonomous cars can travel point-to-point, thus providing an advantage over trains and buses that travel pre-defined fixed routes. Fewer taxis, or at least taxi drivers, will be required. In fact, all driving professions are likely to be negatively affected.

Other industries come to mind. Courier companies may face new competition from autonomous package delivery outfits, exemplified today by the drone-based delivery model of companies such as SF Express.[10] Hotels may be faced with more empty rooms as people sleep in autonomous cars on long journeys. Airlines may lose customers for the same reason. Insurance companies will have to rethink their underwriting of automotive policies, and they'll battle with lower demand and lower prices resulting from declining accident rates. The healthcare industry will have fewer injuries to deal with, and law enforcement will devote less time to writing tickets.

Other impacts are less obvious. For example, fewer cars constantly on the move will mean a reduced need for parking spaces. This will dampen the profitability of parking garages and affect government coffers. The additional space opened up by fewer parking spaces (one-third of space in many cities) could lead to urban renewal and spark a real estate boom (or a correction).[11] On the subject of space, autonomous cars can allow people to work as they drive, partially obviating the need to live close to work, and thus raising the attractiveness of rural living. With drivers freed from the responsibility of watching the road, autonomous cars could become media and entertainment hubs. Autonomous cars could deliver your food or shopping, thus affecting restaurants and retailers. The advent of autonomous cars is also widely seen as a boon for the prospects of combating climate change, because of reduced traffic congestion and decreased environmental footprints arising from a total decline in the number of vehicles produced.[12]

Upon consideration, it is easy to see how autonomous cars are bound to impact huge swaths of the economy. In fact, by our reckoning, all the industries in Figure 4 will be affected, some positively and some negatively.

The Encumbered Incumbent

Our survey asked when (if ever) executives expected digital disruption to affect their industry. The average time to disruption (meaning a "substantial change" in market share among incumbents) was approximately 36 months, which represents a clear escalation in the rate of competitive change compared with historical levels.

Incumbents now face the so-called "innovator's dilemma." As Clayton Christensen of Harvard Business School observed, "The reason it is so difficult for existing firms to capitalize on disruptive innovations is that their processes and their business model, [which] make them good at the existing business, actually make them bad at competing for the disruption."[13] Despite this, incumbents *do* have cards to play, even though many are constrained by a predilection for doing things the way they've always been done, as well as shareholder expectations, unwieldy cost structures, and other factors.

Most of the executives surveyed believed "insiders" would be the most likely disruptors, meaning both incumbents and startups from their own industries (see Figure 5). Executives from several industries with long histories of producing innovative startups – media and entertainment, telecommunications, and retail – believed startups would continue to drive disruption. None of this means, however, that companies from other industries don't constitute a threat. As we shall see, "outsiders" can use disruption to strike incumbents seemingly out of nowhere. Whether disruption comes from inside or outside an industry, the momentum toward the center of the Digital Vortex will continue.

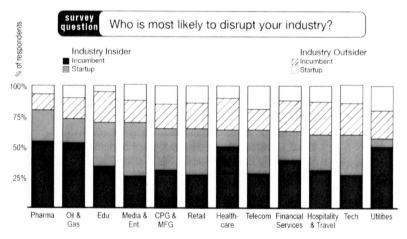

Figure 5: Inside Job vs. Break-in
Source: Global Center for Digital Business Transformation, 2015

Let's look at the role of startups in driving disruption in one of the most traditional industries: higher education. While most education leaders in our survey pointed to incumbents as the primary source of disruption, 41 percent of education leaders also feared the rise of "ed-tech" startups. So-called massive open online courses (MOOCs), such as Coursera and Udacity, are proving that online university-level education can thrive in a low-cost model by combining highly scalable expert knowledge with a community of learners. Pluralsight, the only education unicorn as of mid-2016, used a number of acquisitions to increase its capabilities while seeking to dominate the growing market for "hard" computer science and IT skills. [14] Given the stratospheric costs of higher education in many countries, the value provided by traditional institutions of higher learning is being questioned. Scores of universities, including some of the world's most prestigious, are now compelled to offer competing services at low or no cost.

According to the executives surveyed, startups have a clear set of advantages as they attempt to grow their businesses and unseat incumbents. Although leaders such as Elon Musk are rightly praised for their vision, executives in our survey believe that the real advantage of smaller digital players comes not from a grand plan, but from the following capabilities (see Figure 6):

- Fast innovation
- Agility
- A culture of experimentation and risk-taking

Clearly, the ability to develop new innovations, and to change quickly as conditions dictate, is a critical advantage – and generally a more important one than any specific innovation a startup may bring to market. (We will explore this concept of organizational agility in detail in Chapter 5).

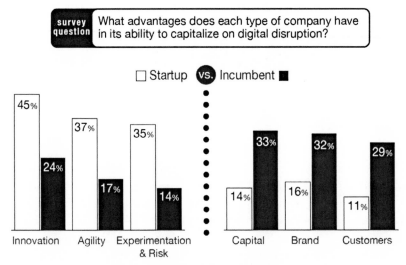

Figure 6: Fortune Favors the Bold
Source: Global Center for Digital Business Transformation, 2015

By contrast, the incumbent advantages cited by executives stem directly from their established market positions:

- Access to capital
- Strong brand
- Large customer base

To be sure, large companies can issue new shares, access corporate debt at historically low rates, and leverage their substantial cash flows in the face of competitive turmoil. Many incumbents have also spent decades promoting and burnishing their brands, many of which are worth billions (according to Interbrand, Apple's brand was valued at $170 billion in 2015).[15] And, by definition, incumbents have large customer bases.

However, many of these incumbent advantages hinge on scale, which is fast becoming a fleeting and commoditized asset. Consider Wells Fargo, the second-largest bank by deposits in the United States.[16] Wells Fargo first offered online banking services in 1995,[17] and now boasts about 25 million[18] active online banking users and 14.1 million[19] mobile banking users. Compared with Wells Fargo's painstaking customer acquisition efforts, MyFitnessPal, a mobile app used with wearable devices (such as Fitbit) for diet and exercise tracking, has amassed more than 80 million users.[20,*]

Meanwhile, Snapchat, a unicorn in the mobile image and video messaging space, is rumored to have more than 200 million active monthly users,[21] roughly the size of Brazil's entire population. In May 2015, Snapchat raised $537 million in capital, valuing the company in excess of $16 billion.[22]

These examples demonstrate that the first lines of defense that have insulated incumbents from previous upstarts can be surmounted with growing ease. This is because, to use terms from the organizational theorist Geoffrey Moore, the "late majority" has now "crossed the chasm"[23] and is exhibiting digital behaviors – e.g., a comfort level with smart mobile devices and apps – that were once the preserve of innovators and early adopters. As seen with WhatsApp, a large customer base is now a sufficient condition to create disruptive business models that can cross another kind of chasm: the divide that has historically separated one industry from another.

---

* Fitness apparel maker Under Armour acquired MyFitnessPal in 2015 as part of a digital strategy that may soon offer sensor-based clothing to track movement and biorhythms. "Under Armour Turns Ambitions to Electronic Apparel Monitoring Apps," *Wall Street Journal*, February 27, 2015, wsj.com/articles/under-armour-looks-to-get-you-wired-with-its-apparel-1425061081

It's the Value, Not the Value Chain

As noted, the trajectory of an object circling in a vortex is highly unpredictable. It can be close to the periphery one moment, and drawn directly into the center the next. Executives in industries now on the outer edges of the Digital Vortex, such as pharmaceuticals, may be tempted to take solace in the idea that their sector is relatively less prone to disruption. While this may be true today, they should also consider the cautionary tale of another industry. Five years ago, few firms seemed less vulnerable to digital disruption than taxi companies. Today their value is under siege. They have been rapidly and forcefully pulled into the digital center, now obliged to compete with digital competitors such as Uber and Lyft.

Let's also look at the utilities industry, recalling that our analysis ranked this sector at No. 10 out of 12 on the list of industries – making it, in our analysis, one of the least susceptible to disruption. Utilities require major capital investment to generate and distribute electricity. However, the ultimate value provided to their customers is power, and significant disruption has already occurred in the area of renewable energy. For example, Germany obtains 26 percent of its electricity from renewable resources (22 percent from solar power),[24] and Scotland gets more than half.[25] The fluctuations and logistical challenges inherent in producing energy from solar, however, in addition to the flexibility required to integrate power from user-generated solar panels, requires an enabling digital technology: a "smart" grid.

Tesla has emerged as a household name and a poster child for digital disruption. Until recently, the primary industry Tesla disrupted was the automotive sector. The company's ability to upgrade the capabilities of electric vehicles via software downloads makes its cars more valuable to their owners over time, presenting a disruptive challenge to mainstream automakers. In May 2015, however, Tesla unveiled inexpensive batteries for the home and business markets, batteries that could store energy generated by solar panels and pull power from the energy grid during cheaper off-peak hours.[26]

The technology that has made Tesla such a formidable threat to automakers – its batteries and software – is highly transferable to power generation and storage. Examples of such disruptions, in particular their applicability to multiple industries and business models, should strike fear in the hearts of incumbents. A single innovation or platform can be used to redefine markets that, on the surface, have little in common. For this reason, it can be difficult for executives to know who their most fearsome opponents will be, and from which industry they will emerge. Thus, executives who feel insulated from attack by outsiders may fall victim to their own lack of imagination.

We also see this dynamic in the way financial technology (FinTech) startups are disrupting banks by unbundling their products and services – seizing a share of their most profitable business, while avoiding the entry barriers associated with being a full-service bank. These startups use a combination of technologies and business models, including analytics and automation, to digitize their offerings, and they may disrupt more than one profitable business at a time while fulfilling unmet needs in the market.

Digitization of products, services, and business processes allows disruptive players to deliver the same value as a traditional competitor, and even augment it, without having to reproduce the conventional value chain. In fact, this is the fundamental objective of digital disruptors: to provide superior value to the end customer while avoiding the capital investments, regulatory requirements, and other such impediments of "encumbered incumbents." For disruptors, it's the new and improved value created for the end customer that matters, not the value chain that produces products or services. We will unpack and explore different forms of customer value in the following chapter.

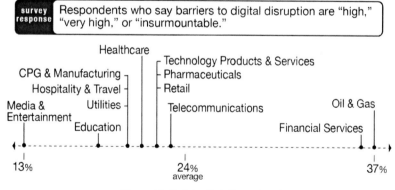

Figure 7: Safety Not Guranteed
Source: Global Center for Digital Business Transformation, 2015

The perceived sense of protection we detected among executives largely depends on the built-in defenses they ascribe to their industries. Of those surveyed, 25 percent believed there were "high" barriers to digital disruption in their industries, with oil and gas (37 percent) and financial services (36 percent) at the top of the list (see Figure 7). These barriers included capital costs, regulatory roadblocks, and the complexity of business processes. Most disruptive players, however, have little interest in competing on these terms.

Implications

Digital disruption is affecting most sectors of the economy and many facets of our lives. In this age of digital disruption, multiple technology transitions (cloud, mobile, social, big data) are converging. What happens when one exponential force collides with another? Is there a doubling of their effects? Or an order of magnitude increase? Do they change direction? Or do they become something completely new?

As they move toward the center of the Digital Vortex, industries frequently collide, decoupling sources of value, and then merging and creating new competitive forms. As the level of digitization increases, industries are unbundling and recombining, so much so that the very notion of "industries" may become meaningless. Competing on the basis of membership in a club of companies that identify as "banks" or "utilities" may seem quaint in the decades ahead. To which industry does Tesla, or Apple, belong?

The 44 percent of surveyed executives who dismissed the threat of digital disruption should ask themselves, "Why will we be spared such a change? When does confidence become complacency?" Exponential change looks remarkably like linear change until it reaches what futurist Ray Kurzweil calls the "knee of the curve" – by which time it is too late to prepare.[27]

Disruptive innovators are digitizing ever more granular pieces of the value chain in virtually all industries. As a result, value is atomizing, and many of the traditional profit pools on which incumbents depend have sprung leaks. Our research reveals executives believe a significant number – as much as 40 percent – of incumbents may be left wounded, perhaps mortally, by digital disruption in the next five years. Nevertheless, all is not lost for incumbents. As we will demonstrate in this book, those that can harness digital technologies and business models can prevail.

However, our survey also highlighted factors that question incumbents' readiness to battle their new digital rivals. What is sometimes called "premature abandonment of the core"[28] (i.e., when successful companies unwisely chase growth in new markets, thereby undermining their principal sources of revenue and profit) has been the road to ruin for many a market leader. Most mature organizations still have considerable value that they can, and should, extract from digitizing their operations and key internal processes. With corporate profits at record highs, moreover, defensive strategies for incumbents actually may seem perfectly appropriate, and often are.[29] We will explore the range of response strategies open to incumbents when confronting digital disruption in Chapter 4.

Sometimes, though, the best defense is a good offense. After a prolonged period of revenue stagnation, the International Monetary Fund now forecasts a return to stable global GDP growth[30] approaching 4 percent per year through 2020.* Yet a recent analysis from McKinsey paints a very different picture. After observing enormous gains in corporate profits over the past two decades, McKinsey projects corporate margins will decline some 15 percent through 2025.[31] They attribute this decline to both emerging-economy competitors and digital disruptors, noting, "High-tech companies are introducing new business models and striking into new sectors. And the tech giants themselves are not the only threat. Powerful digital platforms such as Alibaba and Amazon serve as launching pads for thousands of small and midsize enterprises, giving them the reach and resources to challenge larger companies."[32] Thus the Digital Vortex presents a clear exacerbation of margin pressure that may demand more disruptive strategies from incumbents.

"Disrupting yourself" does not mean discarding what has made you successful. Nor does it require you to mimic in-vogue digital tactics. Instead, it begins with challenging the assumptions that have underpinned past success, and stress-testing the ways in which you deliver value to customers.

---

* Not all observers are so sanguine about the prospects for returning to growth. See, for example, Robert J. Gordon, *The Rise and Fall of American Growth: The U.S. Standard of Living Since the Civil War*, (Princeton: Princeton University Press, 2016).

Chapter 2:
Digital Value and Business Models

Three Forms of Customer Value

As industries move toward the center of the Digital Vortex, where disruption is most intense, it is crucial to understand that this movement is not caused simply by the effects of technologies. What's "different this time" is that digital technologies are enabling new business models that in turn deliver new value to customers in innovative ways.

What is a business model? Like "digital," definitions of the term are legion. For our purposes, the definition used by Alexander Osterwalder and Yves Pigneur in their book *Business Model Generation* does nicely: "A business model describes the rationale of how an organization creates, delivers, and captures value."[1]

Disruptive business models, enabled by digital technologies, can be categorized by the primary type of value they provide. The DBT Center's research reveals there are three main types of customer value* delivered by digital disruptors: (1) cost value, (2) experience value, and (3) platform value.

To understand the workings of digital disruption, we examined the business models of more than 100 digital disruptors, both business-to-consumer (B2C) and business-to-business (B2B), and classified them by form of customer value (see Figure 8). The purpose of cataloging these

---

* Note: customer value is not synonymous with *consumer* value. Disruptors use cost value, experience value, and platform value to create compelling offerings for businesses as well as for consumers. In fact, many of the pre-eminent disruptors we discuss in this book have significant B2B revenues. Google's primary business is B2B, collecting one third of digital ad revenue globally ($67 billion); Apple's enterprise business hit $25 billion in 2015. There are also numerous disruptors that are targeting specific B2B industries, such as logistics, manufacturing, and energy. See Kris Carlon, "Google Makes One Third of All Global Online Ad Revenue, But There's Trouble Ahead," *Android Authority*, March 18, 2016, androidauthority.com/google-makes-one-third-global-online-ad-revenue-680883/ and Daisuke Wakabayashi, "Apple's Business-Related Revenue Hits $25 Billion" *Wall Street Journal*, September 29, 2015, wsj.com/articles/apples-business-related-revenue-hits-25-billion-1443548280

business models is not only to understand from where threats will materialize (if you are being disrupted, it is almost certainly going to come through one or more of these business models), but also to establish a kind of checklist that incumbents can use to create disruption *themselves*. We will explore this issue in Chapter 4.

Let's consider the three forms of customer value in detail, as well as the five main business models used by disruptors for each (for a total of 15 business models). We'll review examples of firms – both startups *and* incumbents – using these business models to effect market change. Successful disruptors rarely employ just one business model, however, and are proficient at blending them to create customer value in a way that deepens market disruption. We'll discuss this notion in the coming pages as well.

Cost Value

Cost value is the area in which the competitive effects of digital disruption are probably most acute. Here, disruptors lower the cost of a product or service for the end customer. Virtualization (also known as "dematerialization") of products and services is one key component of how digital disruptors lower costs. If you don't have to fabricate a physical product, you can obviously charge less than you otherwise would. The Amazon Kindle and other e-readers are examples of the dematerialization of products. The user downloads bits and bytes instead of purchasing a physical book. Virtual meetings are another form of dematerialization. Companies including InXpo, ON24, and Unisfair offer online conferences that replace the need for business travel. This negatively affects hotel

Cost Value

• Free / Ultra-low Cost
• Buyer Aggregation
• Price Transparency
• Reverse Auctions
• Consumption-based Pricing

Experience Value

• Customer Empowerment
• Customization
• Instant Gratification
• Reduced Friction
• Automation

Platform Value

• Ecosystem
• Crowdsourcing
• Communities
• Digital Marketplace
• Data Orchestrator

Figure 8: Digital Business Models by Form of Value
Source: Global Center for Digital Business Transformation, 2015

companies, which often depend on convention travel for a large share of their profits.[2] Virtualization also extends to distribution. Brick-and-mortar retailers have to maintain margins that can support a network of physical stores, along with the labor to staff them, but e-commerce has radically upended this model.

In addition, many digital disruptors use analytics to create or exploit information advantages and optimize operations, which drives cost value. Disruptors use these information advantages to enable customers to "get more for less," as in the case of coupons, rewards, or rebates that generate cost value for the end customer. Finally, digital disruptors tend to embrace unconventional approaches to workforce management, supply chain, and other parts of the business (leveraging cloud technology, analytics, crowdsourcing, etc.) to secure operational improvements that translate into lower costs and greater competitiveness. We discuss this in depth in Section 2 of this book.

But cost value isn't created only when a disruptor can lower the cost of its own offering relative to that of the incumbent. Cost value is also created when a disruptor re-intermediates commercial interactions. For example, online travel-booking sites such as Expedia, LY.com, and Orbitz are not themselves airlines, hotel chains, or car rental agencies, but they exert indirect cost pressure on firms in those industries (as well as direct pressure on competitors in their own domain, namely travel agents). While delivering cost value to customers, the comparison-shopping facilitated by these sites limits the pricing power of companies whose services are sold through this channel, creating cost value for the end customer.

There are five business models (see Table 1) that collectively explain most of the cost-value-creating approaches in today's market. Let's review them in turn.

Free / Ultra-low Cost provides products or services to customers at no cost, at nearly no cost, or at extremely low margins. These are wares for which customers have traditionally paid full or prevailing prices. As the old saying goes: it's pretty hard to compete with free. Examples of things for which customers have historically had to pay but no longer do include university classes (now offered by services such as Coursera) and voice and video calling (offered for free by Skype and many other providers). This category also includes business models built on providing rewards, rebates, or other incentives that extend economic gain for end customers (and for which they don't pay). Two examples of this are iBotta and Shopkick.[3]

Players that use "freemium" pricing, providing basic products or services at no cost while charging users a fee for premium or specialized variations of the offerings, are also included here. Dropbox, the online storage provider, and Spotify, the music streaming service, are well-known examples.

Finally, companies that offer products or services with very small or no markup are also included in this category. Amazon and Jet.com (described in more detail in Chapter 3) fit into this category of firms that compete by eliminating or dramatically cutting their margins, and creating cost value for their customers.

Business Model	Customer Value	Examples
Free / Ultra-low Cost: Providing something for free, rather than requiring customers to pay for it; providing rebates or rewards; no or very low markup; freemiums	Outright elimination of cost; incremental value for loyalty or participation	Coursera, Skype, iBotta, Shopkick, Dropbox, Spotify, Amazon, Jet.com
Buyer Aggregation: Spreading costs over people or time	Amortization of costs over time; group discounts, buying economies of scale	Fon, Groupon
Price Transparency: Extracting better bargains through price comparisons	Greater supplier choice, comparison shopping	Priceline, Shopzilla, NexTag
Reverse Auctions: Reverse- auction-style sales; competitive bidding; "name your own price"	Downward pricing pressure, strategic sourcing	LendingTree, SAP Ariba
Consumption-based Pricing: Paying only for what is used/consumed; subscription services; "X as a service"	Variable cost, lower risk, decreased vendor overhead	Metromile, Salesforce.com, LiquidSpace, ShareDesk, Rolls-Royce Holdings

Table 1: Cost-Value-Driven Business Models:
To compete by offering the customer lower costs or other economic gains
Source: Global Center for Digital Business Transformation, 2015

Buyer Aggregation spreads costs over people or time, or creates economies from "group buying" or volume discounts. Fon, for example, bills itself as the largest Wi-Fi network in the world. The company's members allow users to connect via one of Fon's roughly 20 million hotspots. This strategy poses a threat to Wi-Fi services provided by the incumbent telecommunications companies, as a group of customers leverages a digital business model to cooperate and spread costs.

Although it has encountered its share of difficulties, Groupon, the social couponing site, is another example of how multiple users can collectively drive down costs. The more people who sign up for an offer, the lower the price falls.

Price Transparency spawned many of the disruptors associated with the first wave of e-commerce. Firms such as Priceline (the parent of online travel and hospitality portals Booking.com and KAYAK) and a wide range of comparison-shopping tools, such as Shopzilla and NexTag, improve price transparency for buyers, enabling customers to extract better bargains from purveyors of products and services. These sites can detect price differences across multiple markets. For example, luxury goods such as watches or jewelry are often priced differently in different markets. Many disruptors make these differences transparent, so the items can be sourced at the lowest cost worldwide.

Reverse Auctions turn the tables on commerce, requiring sellers to bid for buyers' business. This competition, exemplified by companies including LendingTree (mortgages and loans) and SAP Ariba (B2B procurement), creates price pressure on suppliers and cost value for customers. A reverse auction introduces uncertainty for the seller over the maximum price that can be charged without prompting the buyer to select a competing offer from another seller. Online reverse auction settings also use sophisticated software algorithms that make the bidding process faster and more dynamic, placing further downward pressure on prices.

Consumption-based Pricing transforms the ways in which customers pay for the products and services they purchase. By switching from flat-rate pricing to an approach that lets customers pay only for what they use, providers deliver increased power (and cost value) to the customer. Examples of Consumption-based Pricing include pay-as-you-drive insurance (e.g., Metromile) and cloud-based software applications consumed through a subscription model (e.g., Salesforce.com, Cisco WebEx). In some cases, customers can move from purchasing goods as capital investments to buying services that are counted as operating expenses, providing greater financial flexibility, predictability, and still more cost value.

In the B2B space, disruptors such as LiquidSpace, ShareDesk, and PivotDesk enable companies to rent unused office space by the hour, day, or month. This is particularly useful for fast-growing organizations or virtual teams that need to come together periodically to work in a physical location. By taking advantage of this consumption-based pricing model, companies are able to pay for only the time they need to use the space. This is a significant benefit given that the average utilization rate for offices is only 45 to 50 percent.[4] Meanwhile, companies such as Rolls-Royce Holdings, the world's second-largest manufacturer of aircraft engines, sell "business outcomes"[5] – namely, propulsion or uptime – rather than equipment as a capital expense, as has been the norm when purchasing jet engines in the past.[6] These performance-based arrangements shift financial risk from the buyer to the seller, a form of cost value for the customer.

Experience Value

Experience value – offering customers more convenience, context, or control, for example – has been central to the rapid ascent of many of today's most disruptive companies. As with cost value, experience value increases as offerings are digitized, because what was formerly physical and indivisible can now be partitioned into only those units that customers want, and then delivered instantly to any device or location.

Disruptors that unbundle incumbents' offerings give customers the power to select (and pay for) only the products or services they value, discarding the "bundled" elements they don't want (and which drive up the price). "Unbundlers" also attack incumbents, such as large financial institutions, that aggregate services. Virtualization allows niche players to provide these services through digital channels, with more personalization and at a lower cost (even for free). This unbundling has banks scrambling to maintain the most profitable parts of their business, such as wealth management and mortgage banking, which are rapidly being attacked by disruptors.[7]

The superiority of experiences offered by disruptors can make it hard for incumbents to maintain market share based on brand or quality, and makes it easy for customers to move their business to an unconventional provider. Recent research we have conducted, for example, reveals that four out of five consumers would trust a company that was not a traditional bank to handle their "banking" needs.[8] To better understand the ways digital disruptors provide experience value, let's explore the five main business models (see Table 2) that give rise to it.

Customer Empowerment removes middlemen who do not add value (or enough value) yet still collect economic "rents" by acting as

Business Model	Customer Value	Examples
Customer Empowerment: Enabling self-service, disintermediation of middlemen, do-it-yourself	Greater independence, control, convenience	PayPal, Netflix
Customization: Personalization of products, services, experiences	Increased customization, contextualization; aesthetic / design improvements	Nordstrom / Trunk Club, New Balance
Instant Gratification: Delivering goods, services, or value-added experiences in real time, or via new devices (e.g., mobile), dematerialization	Relevance, immediacy	Instacart, Shyp, Google Express, Amazon Prime Now, Tesco Click + Collect, Amazon Echo
Reduced Friction: More simplification, greater efficiency, information aggregation	Removing latency or bottlenecks in business processes	Mint.com, Liquidnet, Bitcoin
Automation: Automation of processes using analytics or low-cost labor	Time savings, improved execution quality, wage arbitrage	Wealthfront, TaskRabbit

Table 2: Experience-Value-Driven Business Models:
To compete by offering the customer a superior experience
Source: Global Center for Digital Business Transformation, 2015

intermediaries in transactions. With these middlemen displaced, customers get what they want, avoid what they do not, and often pay a lower price. Circumventing middlemen (going direct), do-it-yourself (DIY), and placing the customer "in charge" are core elements of digital disruption. PayPal, for example, introduced new ways of sending money and making purchases that skirted the traditional payment methods (and fee extraction) long overseen exclusively by banks and credit card companies.

Netflix is another renowned example of Customer Empowerment. Instead of having to purchase an expensive cable package with hundreds of channels that go unwatched, Netflix members pay a small monthly fee to gain access to a huge selection of TV shows and movies. Netflix uses a digitally enabled business model to unbundle television programming from the strictures imposed by middlemen (cable companies) to deliver greater independence, control, and a more convenient viewing experience.*

Customization delivers value by tailoring experiences to a customer's unique preferences.† Value can come from either customization of the product or service itself, or contextualization (i.e., providers intelligently interpreting a user's location and specific needs to create an experience that maximizes value). Our recent research on the retail sector reveals a growing expectation among mainstream shoppers for "hyper-relevant" experiences that go beyond basic personalization capabilities, such as recognizing and welcoming a customer or presenting search results that include items "viewed by customers like you."[9] Omni-channel innovations, by which consumers can enjoy comparable experiences in a channel of their choosing, also fall into the category of Customization.

Trunk Club is a subscription-based personal styling service for men. When they sign up for the service, men are interviewed about their fashion preferences, and their measurement details are captured. Trunk Club then sends them a "trunk" that contains clothing and other accessories that have been personalized according to customers' preferred styles. The subscriber can try on the clothes in the comfort of his own home, and pay only for the clothes that he does not return within 10 days.

Several aspects of the Trunk Club business model enhance the customer experience through customization. First, the contents of the trunk are customized to subscribers' preferences; they choose from a selection already "filtered" by the stylist. Second, customers are realizing experience value through the 2014 acquisition of Trunk Club by department store retailer Nordstrom. Nordstrom has built its differentiation in a cut-throat market for apparel and housewares through world-class personalization.[10] Trunk Club subscribers are now able to use Nordstrom's in-store tailors to make alterations to the clothes they choose to keep from their trunks, creating customization value at multiple stages in the customer experience.

---

* Netflix is an excellent example of a disruptor that "leads with" experience value, even though cost value is clearly part of the attraction. Customers pay less by paying only for what they value.

† The 15 business models presented here do not describe every conceivable way in which a company can compete, but rather how these business models can deliver new customer value and improve competitiveness. For example, boasting a product that is "higher quality" or "better designed" – higher thread-count bedsheets, a juicier steak, a sleeker-looking car – may be critical factors for a customer in making a purchase decision, but are less directly tied to digital disruption itself.

New Balance is now offering shoes that are customized to the size and shape of a runner's foot. A scanner captures an image of the customer's foot. New Balance then uses a 3D printer to produce a sole that fits the foot exactly.[11]

Instant Gratification transforms the fulfillment of products and services, removing time as a dimension in the buying cycle. This business model gives customers the value they want without having to wait, either by delivering physical products very quickly or by providing digital versions instantaneously. Dematerialization plays a role, but as we have seen in countless digital disruptions, the speed afforded by a digital business model can be equally effective.

Instacart customers shop at participating grocers online or with their mobile app, and receive their orders within an hour for just $7.99.[12] Companies such as Shyp use a similar model. Here, customers take a photo of an item to be sent and a "Shyp Hero" comes to the consumer's location to pack and ship the parcel, freeing the customer from waiting in line at a post office or shipping outlet.[13] Google and Amazon have fought a pitched battle over delivery speeds with their Express and Prime Now services, respectively.[14] Amazon has invested in technology that will allow near-real-time delivery of manufactured goods, with delivery trucks equipped with 3D printers. The company has also announced an ambitious drone-based fulfillment program.[15] Amazon Echo is a small connected device for the home with a voice-command-activated artificial intelligence agent that answers to the name of "Alexa" and thus allows for Instant Gratification. This is not just accelerating the speed by which goods arrive at a consumer's door from Amazon (if a customer verbally places an order for an item with Alexa), but also providing instantaneous *information*, such as the answer to questions like "What is the quadratic equation?" or "What is the weather forecast for tomorrow?"[16]

Tesco, one of the most innovative retail market incumbents, has introduced a raft of experience innovations in recent years, including its "Click+Collect" approach to fulfillment: "With Grocery Click+Collect, you can order your groceries online and pick them up at a time you choose and at a location that suits you. There are more than 350 collection locations from which to choose, including Tesco stores, train stations, and local businesses (bringing Click+Collect groceries closer to you)."[17] In the case of Tesco, it's not just that time is collapsed, but waiting (the consumer frustration associated with time) is eliminated.

Reduced Friction is all about making things easy for customers by digitizing physical business processes and using technology to help them overcome obstacles and increase convenience. Mint.com, a subsidiary of Intuit, aggregates user account data from various financial institutions into a single tool. This enables customers to track their expenses, balances, budgets, and goals in a unified portal, rather than having to manually assemble a "true picture" of their finances from all their banks, lenders, and investment managers.

For big banks and asset managers, trading on big public financial exchanges can cost them valuable information advantages. Alternative equity trading systems such as Liquidnet reduce friction in the trading of securities by eliminating inefficiencies in matching buyers and sellers to pools of liquidity (i.e., other institutions that want to transact). By moving trades outside the normal execution of major trading exchanges, for example, the large asset managers that are Liquidnet's customers are able to move very large volumes of securities (the average equity trade on Liquidnet is reportedly around 42,000 shares, more than 100 times the average of any major U.S. stock exchange) directly between buyers and sellers with very fast "low latency" execution (with trading of this scale, information advantages are measured in milliseconds).[18] Institutions can also trade anonymously, preventing other firms from knowing who's selling what (or what positions they hold), and from engaging in predatory trading that exploits this knowledge and negatively affects prices.[19]

A number of digital disruptors are using blockchain technology to reduce friction in financial transactions. Blockchain is a record, or ledger, of digital events – one that's "distributed," or shared among many different parties. It can be updated only by consensus of a majority of the participants in the system. And, once entered, information can never be erased.[20] The consensus-based model makes it extremely difficult to falsify, and thus major crypto-currencies such as Bitcoin use blockchain as the basis for maintaining records of all transactions ever made using the currency. The beauty of blockchain is that it allows trading partners to exchange digital money in a verifiable way without the need for an intermediary, such as a bank, significantly reducing friction of transactions. This promises to completely transform the way that business-to-business payments occur across industries. In addition to hundreds of startups, dozens of the world's largest banks and even national banking systems are investing in tests of blockchain.[21]

Automation provides experience value by using technology to automate tasks or arrange for the completion of activities by others. Wealthfront is an automated investing service that uses advanced analytics to select the right investment portfolio and asset allocation based on answers to a few simple questions. Wealthfront also automatically balances investments across asset classes to maintain an ideal balance based on an investor's goals and risk profile. Finally, it automates the process of "tax loss harvesting," allowing investors to reduce their overall tax bill by realizing or "harvesting" losses when asset values go down. Whereas Wealthfront provides experience value in an area where many customers lack expertise, Automation can also save time and offload the performance of activities that customers may dislike. These activities can be performed by machines or by cheap or specialized labor. TaskRabbit, for example, frees users from drudgework, errands, and other chores they don't have the time or inclination to perform by enabling them to tap into an on-demand pool of low-cost labor.[*]

Platform Value

Although competing on the basis of cost or quality of experience is not novel, platform value is a competitive twist unique to digital disruption. Platform value is disruptive to competitive dynamics because it introduces an exponential element. Platforms create network effects – situations in which the number or type of users affects the value they derive. Network effects are often associated with "Metcalfe's Law," named after well-known technologist Robert Metcalfe. This law states that the value of a network increases proportionately to the square of the number of its users. By itself, for example, an individual telephone is not very valuable. However, as the number of users grows, so does the value of each phone. This largely explains why platforms drive disruption: the market changes that they engender are not linear.[†]

As citizens, consumers, and businesspeople, we encounter network effects in our daily lives. The World Wide Web, communicable diseases, tipping points, the wisdom of crowds, file sharing, social media, user-

---

[*] Automation can of course also introduce significant cost value, as in the case of Wealthfront, where consumers do not need to pay expensive financial advisors. Cost value can also be created through wage arbitrage (using cheaper sources of labor to perform tasks). Despite the potential for cost value benefits, Automation falls squarely into the experience value camp because simplification, efficiency, and convenience are its hallmarks.

[†] Do today's dominant platforms constitute "disruptive" innovation? This has been a source of considerable debate and attention. For an interesting perspective on this issue, see Alex Moazed and Nicholas L. Johnson, "Why Clayton Christensen Is Wrong about Uber and Disruptive Innovation," *TechCrunch*, February 27, 2016, techcrunch.com/2016/02/27/why-clayton-christensen-is-wrong-about-uber-and-disruptive-innovation/

generated content, financial contagion – all of these are manifestations (positive and negative) of network effects. Network effects are a big-tent idea: they span peer-to-peer (P2P) interactions, interdependence, viral patterns, gamification, and feedback loops. In a manner of speaking, a simple network effect is generated when network participants (or "nodes") are connected in a way that makes possible "the whole being greater than the sum of the parts." Hence, platforms represent a higher-order customer benefit with inherent value-amplifying characteristics.

They are also a powerful competitive force. The networked nature of platforms, once successfully established, makes them harder (though not impossible) to dislodge relative to discrete competitive innovations. This can lead to so-called "winner-takes-all" effects [22] in which dominant platform owners disproportionately realize the gains.* This logic is the basis of many of the most dynamic and game-changing digital business models, including those of Facebook, Google, iTunes, Twitter, and Uber. Platform value flows from five major business models (see Table 3).

Ecosystem is a business model in which a company (or a consortium of companies) provides a standardized toolkit, building blocks, environment, or "sandbox" that others can use to create value for themselves, especially monetary value. Apple and Google's developer ecosystems are well-known examples. Another is the video game Minecraft. Players can use visual elements (similar to LEGO blocks) to create visually stunning buildings or landscapes, and interact with other players and their creations. Users can also develop modifications ("mods") that create new capabilities, or games within the game, spawning multiple potential revenue streams for players.[23] Raspberry Pi, the cheap and basic computer that has attracted millions of users, is another example. Sold for $35, Raspberry Pi provides an Ecosystem dynamic for millions of educators, hobbyists, and tinkerers to create innovations at low cost using standard personal-computer components.[24]

Disruptors in the B2B market are also embracing the Ecosystem model. GrabCAD, a company founded in Estonia and acquired in 2014 by 3D printer firm Stratsys, has built an ecosystem of more than 2.9 million members who have collectively collaborated on and shared over 1.25

---

* Research from Citi provides empirical confirmation of market share consolidation as a result of disruption, finding "digital segments are significantly more concentrated than traditional segments with an average of ~80% top-3 share vs. ~45% top-3 share in physical segments." See Sandeep Davé, Ashwin Shirvaikar, and Dave Baker, "Digital Money: A Pathway to an Experience Economy," Citigroup, January 2015, citibank.com/icg/sa/digital_symposium/docs/DigitalMoneyReadinessReport2015.pdf

Business Model	Customer Value	Examples
Ecosystem: Providing a standardized toolkit, building blocks, environment, or "sandbox" that others can use to create value for themselves	Co-creation with other ecosystem participants, repeatability and resource leverage, opportunities to monetize offerings via ecosystem	Apple iOS, Google Android, Minecraft, Raspberry Pi, GrabCAD, Docker
Crowdsourcing: Crowdsourcing inputs from ecosystem of contributors	Larger volume of ideas, greater diversity of ideas, new labor sources, capture of scarce or unique information	Quora, Huffington Post, Kaggle, Innocentive, WikiLeaks
Communities: Dissemination of information through a network or community of recipients; viral content	Optimization of communications / distribution / execution	Nextdoor, Twitter, Reddit
Digital Marketplace: Connecting individuals and groups; creation of marketplace capability; "sharing economy" and peer-to-peer (P2P) dynamics	Revenue from buying, selling, transacting; socialization and mobilization of resources, education of users	Etsy, Airbnb, Cargomatic, Transfix
Data Orchestrator: Combination of sensor / machine data and analytics to create new insights	Real-time data, new sources of data, recognizing patterns in extreme complexity, optimizing decisions	ABB, Cisco, GE, IBM, Intel, Palantir, SAP, Splunk, John Deere

Table 3: Platform-Value-Driven Business Models:
To compete by offering the customer positive network effects
Source: Global Center for Digital Business Transformation, 2015

million open source (free) computer-aided design (CAD) models.[25] Docker is an open-source technology that enables developers to build, run, test, and deploy applications using "containers." Containers enable software to run reliably from one computing environment to another, such as on a laptop or in the cloud.[26] Docker has seen incredible growth in recent years. In the first six months of 2014, there were 3 million downloads, but by December 2014 there had been 100 million.[27] This popularity has led to the emergence of an ecosystem of major technology vendors and developers all working to support the development of the technology and the integration with their own offerings.[28]

Crowdsourcing exploits diversity of contributions as a competitive tool, and benefits platform users in many ways. First, it can lower costs by having users perform work that augments the platform (this benefits both the user and the platform owner). At Quora, users provide expert answers to questions posed by other users. Quora provides the venue in the form of a social network, but not the content, which is sourced from the user base on an unpaid basis. *The Huffington Post* has established itself as one of the most popular news aggregators on the web, largely by publishing content from bloggers and guest columnists who aren't compensated. Unlike many of its media competitors, HuffPost doesn't charge users to access content. It has succeeded because the user base attracts marquee columnists and content providers (such as celebrities) who want to reach its readers, creating a virtuous circle of information supply and demand.

Second, platform users benefit from diverse insights, often where information would otherwise remain obscure. Kaggle and Innocentive are two companies that gamify technical work (predictive analytics, scientific "challenges") to bring sought-after expertise to bear in a competitive, multi-participant setting that can contribute to breakthrough results for deep-seated business problems. WikiLeaks, the site known for "whistleblower" information, is a Crowdsourcing approach that is applied (anonymously) to uncovering scarce insights such as confidential files to which users would otherwise have no access.

Communities is a classic platform-oriented business model. The Communities model seeks efficiency and scale gains from network effects that can translate into positive commercial impacts (or promote other organizational aims, in the case of nonprofits).* We see this model on the web almost every day, frequently in the form of content dissemination (e.g., a YouTube clip or a TED Talk that goes viral), but it can apply to any circumstance in which user value corresponds to efficiency or effectiveness

---

* What is the difference between Ecosystem and Communities business models? In the former, the members of the network use the foundational building blocks provided by the ecosystem owner to generate value for themselves. This can include refining or adding to those building blocks in a way that monetizes the improvement for the benefit of both the contributor and the ecosystem owner (who takes a cut). In Communities, the users of the network are just that: users. Although users may expand on the information they access (e.g., by re-tweeting), rarely does "secondary" value creation – in which the user obtains revenue, for example – occur in a Communities model. In general, the potential for value-added that users generate as a result of Communities is lower than in the case of an Ecosystem business model. To summarize the distinction between *Crowdsourcing* and Communities (as both may employ gamification, for example), the former creates value from diversity of contribution, whereas the latter revolves around efficiency of transmission.

of transmission. Nextdoor, for example, is a social network that focuses on "hyper-local" connections to create a communications platform for neighbors, businesses, and institutions in a local community. Nextdoor members can use its "bulletin board" to engage in commerce with buyers or sellers in the community, participate in civic activism (such as petitions), or exchange information that is valuable within only that locality, such as a missing pet, a school closure, or a broken water main. Allowing only local residents to participate in a community's communications enhances the efficiency of transmission, as broader participation would dilute these interactions.

Economy of scale innate to successful platforms means that users can lower the latency of the information communicated (it can be transmitted faster) and expend fewer resources in "getting their message across" or, conversely, in obtaining information valuable to them. This is instrumental to the success of platforms such as Twitter, where users can reach large numbers of other users at zero incremental cost. "What's trending on Twitter" information improves information utility for users by pointing them to what other users have found valuable. This decreases the likelihood that an individual user will devote resources (time, attention) to accessing information not considered valuable. Twitter's "verification" mechanism also ensures that users are who they claim to be, eliminating uncertainty for other users.

Much of the value that flows to users in a Communities model may not be purely economic. Some of it can be intangible value. Psychologists and behavioral economists tell us we conceive of value in more than purely financial terms. Platform value can include reputational capital, prestige, and relationships (as in a "sense of community," for example).

The spiritual notion of karma revolves around the idea that one's future happiness or success depends on one's own actions and intentions. So-called "digital karma," then, is a quantified measure of the "good behavior" of a user in contributing to a platform. On eBay, sellers' ratings denote their experience as participants on the platform, contributing to a sense of trustworthiness in the eyes of prospective buyers. Reddit, the popular news and information bulletin board site, offers "creddits" to users for particularly compelling posts. Users can collect points for the quality and frequency of their posts. Although Reddit karma has no financial value, it nonetheless conveys a measure of status to users, which affects the value received by a platform user. Communities business models may also rely on gamification and their ability to create social pressure, competitive tension, fun and camaraderie, and the prospect of "success cachet" to motivate community users, foster desirable behaviors (such as customer loyalty), and drive engagement.

Digital Marketplace, which has emerged as a ubiquitous feature of many digital disruptors' strategies, is premised on creating connections among individuals and groups for their mutual benefit. This notion of benefiting multiple "sides" of a market is central to platform value. It is not only the value delivered by the disruptor itself, but also the value facilitated. Digital Marketplace includes capabilities in which a platform provider "makes a market" in goods or services and creates a venue for buyers and sellers to transact. Etsy is an example of a disruptor using Digital Marketplace to create a platform for specialty goods such as handmade and vintage items, art, crafts, jewelry, and clothing. The company reported 2015 sales of over $2 billion[29] and boasts more than 50 million registered users.[30] Merchants on Etsy, often home-based businesses and artisans, benefit from access to buyers they would not have been able to reach through traditional retail channels. Meanwhile, buyers obtain access to merchandise that would otherwise be impossible (or at least cumbersome) to browse and buy. Value is obtained in the form of access, variety, and transaction efficiency.

Digital Marketplace also encompasses so-called "sharing economy" players such as Airbnb, through which individual property owners can market accommodations to travelers. Guests can concurrently shop for accommodations outside the traditional hospitality value chain.

In part, the sharing economy rests on P2P dynamics, which represent another fundamental aspect of platforms. For Airbnb, this means converting an individual property owner (e.g., someone who wants to monetize a spare bedroom) into a service provider, and then connecting the owner with people who wish to make use of the service. Again, neither Airbnb nor the providers of the accommodations are hotel companies. The accommodations providers are largely individual consumers, though some are smaller-scale property managers.

B2B startups such as Cargomatic and Transfix have created digital marketplaces that target the trucking industry, increasing the efficiency of matching drivers to loads. Shippers can list their jobs on these platforms, and truckers can take on jobs they otherwise might not have been aware of. In addition, both parties benefit from other digital capabilities, such as real-time shipment tracking and online payments. In addition to many smaller businesses, large shippers such as American book retailer Barnes & Noble and German manufacturer Bosch are using this type of digital marketplace to arrange the transport of their goods.[31]

Data Orchestrator leverages the disruptive power of IoT and big data analytics to create new opportunities for innovation and value creation, including location-based services, remote monitoring and predictive maintenance, context-aware marketing offers, and video analytics. There are many different definitions for IoT, but the simplest is to consider it the networked connection of physical objects.[32] IoT is about connecting the unconnected: vehicles and other transportation infrastructure, buildings, plant-floor machines, medical devices, apparel, and much more. Whereas the internet has historically focused on connecting *computers* (i.e., machines that facilitate information processing), IoT connects *objects* with a myriad of other purposes. This creates the potential for a vast platform of sensors and embedded systems, with information traveling over networks and analyzed by applications to create new insights.

Many companies own or oversee large asset bases and data streams that are conducive to this kind of connection. Smart buildings, industrial automation, wearable devices, and telematics are all enablers of this business model. The possibility of creating value-added services for end customers via an IoT/analytics platform is appealing to many large companies facing digital disruption or other competitive pressures in traditional, especially product-centric, lines of business. Companies pursuing the Data Orchestrator business model include ABB, Cisco, GE, IBM, Intel, Palantir, SAP, and Splunk.

John Deere, the American manufacturer of agricultural equipment, has pursued the vision of smart farming with a Data Orchestrator business model. The company has launched an online portal, Myjohndeere.com, through which farmers can access a range of data, such as information gathered from sensors on their own machinery as well as third-party financial and weather data. The farmers can use this information to optimize their farming practices, such as deciding when and where to plant. The data also is used for predictive maintenance so that farmers can replace vehicle and equipment parts before they fail. John Deere has even extended its role as a data orchestrator beyond its own company by launching the Deere Open Data Platform, which farmers can use to exchange data with one another and with third-party developers who can build innovative new farming applications.[33]

Combinatorial Disruption

The most successful disruptors in recent years, including Amazon, Apple, Facebook, Google, and Netflix, employ what we call "combinatorial disruption," in which cost value, experience value, and platform value are fused to create new business models and exponential gains.

The term "combinatorial innovation" is most often associated with Hal Varian, chief economist at Google and professor emeritus at the University of California, Berkeley. In his work, Varian develops the idea of combinatorial innovation by citing examples of how, throughout history, technology standardization and convergence have supported the combination and recombination of technologies, resulting in new inventions.[34] Combinatorial *disruption* builds on this principle, updating it for the Digital Vortex era, to show how digitally enabled business models can be combined, and recombined, to enable the delivery of disruptive blends of cost value, experience value, and platform value to customers, whether they be consumers or businesses. This process produces digital disruption, competitive change, and the need for companies (especially incumbents) to transform themselves. Combinatorial disruption is compelling for end customers for obvious reasons – it delivers the goods on multiple fronts – and is the best source of differentiation and competitive advantage for that minority of companies that can deliver on this higher standard of value.

Some disruptors build their organizations around one business model, and on occasion, a single form of customer value. Kickstarter, for example, is a pure platform play for the crowdsourcing of investment capital funding by new ventures. Most disruptors with enduring success, however, practice some form of combinatorial disruption. Let's look at two company examples, one that primarily combines two forms of customer value, the other all three.

Adyen

Adyen is a B2B provider of international payment services based in the Netherlands. Customers such as Uber, Facebook, Airbnb, KLM, and Spotify use the payment platform to accept electronic payments through credit cards, debit cards, bank transfers, and other means worldwide. Adyen is also one of Europe's most highly valued private companies (i.e., "unicorns"), having achieved a valuation of $2.3 billion in 2015.[35] The company has been profitable on an EBITDA basis since 2011, and has processed more than $50 billion in payments since its founding.[36] Below, we have identified a sample of the different types of business models that Adyen is using to offer, in this case, experience value and platform value.

Experience Value

Reduced Friction – Adyen's payment platform connects 250 payment methods, including 17 currencies across six continents. Adyen also enables businesses to receive payments from their customers across multiple channels, including e-commerce, mobile phones (iOS and Android), and in-store point-of-sale (POS) systems. The ability to accelerate the speed of commerce transactions by reducing friction is at the core of Adyen's value proposition for its customers.

Instant Gratification – Adyen offers instant gratification both to its direct customers and to its customers' customers. The company offers pre-built payment integrations, such as hosted payment pages, encryption services, and direct application programming interfaces (APIs) for payment processing, which obviate the need for its customers to build or procure these for themselves. These services offer a significant source of value for the type of merchant that Adyen serves – fast-growing digital disruptors for whom time-to-market is critical. By using Adyen's platform, merchants can bypass the time and effort of constructing their own payment solutions for each local market. For example, in 2015 Uber announced that it would use Adyen's platform to support its expansion into Morocco, eliminating the need for the ride-sharing service to build its own bespoke, local payments agreements.[37]

Adyen also provides instant gratification to the end-users of its payment platform – the millions of consumers who use their credit cards or other forms of non-cash payment to buy services. These consumers increasingly expect one-click ease of payment, regardless of what they are shopping for and how they buy. Adyen has recognized this need by becoming the only payments technology provider to accept Apple Pay in the United States and United Kingdom, both for in-app and in-store purchases.[38]

Platform Value

Data Orchestrator – Adyen's ability to offer retailers a single payment platform through which they can accept in-store and online purchases provides them with the ability to capture valuable consumer data. Retailers and other merchants can use this data to understand shopper behavior across channels (e.g., in-store vs. online) and to launch innovative new services such as the ability to purchase online and pick up in store. In addition, the data that Adyen captures can be used to improve fraud detection and prevention strategies for online merchants.[39]

Adyen's global payments platform employs digital business models to deliver a new combination of value to merchants and consumers. The company provides its services at a slightly lower cost than traditional providers, but its main value is rooted in its service levels and global reach. It reduces friction and enhances customer choice by offering a global payments acquiring solution to businesses that would otherwise have to negotiate a series of contracts with local providers. Its global platform allows it to compete with larger local players who struggle with cross-border commerce.

LinkedIn

LinkedIn is the world's largest business-oriented networking site, with more than 400 million users from more than 200 countries.[40] LinkedIn pursues a strategy of combinatorial disruption through the following business models (among others).

Cost Value

Free / Ultra-low Cost – LinkedIn offers members several features for free, including the ability to build online profiles, connect with others, join interest groups, and publish posts. As of May 2015, more than 80 percent of LinkedIn's members used only the platform's free services.[41] However, the company also offers paid "Premium" services, ranging from the local currency equivalent of US$29.99 to US$119.95 per month, for access to advanced search functionality for profiles, the ability to contact individuals outside of one's own network, and online training.

Experience Value

Customization – LinkedIn members can customize their online profiles to a high degree. This includes not only descriptions of their educational and job experiences, but also the inclusion of awards, publications, and recommendations from their contacts. In addition, members can personalize the appearance of their profiles using their preferred images and can specify which parts of their profiles others can see. However, this user-led Customization represents only a small part of LinkedIn's value. The company makes extensive use of analytics, such as machine learning, to match the content that members receive, including contact suggestions, news feeds, and job postings related to their specific profiles and behaviors.[42]

Platform Value

Data Orchestrator – Hundreds of millions of individuals around the world have freely provided detailed information about their professional backgrounds and related information on LinkedIn. In addition, many of these people spend hours browsing the site, and the company is able to garner insights from this clickstream. LinkedIn has built a business selling valuable intelligence to thousands of companies who are looking to recruit more effectively, or even to get insights into the behaviors within their own workforce, such as identifying employees who are likely to quit. In fact, in 2015 the company derived more revenues from selling such B2B talent and recruiting solutions to employers than it did from advertising and consumer-driven subscriptions combined.[43]

Communities – One of the key aims of LinkedIn is to enable individuals to build communities of members who share similar backgrounds and interests. Since 2004, more than 2 million LinkedIn Groups have been created, allowing users to exchange advice and hold online discussions. These communities have seen tremendous growth – the average member joins seven groups.[44]

Digital Marketplace – In October 2015, the company quietly launched its new ProFinder service, a job-matching marketplace that will compete with disruptors such as Fiverr and Upwork. A key difference between them and LinkedIn ProFinder is that freelancers on ProFinder are "vetted by the ProFinder concierge team" before they're listed on the platform, so those hiring are likely to find a higher caliber, more trustworthy professional than what's typical on the cheaper freelance sites. Online marketplaces such as Fiverr and Upwork and 99designs.com have no such entry requirements for freelancers. With its existing vast platform, LinkedIn is now well-positioned to effect connections between freelance professionals and companies seeking quality contracted work.[45]

Triple Threat

As we have seen through the examples of Adyen and LinkedIn, disruptive companies have many options at their disposal to use digital business models and upend competitors with attractive combinations of value to customers. If you examine a highly disruptive company in any industry today, you will find a similar pattern of combining the 15 business models described here.

Although companies have competed on cost or quality of experience for centuries, digitally enabled business models allow disruptors to combine low costs and superior experiences in ways that previously could not have been done. Moreover, platform value is a new source of competitive advantage that disruptors are brandishing against incumbents.* The ability to scale rapidly, to connect those who need a service with those willing to provide it, and to direct new sources of data to those who can act on it, were not possible just a few years ago. Platforms also provide a powerful mechanism to build complementary business models and practice combinatorial disruption, melding cost value and experience value with a critical mass of customers. For example, the advertising revenue available to platform owners (by virtue of the "eyeballs" they offer) can offset other costs. This allows owners to introduce incremental cost value or experience value, often at no charge or as a freemium-style enticement, that cuts non-platform competitors off at the knees.

What makes digital disruptors so threatening to traditional market leaders is their ability to create vast new troves of value for customers, especially by combining digital business models to mesh cost value, experience value, and platform value. Such combinatorial disruption is the power source of the fiercest, most dangerous digital disruptors, to which we now turn.

---

* For a detailed discussion, see Geoffrey G. Parker, Marshall W. Van Alstyne, and Sangeet Paul Choudary, *Platform Revolution: How Networked Markets Are Transforming the Economy and How to Make Them Work for You* (New York: W.W. Norton & Company, 2016).

Chapter 3:
Value Vampires and Value Vacancies

In the last chapter, we examined the three types of value that digital disruptors deliver – cost value, experience value, and platform value – and the business models supporting each of them. In this chapter, we'll look at the competitive dynamics of the Digital Vortex and introduce two new concepts: value vampires and value vacancies. Value vampires are a subset of digital disruptors that combine compelling forms of cost value with experience value and platform value to undercut incumbents and quickly win significant market share. Value vacancies are short-duration windows of opportunity in tightly contested markets. They can be leveraged by organizations in response to threats from value vampires and other digital disruptors.

Value Vampire
A disruptive player whose competitive advantage shrinks overall market size.

- Places incumbents on the defensive

- Uses cost value to shrink margins and/or revenue of incumbents

- May also use experience value (renders incumbents obsolete) or platform value (rapidly acquires market share)

- Most dangerous value vampires practice "combinatorial disruption" (all three sources of value at once)

Figure 9: "Value Vampires" Defined
Source: Global Center for Digital Business Transformation, 2015

Value Vampires

Simply put, a value vampire is a company whose competitive advantage shrinks the overall revenue or profit pool (or both) in a market (see Figure 9). Value vampires are dangerous for incumbents because they are ruthlessly efficient at creating customer value.

First, value vampires always introduce a form of cost value, employing business models including Free / Ultra-low Cost, Price Transparency, and Buyer Aggregation. These business models drain margin from incumbents. Second, value vampires have a nasty habit of creating innovations that yield new and better experience value for customers. Customer Empowerment, Instant Gratification, and Reduced Friction put customers in control, deliver products and services faster, and eliminate inconveniences. As noted earlier, these disruptors are focused on value, not the value chain. That is, they tend to create experiences that circumvent the *modus operandi* of the "encumbered incumbent" – experiences that can render the most venerable companies obsolete. Value vampires therefore do not merely drink up profit pools; they may disintermediate market leaders completely. Third, value vampires benefit from, and contribute to, exponential changes in markets.

Welcome to life in the Digital Vortex. Don't get too comfortable.

Value vampires can affect any industry, but they are most likely to alight on markets that have not seen much innovation (i.e., new forms of cost value, experience value, or platform value). Why? Because many customers in these markets are dissatisfied with existing service levels. Worse, they may feel abused by incumbents who dictate processes and circumscribe choice. Such established players have often enjoyed high margins for a long stretch.

Going forward, value vampires may promote more frequent and more catastrophic revenue stalls for companies in the Digital Vortex. The most lethal value vampires adeptly practice combinatorial disruption. They simultaneously create cost value, experience value, and platform value. One is bad enough, but when a value vampire kills your margins, makes your value proposition superfluous, and acquires your customers *en masse*, that really sucks.

Napster: The Original Value Vampire

Determining which companies are value vampires and which are more garden-variety digital disruptors involves a measure of subjectivity. It is usually impossible to label a company as a value vampire until you have evidence that the overall size of the market has decreased.*

Perhaps the starkest example of the value vampire phenomenon occurred in the recorded music industry, where waning revenues and profits, and an overall market decline, cannot be attributed to economic cycles or other causes. After more than a decade of digital disruption, this sector represents an object lesson in the effects of value vampires.

In 1999 the music industry was riding high, as global revenues reached $28.6 billion (see Figure 10). The average price of a compact disc (CD) was $14 – the same as in the early 1990s, despite a major drop in the cost of production.[1] Everyone in the value chain benefited from the high prices. When a CD was sold in 1995, for example, 35 percent of the retail price went to the store, 27 percent to the record company, 16 percent to the artist, 13 percent to the manufacturer, and 9 percent to the distributor. Retailers alone earned a 35 percent margin on the sale of a CD.[2] Consumers, however, went from feeling puzzled about the persistence of high prices, as CD technology matured, to feeling exploited as CDs sometimes retailed for over $20. Nevertheless, they kept buying CDs, partly because of their superior sound quality compared with cassettes, and partly because they were more portable than vinyl records. CD sales peaked in 2000, reaching nearly 2.5 billion units.[3]

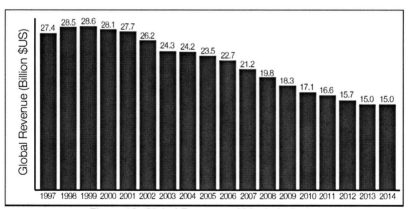

Figure 10: Global Revenue of Music Industry
Source: IFPI, 2015

---

* Careful analysis of a market is of course warranted to ensure that the introduction of the value vampire was causal of, and not merely correlated with, market decline.

Few executives had any inkling that their industry would be thrust into the middle of what we now call the Digital Vortex, but disruption was underway. CDs put studio-quality digital files in the hands of consumers. All that was missing to catalyze the reaction was a file format that could replicate that digital file and make it easy to distribute.

Enter the MP3. Standardized in the mid-1990s, it took the large amount of data from the CD, compressed it, and made it transferable. Through "burned" CDs and the internet, consumers could finally duplicate and share reasonably high-quality digital music files with ease.

Indeed, an estimated 30 billion songs were illegally downloaded on file-sharing networks and torrent sites from 2004 to 2009.[4] This digital disruption had a colossal impact, cutting global industry revenues in half (again, see Figure 10). By 2014, only 46 percent of industry revenue came from physical music sales.[5] The effects on several players in the value chain were swift and merciless, and incumbents who managed to survive are still feeling the reverberations today.

Let's examine what many consider to be the key player in the disruption, and what could be deemed the archetypal value vampire: Napster. While perhaps a familiar story, we will view this example through the lens of cost value, experience value, and platform value to see how value vampires attack, and how they benefit end customers while simultaneously weakening the market.

Launched in 1999, Napster was a file-sharing service that let consumers download music for free and share their music collections with others. By "ripping" digital files from CDs and converting them to the MP3 format, music lovers unshackled their favorite albums and songs from their physical bonds, enabling others to acquire them at will over the internet. Napster provided the platform that connected music fans so they could swap or download files that others had posted. Suddenly, instead of being forced to buy what many considered an overpriced CD, consumers could get exactly the songs or albums they wanted at no cost. Napster's business model is highlighted in Table 4 below, which details the complementary forms of cost value, experience value, and platform value that flowed to consumers.

Napster's business model (it was a "business" in only the loosest sense, of course) placed immense cost pressure on other players in the value chain – notably record labels and retailers – because a product that was sold at a huge markup was suddenly available for free. Cost and consumption were decoupled. Napster users could acquire songs and albums without paying.* At their most disruptive, value vampires fill a significant market need, and scale their offerings quickly. In Napster's case, the unmet needs were 1) the ability to acquire the music customers wanted while avoiding what they didn't want and 2) the ability to acquire it immediately.

	Business Model	Customer Value
Cost Value $	**Free / Ultra-low Cost:** Providing something for no cost or very low markup.	Full decoupling: customers could own a huge volume and variety of music without paying for it.
Experience Value	**Customer Empowerment:** Enabling self-service, disintermediation of middlemen, sharing of content and experiences **Instant Gratification:** Delivering goods, services, or value-added experiences in real time, or via new device form factors (e.g., mobile), dematerialization. **Customization:** Personalization of products, services, and experiences.	Users could pick the artists, albums, and songs they wanted and download them directly, and immediately. In addition, they no longer had to pay up to $20 for a CD, when all they wanted was an individual song—which they could not buy as a single in the existing music distribution model.
Platform Value	**Digital Marketplace:** Dissemination of information through a network or community of recipients; creation of marketplace capability. **Communities:** Ability to scale quickly; acquire and disseminate content through peer-to-peer dynamics; viral content.	Connected millions of music fans who distributed content from their own machines using P2P sharing. P2P allowed Napster to quickly scale the number of songs and albums, and enabled a very low-cost structure.

Table 4: A Free Lunch with Millions of Dishes
Source: Global Center for Digital Business Transformation, 2015

---

* While the ethics of this were openly questioned at the time, online users were becoming accustomed to receiving for free content they had formerly paid for, such as newspapers and magazines.

In the world of CDs, music fans had to make a sizable investment – $14 to $20 – even if they wanted merely a single song. There was rarely an option to buy a low-cost single. Moreover, consumers had to travel to a retail store, which may not have had the desired CD in stock. With Napster, they could pick songs or albums and download them immediately. Users could also use Napster to discover new music beyond the limited selection offered by most FM radio stations, music video programming, or retail outlets.

Most important, Napster's P2P file sharing allowed it to scale incredibly fast (at one point, Napster was the fastest-growing application in the history of the internet, rising from 1 million to 50 million users in just seven months).[6] At its peak, the service boasted some 80 million customers, or nearly one in five internet users at the time.[7] Users shared their music libraries, and attracted others who did the same. This created a virtuous cycle for Napster: the platform acquired customers *and* content exponentially. In short, it was combinatorial disruption – a combination of cost value, experience value, and platform value – that made Napster so supremely disruptive.

The New Blood: ClassPass, Jet.com and Freightos

Digital disruption over the last decade has tended to be most severe where the core product or service is highly "digitizable," as was the case with music and other information-centric offerings. We often hear this from executives whose companies market "physical" offerings, such as pharmaceuticals, apparel, fossil fuels, and transportation. While it's true that the technology and media and entertainment sectors are the most vulnerable to digital disruption, thanks in part to the "digitizability" of their products and services, our research has found that digital disruption is accelerating for all industries, regardless of the digitizability of offerings. This means that disruptors are using digitally enabled business models to upend the status quo. Uber is an oft-cited example in which the product – automobile rides – is physical.

Can value vampires create cost value, experience value, and platform value when offerings are less conducive to digitization? In the Digital Vortex, everything that can be digitized *is* digitized. So, in the value chain of industries where products are inherently physical, "what can be digitized" may often be a channel or a step in the customer lifecycle, not the product itself.

To understand the applicability of the value vampire beyond so-called "information industries," let's examine three relatively new companies –

ClassPass, Jet.com, and Freightos. Despite their youth, all three exhibit telltale signs of value vampirism.

With a valuation reportedly topping $400 million in mid-2016,[8] ClassPass bills itself as a new kind of fitness membership: "Thousands of classes. One pass." Rather than paying to join a single gym, ClassPass members pay a flat monthly fee to access all gyms in the ClassPass network on an unlimited basis (with a maximum of three classes per month at any one gym). This feature creates cost value for customers: the flat fee (roughly $125 per month in most cities where the service is offered) is cheaper for anyone who even occasionally takes exercise classes (e.g., five or six "drop-ins" per month).[9]

As with online travel-booking sites, which are not actually providers of flights or hotel rooms, ClassPass is not a gym, but has re-intermediated a well-established commercial relationship between gyms and members. Gyms depend on low levels of utilization for profitability (fewer customers using their facilities translates into lower variable costs to operate), so this places gyms in a tough competitive position when ClassPass members fill up workout sessions, increase utilization, and prevent other higher-paying clientele from taking a class.

ClassPass provides experience value because users enjoy dramatically more choice in where they exercise, the times classes are offered, and the types of classes they take, including yoga, pilates, cardio kickboxing, dance, and indoor spin cycling – a menu of offerings that would not typically be feasible under one roof.

Platform value is generated via the network effect of its 8,000-plus participating gyms and fitness studios. ClassPass creates competitive pressure for gyms and fitness studios to sell their classes through the ClassPass platform, lest they be sidelined by the evolving market expectations of gym-goers. In fact, consumers can "recommend" to ClassPass that their gym be added to the network. In a classic pathology of value vampirism, this can lead to a downward spiral in margins for incumbent providers as the network grows.[10] The company has reportedly booked more than 15 million exercise sessions since launching in 2013, claims it is growing its user base by 20 percent per month, and is now offered in nearly 40 cities worldwide.[11] While the company said it would pay out more than $100 million to participating gyms in 2015,[12] it will be intriguing to see how overall gym and fitness studio revenues change in the years ahead.*

Jet.com is a striking example of another digital disruptor that may spawn value vampire effects, this time in a multi-segment market that cuts across different retail categories. Jet describes itself as "the shopping membership that gets you club price savings on just about anything you buy." It combines the Free / Ultra-low Cost and Price Transparency business models to offer significant discounts on a vast array of products, ranging from groceries to appliances to jewelry.

Its strategy initially was to promise consumers the lowest prices on the internet (generally 10-15 percent lower than elsewhere online),[13] charge no margin on goods (in fact, it frequently incurred negative margins), and earn revenue through an annual club membership fee of $49.99. This fee was reminiscent of those charged by the incumbents the company is targeting: Costco and Amazon Prime. In October 2015, the company announced it was eliminating the annual membership fee[14] and would instead charge retailers "commissions" on sales through the Jet channel.

Jet buys goods from merchants who then fulfill them directly to the consumer. When reporters from *The Wall Street Journal* tested Jet in July 2015, buying a basket of 12 items, they found "Jet's prices for the 12 items added up to $275.55, an average discount of about 11 percent from the prices Jet paid for those items on other retailers' websites. Jet's total cost, which also includes estimated shipping and taxes, was $518.46. As a result, Jet had an overall loss of $242.91 on the 12 items."[15]

Jet also offers impressive experience value, especially Customization (greater choice) and Reduced Friction (eliminating process inefficiencies). An explicit component of its business model is "Unbundled costs to give you choice. We took apart the traditional retail model, letting you avoid costs normally baked into prices. For example, if you don't need free returns on an item, we give you the choice to waive returns, so you save more."[16] This unbundling is a perfect illustration of the idea of "value, not the value chain." Consumers don't care about how incumbents have always done things or their operational constraints. They just like lower prices.

Jet uses algorithms to create information advantages, such as grouping products to create shipping efficiencies that can translate into lower costs, more choice, and more flexibility in providing what the consumer wants. Jet's ability to yoke cost value with experience value shows how long-

---

* This business model is having knock-on effects in other markets as well. See, for example, Laura Entis, "Meet Cups, the ClassPass of Coffee Shops," *Entrepreneur*, September 3, 2015, entrepreneur.com/article/250183

standing competitive strategy constructs such as "cost leadership" versus "differentiation"[17] go out the window when firms practice combinatorial disruption. It also underscores why this form of customer value is so disruptive, because the consumer isn't forced to choose between low cost or quality of experience.

Jet's model is especially interesting because retailers are not losing margin directly (although they're now reportedly paying Jet referral fees, as noted above). On the contrary, Jet's "Smart Cart" algorithms can actually translate into larger basket sizes as customers realize more savings when they add more items to their carts. On the surface, the relationship is symbiotic – Jet amounts to another channel for other retailers, as well as a platform intermediating a "two-sided market" of merchants and consumers. However, the bigger-picture question is whether Jet is waging a stealth price war on the entire retail industry by creating cost value on a grand scale, further conditioning buyers to expect a rock-bottom price for absolutely everything. Boomerang Commerce, a provider of e-commerce pricing software, estimates that Jet's prices are less than Amazon's on fully 81 percent of products.[18]

Since its launch in July 2015, the company has acquired more than 100,000 users and is seeking a valuation north of $3 billion.[19] The company concedes it has no plans to turn an operating profit for at least five years, but says it will do so after reaching a threshold of 15 million users (how its path to profitability is affected by the recent move to stop charging for memberships is unclear).[20]

These plans raise questions about the sustainability of such a model. Can it be said, though, that a value vampire such as Napster ultimately "won"? It's the disruption, not the disruptor, that matters: it is unlikely that companies will collectively stop using analytics to wring margin out of prices (if anything, this seems sure to intensify), no matter what happens to Jet.com. Nonetheless, with this disruption, incumbents may be compelled to engage in a competitive "race to the bottom" that counts many among their number as collateral damage.

As we have seen, value vampires have the effect of permanently sucking profit margins dry, and often total revenues as well, with combinatorial disruption that is led by aggressive cost value. While the most commonly known value vampires stalk industries that serve consumers directly, bloodthirsty startups are making inroads into huge B2B markets too.

For example, logistics is a $4 trillion industry globally,[21] with several highly profitable sub-segments that are ripe for disruption. Predictably, investors have been pouring money into startups in this sector at an unprecedented rate. One of the biggest targets is freight forwarding, a $160 billion market with a few global players such as Kuehne + Nagel and DB Schenker, but which is otherwise highly fragmented.[22] Most freight forwarders do not ship goods themselves, but act as middlemen, coordinating shipments on behalf of their customers. As supply chains have become more international and complex, the role of freight forwarders has increased, but most rely on antiquated technology such as email, spreadsheets, and fax machines. It takes an average of three days for a company to get a quote from a freight forwarder, and the lack of competition and transparency means that companies pay high margins. *Ad hoc* shipments, which fall outside of normal shipping contracts and are often handled by freight forwarders, can account for under 1 percent of a company's shipping volume, yet total 30 percent of its shipping costs.[23]

An Israel-based disruptor called Freightos is using a Digital Marketplace business model to cut the costs of freight forwarding by making the process transparent and competitive. Freightos collects unstructured data on shipping costs from the Web, analyzes it, and condenses up to 20 different fees into a single quote, which includes optimal routing for the entire shipment. The entire process takes less than one minute. Costs are lower because multiple freight-forwarders compete for bids in a Reverse Auction model. In addition to lower costs and faster quotes, companies can use the Freightos platform to track their shipments as they change hands from forwarders, to airlines, and on to their final destination.

Freightos is an example of a potential value vampire using a combinatorial disruption of cost value, experience value, and platform value to suck margins from freight forwarding.* While value vampires do not need to provide platform value to disrupt a market, platforms that link two sides of a market (Digital Marketplace) and use data analytics to uncover opportunities (Data Orchestrator) can generate low costs value vampires need to displace incumbents, making the entire market less profitable.

The New Paranormal

The term value vampire is meant to be descriptive rather than pejorative. Whether value vampires are good for the economy overall is an interesting

---

* Another logistics startup, Transfix, which we touched on in Chapter 2, uses a similar business model to match truckers with empty trailers with goods that need to be moved, charging a 10 percent commission – far lower than traditional logistics firms. Source: "The Appy Trucker," *Economist*, March 5, 2016, economist.com/news/business/21693946-digital-help-hand-fragmented-and-often-inefficient-industry-appy-trucker

question. One school of thought is that they may help keep a lid on inflation by creating cost value (i.e., making products and services less expensive). The low interest rate environment of the last 20 years has resulted in two massive asset bubbles, wealth effects from appreciating stocks and real estate, and an upswing in consumer and business spending. These developments are arguably evidence of value vampires unlocking potential in the economy as a whole. Whether or not you accept the proposition that digital technologies are driving productivity, customers are undeniably realizing major value from digital disruption, especially in the form of lower costs. Therefore, the low levels of inflation we have enjoyed in recent decades may be attributable, at least in part, to cost value created by digital disruptors, some of whom exhibit "vampirish" tendencies.

Another school of thought is that value vampires are a bad thing. Their margin-compressing effects can lead not just to low levels of inflation, but also to debilitating deflation, especially in sectors beset by value vampires. This deflation constrains investment, compresses wages, slows economic growth, and results in structural unemployment, especially when market incumbents that employ a lot of people are displaced.

Value vampires can wring costs from products and services by eliminating layers of physical production, distribution, and overhead. In doing so, they also reduce the size of the industry ecosystem, as well as the number of companies that can profitably subsist on it.

Although we contend value vampires are unquestionably real (leaders discount their existence at their own peril), some observers might maintain they are a transitory phenomenon fueled by "easy money." When access to capital dries up, the thinking goes, the ability of digital disruptors to create new cost value, experience value, and platform value may diminish.

Earlier, we discussed how many advantages of incumbents flow from size – their balance sheets, number of customers, brand strength, and more. We pointed out, though, that disruptors can easily acquire these advantages of scale (citing examples of MyFitnessPal and SnapChat). Value vampires, on the other hand, are particularly pernicious for incumbents because they benefit from *diseconomies* of scale – meaning it is better to be small.

Value vampires do not need to capture all existing profits in a market. They need only enough margin (or equity proceeds) to make their owners and investors rich. Many startups would not think twice about wiping out a multibillion-dollar industry segment if it meant they themselves could make a few million dollars, either from cash flows or an IPO (in fact, many would argue this is the *raison d'être* of today's entrepreneur).

The question of whether these competitive dynamics can be sustained is, therefore, very different in this light. We noted earlier that for disruptors, it's the value, not the value chain. By the same token, for the incumbent, what matters is the disruption, not the disruptor. The ultimate fate of any one particular disruptor does not negate the competitive effects of the disruption. Indeed, today's digital disruptors could simply be a new incarnation of the famously unsound businesses of the dot-com epoch. Although shrewd incumbents can (and do) defeat digital disruptors, the revenue declines, margin compression, and customer flight that value vampires generate can make mere survival a challenge for many big players.

Most incumbents who have the misfortune of confronting a value vampire in their core business tend to acquire an unhealthy pallor. From there, they either die quickly or become the stumbling undead, never to regain their vitality. Customers are also unwilling to relinquish new forms of value, making it hard to put the vampire "back in the coffin."

Value Vacancies

For incumbents, digital disruption is not all bad news. In fact, as industries move toward the center of the Digital Vortex, another scenario may arise: the possibility of capitalizing on "value vacancies."

In the past, markets have presented instances of "white space" – situations in which competition lags behind opportunity; a firm could get a leg up on rivals or help create a new market. Traditionally, markets were neatly defined in a kind of mosaic of competition: this is what *we* do and how *our* market creates value for customers; that is what *you* do and how

Value Vacancy

A market opportunity that can be profitably exploited via digital disruption.

- Allows incumbents to go on offense; represents the upside of digital disruption for established players
- Can be in adjacent markets, entirely new markets, or digital enhancements to existing markets
- Tends to be temporary due to competitive dynamics of Digital Vortex (industry unbundling, recombination, exponential change), rather than long-lasting
- To occupy a value vacancy, incumbents must move rapidly and practice combinatorial disruption that creates customer value on multiple fronts

Figure 11: "Value Vacancies" Defined
Source: Global Center for Digital Business Transformation, 2015

your market creates value for customers. In this environment, the recipe for success was straightforward. Companies competed fiercely within contested markets, but could generate growth and boost profit margins by "seizing the white space,"[24] the gaps in the mosaic.

In the Digital Vortex, however, industries collide and recombine in new ways, yielding new competitive forms – and the rate of change increases exponentially as industries converge toward the center. The resulting landscape is less like a mosaic of clearly demarcated players and more like an ever-shifting kaleidoscope of forces. More (and more diverse) companies can vie for a given market opportunity. It is, therefore, dramatically harder to a) maintain one's position as an incumbent after seizing white space; and b) "see around corners" – i.e., predict what will happen and catch the resulting market transitions. In this environment, certainty is scarce.

In the chaotic swirling of the Digital Vortex, opportunities *do* emerge for savvy firms, but they can close quickly as fast-moving rivals join the pursuit and customer options proliferate. This is why we call such opportunities "value vacancies." A value vacancy is a market opportunity that can be profitably exploited via digital disruption (see Figure 11). Companies can enjoy a period of fast growth, high margins, and a privileged market position, but these are increasingly short-lived. Established competitors from other industries, startups, and value vampires soon intrude. To maintain growth, companies must find and exploit a succession of value vacancies.

If value vampires illustrate the threat posed by digital business models, value vacancies represent the upside. While incumbents react defensively to value vampires, they can go on the offensive to pursue value vacancies.

The ability to detect and occupy a value vacancy plays an enormous role in the success of an incumbent that finds itself in the center of the Digital Vortex. The industry unbundling and recombination characteristic of the Digital Vortex means many different types of firms, from many sectors, can pursue market opportunities and win the day. This is partly what makes value vampires scary – they can come after your market seemingly out of nowhere – but it's also what makes value vacancies so crucial to competitive success.

As with a hotel vacancy, would-be occupants of a value vacancy must recognize that the space is theirs on a temporary basis. Eventually, someone else will want the room. Unlike classical competitive constructs of white space, value vacancies are fleeting by their very nature. As Rita Gunther McGrath notes in her book *The End of Competitive Advantage*, managing amid perpetual change is a formidable task: "Basing your strategies on a new set of assumptions can seem daunting, even if you know it's the right thing to do. Even more challenging is shifting the ultimate goal of your strategy from a sustainable competitive advantage to a transient one – you can no longer plan to squeeze as much as you can out of any existing competitive advantage unless you are already well into exploring a new one."[25]

As noted, the competitive landscape of the Digital Vortex resembles a kaleidoscope of ever-changing pieces, rather than a stable mosaic. This aspect represents a corrective to a so-called "blue ocean strategy" approach in which innovators assume a level of incumbency that "makes the competition irrelevant."[26] Ideas such as "market boundaries" (the spaces between opportunities, firms, and their competitive positions) and "barriers to imitation" are less and less relevant.[27] As we described in Chapter 1, the advantages of incumbency – brand, balance sheet, and a big customer base – seem decidedly flimsy when digitization and re-combination of value chain components are so prevalent. Thanks to digital technologies such as open source software and cloud computing, firms of every size and from all geographies have access to innovation-creating capabilities and applications that were once the exclusive preserve of global multi-national corporations. This accelerates the rate of innovation in the Digital Vortex and shrinks the lifespan of value vacancies as competitive offerings can be formed, tested, and deployed at high speed.

Value vacancies are not necessarily competitive voids. They don't necessarily require fresh market formation, and can be found in adjacencies and digital enhancements to existing markets as well. Instead, they are best understood simply as opportunities to create new cost value, experience value, or platform value and extract competitive gains by exploiting digital tools and business models.

Like the most dangerous value vampires, companies must be well-versed in combinatorial disruption – using different digital technologies and business models to create new markets and synergies – in order to occupy value vacancies. Offering this level of customer value is often the price of dwelling in a value vacancy. We will discuss this idea in more detail in Chapter 4.

Apple: The Value Vacancy Expert

Previously, we highlighted Tesla as an exemplar of combinatorial disruption – one that leverages its innovative offerings in software and battery power to disrupt multiple industries. Indeed, Tesla is a great illustration of how to use digital technologies and business models to

	Business Model	Customer Value
Cost Value $	**Price Transparency:** Tough negotiations with music labels, which needed to monetize digital music **Consumption-based Pricing:** Paying only for what is used / consumed	Customers could pay only for the music they wanted (singles, albums) Digital music prices significantly lower than physical, even for full album
Experience Value	**Customer Empowerment:** Self-service **Instant Gratification:** Immediate gratification (immediate purchases) and music could be enjoyed anywhere (iPod, iPhone) **Customization / Automation:** Genius-created playlists automatically using analytics; suggests songs and artists for purchase on iTunes store that align with personal tastes **Reduced Friction:** Pay by entering Apple ID	iTunes and iPod / iPhone made it easy to obtain, organize, and consume music
Platform Value	**Communities:** Infinitely scalable one-to-many distribution model **Digital Marketplace:** Connected music buyers and labels / artists via an e-commerce platform	Customers could acquire a broad range of songs and albums, legally and with high file quality

Table 5: What You Want, Where and When You Want It
Source: Global Center for Digital Business Transformation, 2015

occupy value vacancies.* But, let's now consider another company famous for capturing new markets. It's not a "dorm room disruptor" like Napster, but a Fortune 500 company: Apple. Apple provides a clear example of how a large enterprise can be a disruptor, rather than the "disrupted."

---

* It's even better when you can persuade your customers to fund your pursuit of value vacancies. Tesla, in launching its Model 3, a mass-market addition to their existing line-up of high-end electric cars, received nearly 400,000 pre-orders within 10 days of unveiling the product. With a $1,000 deposit for each, this sum represents some $400 million in interest-free investment, and a pipeline of $14 billion in sales, despite the fact that many customers will not receive their cars until as late as 2020. See Katie Fehrenbacher, "Tesla's Model 3 Reservations Rise to Almost 400,000," *Fortune*, April 15, 2016, fortune.com/2016/04/15/tesla-model-3-reservations-400000

In 2010, Apple had become the world's largest retailer of recorded music.[28] A decade earlier, such a statement would have been unthinkable. The company wasn't even in the music business, and was viewed by some as a niche player in the technology industry.

Today, Apple is also a leading incumbent in the smartphone business, a market it revolutionized from the position of an outsider. Throughout the past decade and a half, Apple has shrewdly invested in cost value, experience value, and platform value in a synergistic way that protects its most prized profit pool: device hardware.

Apple cemented its position as a market leader in personal computing, not just by adding features and functionality to core products (Mac desktops and laptops), but by revolutionizing an entire category of computing: tablet devices. There's no need to revisit the meteoric rise of Apple under the leadership of Steve Jobs. Instead, let's consider Apple from the standpoint of how it has exploited value vacancies by returning to disruption in the recorded music business.

Apple astutely recognized that the music industry was ripe for disruption, not simply because incumbents were charging too much, but because they didn't sell music the way customers wanted to buy it – by the song and in a format that made it easy to listen wherever and whenever they wanted. The market had already undergone some early-stage disruption in the form of digitization and dematerialization (CDs, MP3 file format, P2P file-sharing), which suggested opportunities to create cost value, experience value, and platform value.

At its Macworld event in 2001, Apple introduced iTunes, ushering in a new phase of digital disruption. What was then a venue for digital music sales (added later were movies, television shows, books, and other categories) was not merely an e-commerce front-end. Apple created a digitally enabled ecosystem that monetized digital music and offered customers an integrated, elegant device (the iPod, and later the iPhone and iPad) on which to enjoy it, from any location. This ecosystem approach would prove instrumental in the company's ability to occupy future value vacancies, such as when the company introduced the App Store. Although iTunes didn't offer free music, it sold albums for less than CDs ($6.99 to $9.99), and unbundled songs from albums, selling them for 99 cents to $1.29 apiece.

iTunes also let customers organize their music and create their own "albums" with playlists. In subsequent years, it added analytics with Genius, which intelligently paired songs that go well together, based on data from millions of iTunes customers (i.e., platform value). Most important, iTunes assembled everything that music customers wanted to buy in a single online store. Customers could pay by entering their Apple ID, which was connected to a credit card, removing the "friction" of purchasing music from multiple sources. Apple combined digital music with a device that made it portable, along with a method for acquiring the music and organizing it. In the process, it seized a value vacancy that disrupted the physical music value chain. These developments dealt a crippling blow to incumbent consumer electronics firms and retailers.

Apple was able to move into a value vacancy in digital music distribution because it satisfied a market need that music labels and retailers had an interest in *not* meeting. If digital disruption means just one thing, it is the end of "artificial" revenue in which customers are forced to pay for things they don't value (see Table 5).

Apple's music sales have slowly but steadily declined over the past three years as the value vacancy it inhabited created a wave of new innovators. To fend off attackers such as Pandora and Spotify, Apple introduced its own streaming service, Apple Music, and a 24/7 radio service called Beats 1 to provide new sources of revenue (such as advertising) and create or extend cost value, experience value, and platform value for customers. [29] With Pandora and Spotify both threatening the music business in a way not seen since Napster (and iTunes), Apple – the music-industry incumbent – must respond. Winners in the Digital Vortex know they must constantly pursue and occupy value vacancies, lest they themselves face revenue stalls, margin compression, or obsolescence. Apple's 2014 announcements launching the Apple Watch and Apple Pay (even a rumored incursion into the automotive business)[30] are the latest in a series of strategic moves to continue investing in value vacancies and secure its position in the future.

House Hunters: Dollar Shave Club, WeChat, and GE

As with taxi companies, firms selling razor blades can be forgiven for believing, in years past, that they weren't on a high-velocity trajectory to the center of the Digital Vortex. Historically, the U.S. market has tended toward stability, dominated by two giants – Procter & Gamble (which owns the Gillette brand) and Schick, a division of Energizer Holdings. For its part, P&G *is* a world leader in using information technology to create business value. Its disruptive innovation processes have become leading case studies of business transformation.[31]

Today, however, several innovative companies are battling for the $3.3 billion U.S. men's grooming products market, and a major shake-up may be in the offing.[32] Dollar Shave Club is one disruptor challenging the U.S.

Gillette-Schick duopoly with a deft combination of cost value and experience value. Customers of Dollar Shave Club pay a monthly subscription price starting at $1 for the most basic option.[33] Instead of purchasing a pack of razors at a store – an experience that can be cumbersome and exasperating, as the products are often under lock and key – customers pay on a recurring basis to have razors delivered to their door.

The rapid success of Dollar Shave Club has caught the attention of analysts and investors, and the company was valued at over $615 million as of mid-2015.[34] More important, the business model that Dollar Shave Club has championed is rapidly winning market share. Dollar Shave Club now sells 8 percent of all razors sold in the United States, and similar models (such as Harry's) have grown from virtually zero in 2012. Already, Dollar Shave Club has reportedly supplanted Schick as the #2 razor blade manufacturer by market share in the U.S.[35]

Online razor sales are expected to increase by 25 percent per year for the next five years – an ascent that has caught P&G and Schick by surprise. As one P&G executive recently said, "The growth has been very significant, and consumers' needs and habits are changing."[36] The success of Dollar Shave Club further underscores the point that the physicality of a firm's products is no guarantee of safety. Digital disruption can impact all sectors.

As we saw with other value vacancies, the hunters are becoming the hunted. In response, P&G has introduced a Consumption-based Pricing model for buying razors[37] and has introduced new packaging to bring razors from behind locked counters,[38] in an effort to attack the value vacancy associated with subscription-driven purchasing of shaving products.*

WeChat, a mobile messaging app developed by Chinese social media giant Tencent, is used by 700 million people.[39] Sensing a value vacancy in the consumer financial services market, an industry completely different from its own, WeChat launched a new service to offer consumer loans via its app. The service, called Weilidai ("tiny loan"), lets users borrow up to 200,000 yuan ($31,350, a not-so-tiny sum) and receive approval within minutes.[40] Users provide their bank account information and other basic personal information, which Weilidai uses to assess creditworthiness, utilizing its own data and loan status information from the People's Bank of China.

The Weilidai service offers cost value by providing certain advantageous loan terms such as not requiring collateral. It offers

---

* As part of their strategic response, P&G has also filed suit against Dollar Shave Club: Paul Ziobro and Anne Steele, "P&G's Gillette Sues Dollar Shave Club," *Wall Street Journal*, December 17, 2015, wsj.com/articles/p-gs-gillette-sues-dollar-shave-club-1450371180

significant experience value because borrowers can pull out their phones, enter a few details, and obtain a loan in moments. There's no need to travel to a bank office, or even sit down in front of a computer. This is a much better experience for borrowers than the lengthy, paper-intensive process of obtaining a loan found in most Chinese financial institutions. Because the app integrates many other functions (such as messaging and e-commerce), users benefit from being part of a larger platform – a "one-stop shop."

In the longer term, WeChat's owner, Tencent, stands to benefit from the new offering by building relationships with consumers in the financial services arena. By gaining a foothold there, the company is in a position to cross more industry boundaries in the future.

Incumbents don't get any more entrenched – or encumbered – than GE, a 124-year-old conglomerate with businesses spanning industrial equipment, power generation, financial services, and durable consumer goods, among others. In the wake of the global financial crisis, GE's stock plunged to under $6, from a high of $60 in 2000.[41] GE was forced to seek FDIC protection for GE Capital, a former earnings machine and a heavyweight in commercial real estate debt; its portfolio took a beating. The company has also faced intense competition in its consumer appliances business. As a result, GE is shedding GE Capital's assets[42] and has sold its Appliances division to China's Haier[43] (see our discussion of GE's strategy in Chapter 4). In all, the company is exiting businesses that in 2015 brought in $19.6 billion in revenue, or nearly 17 percent of GE's total revenue.[44]

Such a massive divestment could turn into a damaging long-term revenue stall unless GE can move swiftly into growing markets. To this end the company jumped with both feet into a high-potential value vacancy – software that connects industrial equipment including jet engines, wind turbines, and plant-floor robots to the internet, and collects and analyzes the data they produce. GE calls this the "Digital Industrial" market. The company already has $5 billion in software revenue, and aspires to be a top 10 software company globally by 2020 on the strength of cloud-based IoT platforms such as GE Predix.[45]

Predix plans to become the biggest software platform for industrial equipment, just as iOS and Android are major software platforms for smartphones.[46] GE is using Predix to develop applications of all kinds to enhance the value of its products and to create new revenue streams. For example, GE is using Predix to help customers anticipate breakdowns and schedule proactive maintenance of GE equipment. GE is also using Predix to optimize the positioning of wind turbines in real-time, as conditions change (see Chapter 7). And using Predix, GE launched railroad applications such as GE Trip Optimizer that analyze data from hundreds of sensors on GE locomotives to automate speed and braking, helping them operate more efficiently and save fuel.[47]

GE is extending Predix to customers who build their own industrial equipment, selling it as a software platform instead of simply an "add on" attached to GE's equipment. Pitney Bowes, which manufactures and services high-volume mail equipment, uses Predix to avoid unscheduled shutdowns and improve the performance of its machines.[48] This strategy is putting GE in direct competition with tech titans such as Google and Amazon, and enterprise software firms including SAP and IBM, which also see IoT as a source of growth.[49] Whether GE successfully occupies this value vacancy remains to be seen. But Predix is exactly the type of offering the company needs to compete in this nascent market, and to pursue growth as it exits its traditional lines of businesses.

Chapter 4: Strategic Response Options

Competitive Strategies

When facing a digitally disruptive threat, many firms just freeze. They understand conventional competitors and are comfortable when operating in tough markets, but they do not know how to cope with new forms of competition or digitally enabled threats. We believe that a structured approach to facing digital disruption based on four competitive strategies – what we refer to as the "strategic response playbook" – is required. Two of these strategies are defensive (shown in Figure 12 on the left), and two are offensive (shown on the right). These strategies dictate how a firm creates new customer value through digital means and how to maximize revenues and profits from pre-disruption operating models (which can be substantial for many incumbents). *Defensive* strategies are used to fend off value vampires, as well as more modest threats, and to maximize the useful lifespan of the businesses under attack. *Offensive* strategies are those

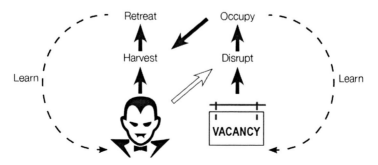

Retreat
A defensive strategy aimed at strategic withdrawal from threatened business segments

Harvest
A defensive strategy aimed at blocking disruptive threats and optimizing the performance of threatened business segments

Occupy
An offensive strategy aimed at sustaining the competitive gains associated with disruption

Disrupt
An offensive strategy aimed at disrupting one's own core business or creating new markets

Figure 12: Strategic Response Playbook
Source: Global Center for Digital Business Transformation, 2015

71

associated with the pursuit of a value vacancy. Companies can pivot from defensive to offensive strategies, an idea we explore in the following pages.

Harvest: Maximizing Value from Disrupted Businesses

When disruptive competitors menace a business, the appropriate strategy for incumbents can be **Harvest**. This is a defensive strategy designed to maximize gains from a declining business. Harvest strategies frequently begin with "blocking tactics," drawing on the benefits of incumbent status with customers, partners, regulators, opinion-makers, and providers of capital. These countermeasures are intended to slow a disruptive player or buy time for an incumbent to muster a fuller response. Tactics may include legal action to halt the disruptors' operations, marketing activities to challenge disruptor claims, or the use of financial resources to undercut disruptor pricing. (Note: this gambit can sometimes backfire, hastening margin decline). Rarely, however, do such blocking tactics thwart the disruption entirely.

A Harvest strategy tries to make the best of a bad situation, optimizing the margin that can be extracted during the period of decline. It involves significant organizational reconfiguration to adapt the business to this new reality – reconfiguration that may include: consolidation of operations; cost optimization and streamlining of processes; stepping down production; locking in loyal or dependent customer segments; emphasizing quality and brand equity in marketing; and pruning portfolio elements that no longer contribute enough to value creation. The strategy is executed through a series of moves that yield competitive ground intelligently. In other words, a territory isn't ceded until the company passes the point at which the costs of maintaining that component outweigh the financial or strategic benefits. "Digital," therefore, plays an important role in Harvest – not just in sparking disruption, but also in mounting a strong defense (such as driving the increased efficiencies required in Harvest).

Unfortunately, most incumbents are bad at Harvest strategies, and one of the biggest reasons is that they require the firm to acknowledge that a given business is in decline. As a rule, companies are reluctant to admit this because it conjures up images of organizational demise. No executive relishes the idea of presiding over a company's "sunset" phase. For many, doing so suggests a breakdown in leadership or vision, the very things they are expected to provide. Financial markets may also punish incumbents perceived as entering a Harvest period because investors often interpret this as a signpost of coming hardship. This in turn hardens resistance.

Harvest shouldn't be equated with failure. It's a natural progression of a mature business confronting commoditization, customer attrition, margin compression, and other unpleasantness arising from digital disruption. Leaders who are clear-sighted enough to accept this are best positioned to steer their organizations through the transition.

Digital disruption is painful and frequently irreversible. The disruption we see in the Digital Vortex doesn't typically allow an incumbent to "weather the storm," as it might with a recession, a botched product launch, or negative press coverage. This is especially so in the case of value vampires, the most extreme and ruinous form of disruptor. Value vampires introduce so much value for customers that buyer expectations for this value become hard-wired, eliminating the possibility of returning to the competitive hierarchy of yesteryear. Incumbents can prevail, but not by battening down the hatches and doing what they were doing before.

Most observers would not consider Netflix an incumbent. In fact, the company is often viewed as the quintessential digital disruptor. That being said, Netflix *does* have a mature, declining business that has been disrupted: mail-order DVD subscriptions.

Streaming video – a disruption Netflix has helped make ubiquitous – is growing impressively. In January 2016, streaming customers stood at 75 million, spanning more than 190 countries, virtually everywhere but China. At the same time, the company's DVD-by-mail offering still serves more than 4.9 million members in the United States, generating $80 million in profit (or 23 percent of the U.S. total) in Q4 FY2015.[1]

To maximize the margins it can garner (DVD subscriptions peaked at 20 million in 2010, and declined 18 percent in the latest fiscal year), Netflix undertook a Harvest strategy by introducing multiple efficiencies to the management of its legacy business, including streamlining and automating warehouse operations. Some of these steps were detailed in an article in *The New York Times* about the company's Fremont, California, distribution center: "About 3,400 discs zip through the rental return machine each hour, five times as many as when teams of Netflix employees used to process the discs by hand. Called the Amazing Arm by engineers here, the machine symbolizes the way Netflix has managed to maintain a profitable physical DVD operation even as it transforms itself into a global streaming service."[2]

It's vital to understand, however, that Harvest is not the only response available to incumbents when confronting a threat in the Digital Vortex. Incumbents can go on the offensive, fighting disruption with disruption (see "Disrupt" strategies below).

Harvesting and disrupting in tandem is a delicate maneuver. Research we have conducted on the manufacturing sector reveals that the complexity associated with such a "two-front war" is the single greatest inhibitor for manufacturers attempting to transition from mature product-centric lines of business to higher-growth service-oriented revenues.[3] This occurrence is common in organizations seeking to protect legacy revenue streams while launching disruptive new businesses. Cannibalizing the existing business is sometimes a risk. Beyond this complexity, organizations must carefully weigh competing investments in Harvest and Disrupt strategies, and assess where resources can be most profitably deployed.

Harvest: Questions for Leaders

- Which blocking tactics can help us slow down disruptors?
- Which elements of the disrupted business represent sustainable profit pools?
- What can we learn from the disruptors to help us improve our current business?
- Which steps should be taken to reconfigure the organization so that we can adapt to the new competitive reality?
- Should we pivot from Harvest to Disrupt (see below) and then go on the offensive?
- When and how fast should we consider Retreat? (see below)

Retreat: Strategic Withdrawal

Harvest is about improving customer experiences and operational efficiency in threatened segments, but when the costs of maintaining a business clearly outstrip the benefits, companies should focus on **Retreat**. This strategy emphasizes withdrawal into a market niche that serves a small subset of existing customers with specialized needs. Usually, the niche is a market that the incumbent has dominated in the past and, in most cases, is expert in managing for profitability. The niche market often requires the creation of a level of experience value (especially Customization) that is unappetizing for disruptors to pursue.

As with Harvest, Retreat strategies are not always a sign of failure. In fact, they can allow a company to take advantage of new value vacancies that will replace the revenue streams coming to an end, and where returns on capital are stronger. Retreat strategies are different from Harvest because they mostly denote "wrapping up" the core business, rather than expending the firm's energies and resources on "wringing out" remaining value. With Retreat, the market opportunity has essentially been exhausted, and only a niche profit pool remains.

Kodak provides an interesting example of a Retreat strategy. The rise and fall of Kodak as a photography giant is well known. At its height, the company was a revenue and profit powerhouse and a leading global brand commanding a dominant presence in many of its markets. The common understanding is that digital killed the company. However, this is not completely true. Kodak still exists, albeit in a much smaller and more specialized form. Today, Kodak operates mainly as a B2B provider of high-end imaging solutions. For example, the company provides the film stock for many Hollywood movies.

There are many similar examples in industries one might assume have been completely disrupted. Specialized travel agents, for example, still profitably focus on complicated itineraries and/or corporate markets. A number of companies are now producing and selling vinyl records. It may come as a surprise that, in the U.S. in 2015, vinyl records were the music industry's *fastest*-growing segment (double the rate of growth in streaming) and accounted for nearly half a billion dollars in sales. [4] Some taxi companies are moving into specialized areas, such as secure transportation, which is difficult for Uber or other ride-sharing companies to manage. Retreat opportunities clearly abound. However, for an incumbent, pursuing a niche strategy almost always results in a line of business that is significantly smaller than before.

Retreat strategies also encompass market exit, where no further value can be created in excess of cost, or where continued allocation of capital is obviously unattractive. Finding the right time to exit a market segment can be a very important decision. Too early, and you risk leaving money on the table. Too late, and the value has disappeared. As noted in Chapter 3, GE has made a dramatic change of strategic direction toward what it calls the "Digital Industrial" market. In making this move, the company decided that parts of the organization that did not fit the new focus would have to be transformed or sold. As part of this transformation, GE pledged to divest more than US$200 billion of assets, including its NBCUniversal news and entertainment properties, its consumer appliances business, and what many considered the firm's crown jewel, GE Capital. [5] For many observers, the sale of GE Capital is an especially radical move. For decades, GE Capital had been a key growth and profit engine for the company. Yet, selling GE Capital while it has a high valuation could prove to be a clever and prescient move.

Harvest and Retreat are both defensive approaches designed to adapt an organization to changing marketplaces and digital disruption. To take advantage of value vacancies, and find growth that can offset declines in disrupted businesses, organizations need to go on the offensive.

Retreat: Questions for Leaders

- What are the opportunity costs (strategic and financial) of continuing Harvest-oriented investments?
- Are there profitable niche markets we can enter that disruptors will find it hard to compete in?
- Does a viable legacy business remain?
- Should we divest of the legacy business?
- How should we divest (consolidate, sell, or shutter)?
- What learnings can be gleaned to drive new business (i.e., find value vacancies)?

Disrupt: New Customer Value through Digital Means

When a value vacancy is detected, companies should pursue a *Disrupt* strategy. Disrupt strategies focus on creating cost value, experience value, and platform value for customers (ideally all three) using digital technologies and business models. This involves a thorough analysis of evolving customer needs; consideration of competitor capabilities and moves; and a critical examination of organizational readiness to pursue the opportunity.

Disrupt is about finding new ways to create the three forms of value in order to alter competitive dynamics. In Chapter 2, we outlined 15 disruptive business models that give rise to cost value, experience value, and platform value. These business models provide a guide to the customer value creation needed for a Disrupt strategy.

Disrupt strategies depend on a rich sense of the business environment to understand:

- Where costs (prices) are headed
- Current state of customer experiences, and options for improving them (increasing personalization, convenience, control, speed)
- How stakeholders in and around the market – customers, partners, employees, third-party contributors – are currently connected (or not), and how platforms could bring about new or more value-adding connections

As we have stressed, digital disruption is about the value, not the value chain. Companies pursuing Disrupt strategies must step outside their roles as providers and consider the market through the eyes of the customer, focusing on outcomes instead of inputs.

As bad as companies are at Harvest, most incumbents are even worse at Disrupt. The essential problem is that the strategic advantages that made incumbents successful serve them poorly in creating and capitalizing on disruptive innovations. For this reason, many incumbents do little to pursue value vacancies without prodding. According to our own research, just one in four companies is aiming to be a disruptor itself. Hence, reactive implementation of Disrupt strategies, in which the incumbent seeks to copy or outmaneuver a disruptor in response to threats, tends to be the norm. Proactive attempts at large-scale disruption by incumbents targeting value vacancies appear to be less common, which may not serve incumbents well in the Digital Vortex.

Disrupt strategies also tend to flounder when incumbents make ill-advised acquisitions in an attempt to reposition themselves, often with great fanfare, as innovators in a new market space. These acquisitions may actually accelerate competitive decline if they are strategically flawed or poorly integrated (or both). Disrupt strategies undertaken as long-shot curatives for mismanaged or moribund business lines are usually doomed from the start. Even prudent acquisitions often fail, when an incumbent lacks the pre-established processes, systems, and skills necessary to adapt to changing commercial priorities.

There is no one-size-fits-all model for Disrupt. Some incumbents find success in acquisitions, some in joint ventures, and some in a "newco" spinoff or spin-in. Others act as venture capitalists themselves, creating a portfolio of investments that can incubate innovations for their advantage.

Combinatorial disruption – creating cost value, experience value, and platform value simultaneously – heightens the challenges of succeeding at Disrupt strategies. Cost value and experience value, for example, have generally been conceived as competing alternatives. As we have shown, however, digital disruptors smash this paradigm. Most incumbents grew up in a world where you primarily do one or the other, and trying to do both is a recipe for dilettantism and decline. Platform value formation is also mysterious to incumbents, as many of them have built-in incentives to perpetuate traditional, non-platform modes of interaction and commerce.

Disrupt: Questions for Leaders

- How can we create new forms of cost value, experience value, and/or platform value for customers?
- Can we create combinatorial disruption that is even more compelling, i.e. can we disrupt the disruptor?

- What is the return on investment (including the risk of cannibalizing existing businesses) of the disruption, and does it outweigh competing Harvest-oriented moves?

Occupy: Prolonging Time in a Value Vacancy

Where Disrupt represents catalytic activities that introduce market disruption, **Occupy** strategies focus on sustaining the competitive gains associated with that disruption. Occupy rejects the Silicon Valley trope of "build it and they will come," and is premised on the reality that the company that introduces a disruption may not end up winning in the end. Instead, it recognizes that value vacancies are fiercely contested market opportunities, often marked by increasing customer choice, and that maximizing the upside from these opportunities requires a deliberate strategy to extend the disruption and prolong the longevity of the company's standing in the value vacancy. It is, therefore, the key component of competition and growth in the Digital Vortex.

As with Harvest and Disrupt, incumbents also typically struggle with Occupy strategies. When people speak about the challenges incumbents face in "becoming disruptors," they're often referring to their inability to succeed with Occupy strategies. Here, the problem is that the incumbent is frequently on unfamiliar terrain. As noted earlier, value vacancies can be born of market adjacencies, new market creation, or digital enhancements to existing markets. In all three cases, the incumbent is operating in *terra incognita* – a land where managers and individual contributors have built no rules of the road, no tried-and-true approaches, no go-to mental models, no coping mechanisms, or other organizational behaviors that have historically led to success. Because Occupy involves managing the "new" part of the business, it's often afflicted by the complexity challenges described above, when companies attempt to manage declining businesses (Harvest, Retreat) and growing businesses (Disrupt, Occupy) at the same time.

Because value vacancies have a limited shelf life, occupiers typically find that insurgents sooner or later assail the market opportunity, and introduce competitive forms of cost value, experience value, or platform value. As the value vacancy matures or is itself disrupted, companies must shift from an offensive footing in Occupy to a defensive Harvest strategy in order to maximize revenue and profits.

KONE, a Finnish manufacturer and servicer of elevators and escalators, is probably not the first company that comes to mind when one thinks of digital. Its products move people in a distinctly mechanical, non-digital way. In 2015 KONE, like many companies, faced a growing set of strategic and tactical challenges, such as low-cost competition from China, and a slowdown in new construction in many countries and regions. None of these challenges was particularly digital in nature, but dig a little deeper and digital opportunities and threats emerge.

For example, technology companies such as IBM, Toshiba, Honeywell, and Samsung were seeking to disrupt the construction industry by building smart cities, communities, and buildings. As part of this change, they were digitally connecting infrastructure, including elevators and escalators. Facilities management companies were taking on increasing responsibility for the maintenance of building infrastructure through digital enablement. Elevators and escalators were becoming connected devices that could be monitored, assessed, serviced, and repaired remotely. KONE was aware that these shifts created a number of value vacancies and, as a result, saw digital as a key to future revenue and profit streams in its new equipment, modernization, and maintenance business lines.

KONE realized that it could not occupy the value vacancies or respond to the threats alone. It needed a partner. So, in February of 2016, the company announced a strategic partnership with IBM to jointly develop and deploy cloud services, connected devices, and advanced analytics technologies.[6] KONE's CEO Henrik Ehrnrooth said, "We operate in a connected world and by working with IBM, new solutions like improved remote diagnostics and predictability means we will deliver better services for our customers and great experiences for the people who use our equipment." For KONE, the battle to occupy newly created digital value vacancies required a different approach: to cooperate with an organization that could otherwise have become a powerful competitor.

Occupy: Questions for Leaders

- How do we differentiate our disruptive offering and extend the cost value, experience value, and platform value it delivers for customers?
- Should we build, buy, or partner to occupy the new value vacancy?
- How do we use platforms to create scale?
- Can we erect barriers (e.g., platform status, intellectual property protections) that can inhibit competitors?
- Is the value vacancy reaching maturity, making it necessary to transition to Harvest?
- What learnings can be gleaned to drive new business (i.e., additional value vacancies)?

Occupy Case Study: A Tale of Three Incumbents

Let's take a closer look at Occupy, a strategy that should be top of mind for executives in the Digital Vortex. In particular, let's drill down on three approaches to Occupy – build, buy, and partner – and how they are playing out in the financial services industry, a sector that our research rated as one of the most likely to be significantly disrupted in the next five years.

Investment management is a key pillar of both growth and profitability for incumbent financial institutions. Globally, professionally managed assets have reached more than $74 trillion in value, with profits cresting the $100 billion mark.[7] Accordingly, banks, insurers, securities firms, and financial advisors covet investment clients, especially high net-worth and so-called "mass affluent" customers, and fees for providing advice. To the chagrin of most incumbents, the phenomenon of the "robo-advisor" – digital disruptors that use algorithms to automatically manage money without human advisors – has emerged as a viable alternative for hundreds of thousands of investors, jeopardizing a crucial source of revenue. The robo-advisor is the disruption, and now the battle is on for occupation of this new value vacancy.

Companies including Betterment, FutureAdvisor, and Wealthfront have headed a pack of disruptors looking to attack the value chain of incumbent firms. The robo-advisor's business model introduces value for investors in a combinatorial way. First, the model creates cost value by eliminating high fees for investment advice. It charges a small fee as a percentage of assets under management, generally in line with banks' lowest-price investment vehicles (such as index funds). Second, it delivers experience value to clients by reducing the burden of managing their portfolio – "set it and forget it."[8] Experience value is also delivered through, among other things, automatic rebalancing of portfolios and dividend reinvestment.

No one yet knows whether robo-advisors are, in fact, value vampires with a competitive advantage that will shrink the overall market. So far, they have not. It's perfectly conceivable that robo-advisors are not value vampires at all. It's possible that robo-advisors could render the provision of financial advice to underserved markets more economical, and even grow the total pie. In the short term, however, there is a very real risk that the disruption they represent will erode a bedrock business for incumbents: analysts project robo-advisor assets under management will grow to as much as $450 billion by 2020.[9] Although this is a relatively small slice of the multi-trillion-dollar global asset management business, robo-advisors' business models have grabbed the attention of incumbents.

The severity of the disruption posed by robo-advisors has been a source of debate, but there is consensus among industry observers that elements of the model – analytics and automation, for example – are likely to persist and find their way into the mainstream delivery of financial advice. The robo-advisor disruption also presents an interesting case study of Occupy strategies for incumbents. Let's now examine how three different incumbents in investment management – Charles Schwab, BlackRock, and Fidelity – have pursued three different versions of Occupy strategies – build, buy, and partner, respectively – to deal with the threat posed by robo-advisors.

Charles Schwab: Build

In the 1970s, the Charles Schwab Corporation emerged as the first major discount brokerage. By the 1990s, it was at the forefront of electronic trading. Now the threat posed by robo-advisors has spurred Schwab to take action again. In October 2014, the company announced the planned launch of Schwab Intelligent Portfolios, its own version of a robo-advisor service. Unlike the models of smaller disruptive rivals, Schwab Intelligent Portfolios charges no fees. According to the company, "Schwab Intelligent Portfolios is an automated investment advisory service. This sophisticated technology builds, monitors, and rebalances your portfolio – so you don't have to. And, Schwab Intelligent Portfolios doesn't charge advisory fees, commissions, or account service fees."[10] After its first full quarter of marketing Intelligent Portfolios, Schwab reported that the service had 39,000 accounts and some $3 billion in assets.[11]

By eliminating fees, the company is creating new cost value for customers. By offloading responsibility to monitor markets and rebalance investments, Schwab is removing inconveniences and adding intelligence, two components of new experience value that disruptors have used to great effect. And using the Apple App Store and Google Play as channels for customers to sign up makes it easy to join, rather than having to endure the frustrating, paper-based sign-up processes typical of most investment managers.

Schwab has also introduced a version of the offering that it markets to the more than 7,000 registered investment advisors (RIAs) in its custodial network; in six short months, more than 500 signed on.[12] A recent article in *Investment News* noted the application "will be customizable for advisors, who can use it to create their own investment strategies and add their own logos to the interface."[13] When the disruption extends to "enablement" of a channel or customer segment in this way, we can say that the obvious cost value and experience value improvements associated with robo-advisors are now accompanied by platform value as well, further amplifying the effects of combinatorial disruption.

Schwab Intelligent Portfolios illustrates one approach to Occupy strategies: *build*. Here, Schwab is using its incumbent status as a competitive sword rather than a shield – a great example of a market leader pivoting from defense to offense when confronted with disruption.

In addition, Schwab is clearly looking at the implications for its existing advisory businesses. When launching Intelligent Portfolios, CEO Walter Bettinger unflinchingly said, "We've never been afraid to cannibalize parts of our business historically." But he added, "That said, this is a very different solution for clients than the majority of our other relationship-intensive advisory solutions. We believe to a great extent it will appeal to people who are less interested in a relationship-driven model than our other solutions."[14]

Schwab will need to manage legacy advisory businesses alongside disruptive plays like Intelligent Portfolios. It's clear, though, that Schwab's strategy is to undercut disruptive players – to beat them at their own cost-value game by eliminating fees and tying off other key profit pools so they aren't infected by the disruption. By compartmentalizing in this way, Schwab can maximize value from its diversified portfolio of businesses. This also puts disruptors on their heels, as they now must attempt to move from Disrupt to Occupy.

BlackRock: Buy

Schwab's build model for dealing with the robo-advisor disruption is one approach. Another incumbent has a different take on Occupy: *buy*.

BlackRock, Inc., a subsidiary of bank holding company PNC Financial, is the largest investment manager in the world, serving corporations, governments, pension funds, and individual investors, with more than $4.6 trillion in assets under management.[15]

In August 2015, the company announced the acquisition of robo-advisor FutureAdvisor, a venture-backed startup managing $600 million in assets.[16] FutureAdvisor is being integrated into BlackRock's investment and risk management division, BlackRock Solutions, which will market the service to banks, insurers, and other investment advisors who want to include robo-advice in their offerings.

Without commenting on the merits of the BlackRock case, the "buy" approach can be especially appealing for incumbents who don't have the right DNA to incubate and launch disruptions in-house. Keeping pace with the rapid evolution of digital technology, moreover, can make acquisitions of disruptors attractive to incumbents, a point reportedly made by BlackRock's leadership at the time of the FutureAdvisor purchase.[17]

BlackRock acquired FutureAdvisor for $152 million.[18] In a release announcing the purchase, BlackRock referred to the financial cost of the acquisition as "not material to BlackRock's earnings per share,"[19] evidence that disruptive innovations can be brought into the business from outside at a price that, for a goliath like BlackRock (even at an estimated 50-times-revenue multiple), is palatable.[20] In absorbing a "mere" $600 million in assets, the FutureAdvisor move appears to be motivated by digital technology and speed, more so than customer accounts.

It's worth noting that the FutureAdvisor business will be embedded within BlackRock Solutions, the company's B2B arm, in what BlackRock refers to as the "analytical core of the firm."[21] By marketing the robo-advisor service to advisors and financial institutions, BlackRock is turning the disruptive threat to advice for individual investors (B2C) on its head – "out-commoditizing the robo-advisor commoditization."[22]

In essence, the company is making the robo-advisor platform a distribution channel that can grow one of its most strategic businesses, BlackRock iShares, a family of ETFs sold through the advisor channel the company is enabling with its robo-advisor tool.

Fidelity Investments: Partner

Finally, let's review a third approach to Occupy – *partner* – through the lens of another investment management incumbent.

With assets under management in excess of $2 trillion, Fidelity Investments is a leader in multiservice investment management, with lines of business in mutual funds, retirement planning, wealth management, discount brokerage, securities execution and clearance, and insurance.[23]

In October 2014, Fidelity entered into a strategic alliance with Betterment. As of April 2016, the latter stood as the top pure-play robo-advisor in total assets, at $3.9 billion.[24] The partnership allowed Fidelity Institutional Wealth Services (IWS) to "white label" Betterment's advisor-facing offering, Betterment Institutional, to the nearly 10,000 advisory firms that work with Fidelity. Fidelity and Betterment positioned the offering as a hybrid of human advisor and technology – a way to make advisor practices more efficient and effective. This enabled them to acquire and onboard clients (especially younger investors with lower asset levels), and allows advisors to focus on high-touch client work such as trusts or inheritances.[25]

One month later, in November 2014, Fidelity partnered with yet another disruptive player, LearnVest. [26] (LearnVest was subsequently snapped up by another incumbent, Northwestern Mutual, in March 2015).[27] Fidelity's tie-ups with robo-advisors and other FinTechs represent the partner approach to incumbents' Occupy strategies – the idea that, as one wry observer put it, "If you can't beat the robots, join them."[28] For Fidelity, the ability to create cost value, experience value, and platform value by leveraging the disruptors' own momentum was compelling.

Partner strategies can also serve as a Petri dish for Disrupt and Occupy strategies, which may then be ported to a build model in which the incumbent develops a disruptive offering with its own resources when it believes the time is right. Michael Durbin, president of Fidelity IWS, explained the possibility of converting from partner to build: "We have a front-row seat on what the market is looking for, and we're monitoring it very quickly to see what we could do on a proprietary basis. The market should not be surprised if we serve up these capabilities more natively through time."[29] Indeed, in November 2015, the company announced it was piloting a new service, Fidelity Go, which provides automated advice.[30]

Incumbents may use build, buy, or partner approaches to weaken upstart rivals in the longer term. There may also be more market consolidation ahead, as we have seen with BlackRock's purchase of FutureAdvisor, and with acquisitive moves into the space by incumbents such as Northwestern Mutual and others. On the other hand, the proliferation of robo-advisors by incumbents may actually create market acceptance and uplift for disruptors such as Betterment and Wealthfront. No matter how it evolves, the investment management sector is sure to be a competitive crucible of digital disruption effects.

Forms of Customer Value and Strategic Responses

How do cost value, experience value, and platform value figure into the strategic response playbook? Let's consider each strategy in turn to understand which forms of value must be prioritized (see Figure 13).

When a disruptive threat emerges and a company enters Harvest mode, cost value and experience value are primary considerations. Companies must ratchet down costs to make their offerings as competitive as possible, while stressing quality of experience to encourage customers to remain loyal.

When the market declines past a certain juncture, companies shift to Retreat, which entails continued cost-cutting, but especially experience value-oriented enhancements that preserve differentiation in the eyes of remaining customers. These customers often have highly specialized needs, which should be cultivated by the company as it retreats into serving them as a niche market. In the case of both defensive strategies – Harvest and Retreat – platform value creation is unusual.

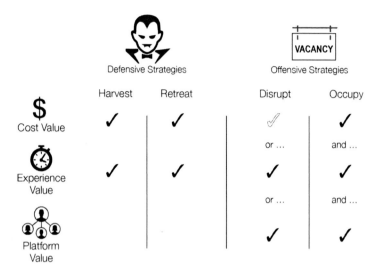

Figure 13: Forms of Customer Value by Strategy
Source: Global Center for Digital Business Transformation, 2015

A Disrupt strategy may be dominated by one form of value, with support from another. For example, as with Uber, the strategy may be based on a significantly better experience at a comparable or lower cost. Or, it may be based on a good-enough experience at a radically lower cost, such as Skype for voice calling or WhatsApp for text messaging. The role of cost value depends to some degree on the starting point – whether a Disrupt strategy is employed by an incumbent in response to a threat or is a proactive move to initiate a new market disruption. If the former, there may be greater emphasis placed on cost value to challenge the upstart competitor directly, potentially outlasting the foe because of the comparative strength of the incumbent's balance sheet. If the latter, cost value is unlikely to be a chief component – rarely does an incumbent disrupt itself of its own volition by creating widespread cost value for customers.

Whereas Disrupt strategies can come about via the introduction of just one form of customer value, Occupy typically requires all three. With Occupy, companies find themselves in an all-out war to win the value vacancy, and practicing combinatorial disruption spanning all three forms of customer value is frequently the necessary standard to compete. Platform value is the key differentiator, as it helps establish longer-term "tenancy" in value vacancies by raising (but not eliminating) barriers to market entry, creating "stickiness" for participants, and providing the basis for ancillary revenues that leverage the platform.

Vampires Killed the Revenue Source

The strategies outlined in this playbook are designed to be used repeatedly. A company will not permanently occupy one value vacancy, and if it's successful, it will not be relegated to living out its remaining days in a marginalized state as a result of Retreat. Instead, the company must progress through these strategies again and again over time, extracting revenue and profit at each step. There's plenty of opportunity available in the Digital Vortex. The question for business leaders is how much of that opportunity their firms will capture.

Let's then consider how these strategies intersect with some of the competitive dynamics we have described, again returning to the evolution of the recorded music business. In Chapter 3, we discussed digital disruption in the music industry, which began with the digitization of music and Napster's free download service. As we saw, Napster caused the initial disruption, but when it was shut down by the music industry in a classic "blocking tactic," there was a vacuum in the market. Consumers clearly wanted to download music files. While many flocked to illegal torrent sites such as Pirate Bay, Apple bet that millions were willing to pay what they considered a reasonable price to legally own good quality music files. The success of iTunes proved they were right.

Thus, while Napster caused disruption in the music industry, it was unable to occupy the value vacancy of digital distribution. Apple, with its combination of intuitive hardware and software and the platform value derived from agreements with most major labels and artists, was the successful occupier. The difference between disrupting a market and occupying it is critical for companies to understand. The firms that occupy value vacancies excel at combinatorial disruption, especially the ability to pair rapid scaling (platform value) with a business model that generates sufficient revenue and profit margin, while undercutting competitors (cost value). Apple did this, making iTunes the dominant force in digital music sales.

To Apple's consternation, but to the delight of music fans, the Digital Vortex did not stop spinning. Apple had what, in the pre-Digital Vortex era, would have been nearly insurmountable advantages, including a virtual distribution platform that had nearly 900 million customers*(iTunes), and tight integration with mobile devices (the iPod, then the iPhone) with well over 1 billion cumulative unit sales.[†]

But streaming music services such as Pandora and Spotify have disrupted iTunes with services that bear the marks (if you will) of value vampires. In the U.S. alone, music streams doubled in 2015 to over 317 billion songs.[31] Both services offer unlimited access to music for free for customers willing to listen to ads, with higher quality, premium access for about $10 per month – the cost of buying 10 songs on iTunes. The vast majority choose the free, ad-supported option.[‡]

Though consumers like to stream music, they don't want to pay a subscription fee: 78 percent of U.S. consumers say they are "unlikely" to do so because the availability of free services makes $10 per month seem expensive by comparison.[32] This raises the question of how much lost revenue Apple can truly recoup even if it can catch market leader Spotify in adoption. The entire arc of disruption in the music business shows us the relentless pressure on companies to innovate, to find value vacancies, and to occupy them. Even when incumbents succeed in fending off value vampires – Apple won an initial round only – revenues do not rebound. Companies must be positioned for the next big thing. It also shows the movement toward a "zero marginal cost"[33] end-state in offerings that can readily be digitized.

Let's now look at Apple's response to the streaming music disruption through the lens of our strategic response playbook. Apple opted for a multi-pronged approach:

Harvest: Apple is maximizing revenue from its declining iTunes business by integrating it with Apple Music, its new streaming offering (see below).

---

* In September 2014, iTunes had 885 million iTunes accounts. Source: Yoni Heisler, "Bono Talks 885 Million iTunes Accounts, New Music Format, and 'Haters'," *Engadget*, September 22, 2014, engadget.com/2014/09/22/bono-talks-885-million-itunes-accounts-new-music-format-and-sa/

† As of October 2015, Apple has sold over 400 million iPods. Source: Sam Costello, "This Is the Number of iPods Sold All-Time," *About.com*, October 13, 2015, ipod.about.com/od/glossary/qt/number-of-ipods-sold.htm
The company has sold nearly 822 million iPhones as of the second quarter of 2015. Source: Evan Niu, "How Many iPhones Has Apple Sold?" *Motley Fool*, November 14, 2015, fool.com/investing/general/2015/11/14/iphones-sold.aspx?source=isesitlnk0000001

‡ For example, only 5 percent of Pandora listeners are paid subscribers. Source: Trevis Team, "Why the Subscription Business Is Important for Pandora and Where Is It Going?" *Forbes*, September 4, 2015, forbes.com/sites/greatspeculations/2015/09/04/why-the-subscription-business-is-important-for-pandora-and-where-is-it-going/#4e3a4a0265ce

A good Harvest strategy can help a company maintain a profitable business even as demand declines. In fact, 2014 was the first year that digital music sales actually outstripped physical CD sales. * And, according to PricewaterhouseCoopers, digital downloads are forecast to decrease by 10 percent per annum between 2015 and 2019,[34] unquestionably a marked decline, but enough for Apple still to milk millions from the business before shifting to Retreat.

Disrupt: Even in the jaws of value vampires, music is an extremely important business for Apple. Apple still makes billions from music downloads, and has every interest in preserving this revenue. While streaming services make music more device-agnostic than ever, requiring just an app and a broadband connection, Apple would not give up the tie between music and mobile devices without a fight. iTunes has been critical to the success of Apple's hardware business, in terms of both the number of units sold and the profit margin.

Apple passes 65 percent of the revenues from iTunes sales to content owners,[35] while selling songs for 65 or 99 cents. When asked years ago why Apple did not try to charge more per song, Steve Jobs said, "Because we're selling iPods."[36] In the notoriously competitive consumer device market, Apple was able to sell iPods for $399 – far more than the competition – and reap a 30 percent profit margin.[37] In fact, digital content from iTunes has been called "the mortar in Apple's financial empire" because it defines the user experience and keeps customers coming back, device after device.[38] In short, iTunes makes Apple hardware more valuable, and has been integral to its corporate strategy.[39] Platforms provide a valuable foundation on which to build ancillary (or, in the case of Apple, core) revenues. In some instances, the platform business itself may serve as a loss leader.

Although the size of the music industry pie was shrinking,† Apple wasn't content with a Harvest play by itself, and opted to take up the high-stakes challenge presented by streaming music value vampires to create still more cost value, experience value, and platform value for customers. This

---

* As we have noted, this is primarily because consumers have adopted free streaming services, and largely stopped paying for music. See Ethan Smith, "Music Services Overtake CDs for First Time," *Wall Street Journal*, April 14, 2015, wsj.com/articles/digital-music-sales-overtake-cds-for-first-time-1429034467

† Global music revenues are still in decline, accounting for under $15 billion in 2015 after reaching a peak of $28.6 billion in 1999, and global digital music sales – downloads and streaming – amount to $6.85 billion. *Recording Industry in Numbers 2015*, International Federation of the Phonographic Industry (IFPI) ifpi.org/news/IFPI-publishes-Recording-Industry-in-Numbers-2015

amounted to disrupting itself, and (presumably) knowingly accelerating the demise of iTunes – a move that would have been inconceivable just five years earlier.

In June 2015, Apple launched its own streaming service, Apple Music.[40] By January 2016, it had 11 million paid subscribers, less than half of Spotify's 30 million,[41] but it acquired them in just seven months.[42]

Occupy: Since deciding to fight value vampires, Apple is battling fiercely to occupy the market. Apple is trying to attract paid subscribers to Apple Music through exclusive releases* and over 10,000 playlists that have been curated by musicians, DJs, and other tastemakers.[43] In particular, Apple is aiming at millennials, many of whom have not stuck with the service after initial trials.[44] For example, the company recently signed an agreement with Dubset Media Holdings to stream DJ mixes and mashups, which sample multiple songs and have been a headache because of copyrights issues.[45] Young music fans love them, but they had not previously been available through commercial music services.

Perhaps Apple's biggest move to differentiate its streaming music service has nothing to do with music, but with video. Apple is teaming with another millennial favorite, Vice Media, to produce an exclusive video series called "The Score."[46] Netflix and Amazon have had huge success gaining subscribers by launching their own TV series, and Apple is keen to do the same. And because young people prefer to watch on-demand shows on smartphones or computers rather than television sets,[47] Apple Music is the logical choice for launching video content over Apple TV, the company's digital media player for the home.

Apple Music is gaining paid subscribers at a fast rate, and is putting pressure on Pandora, the former innovator and market leader – proof yet again that disrupting a market does not guarantee occupation.[48] This fight is far from settled, though, as a variety of players realize that the real value in streaming music is not as direct revenue, but as an entrée to other value vacancies.

Amazon, for example, has designs on occupying the new value vacancy of streaming music through Amazon Echo, a device that combines artificial intelligence with an always-on connection to Amazon's media and e-commerce businesses. Amazon Prime members can use Echo to play free

---

* Some exclusives are big sellers, driving users to Apple Music and iTunes downloads. See "Apple Music, iTunes Exclusive Album Tops Music Charts," *MacNN*, February 16, 2016, macnn.com/articles/16/02/16/rapper.future.hits.top.spot.with.apple.exclusive.release.for.seco nd.time.in.six.months.132571/

music from Amazon or from their Spotify and Pandora accounts. In a strategy not dissimilar from Apple's, Amazon's goal is actually not to make money from music – it is giving it away – but from the purchases a customer will make while listening to music. With Amazon Echo, customers can ask Alexa, the artificial intelligence "agent," to play music from the customer's Amazon Prime account, or listen to another streaming service. But while they're in the kitchen listening to music and cooking, customers can tell Alexa to send another bottle of olive oil and a can of Italian tomatoes.

A casino owner never wants customers to leave the premises, and therefore offers all manner of inducements to customers to continue gambling where they sit. Far from supercharging a music industry renaissance, streaming music and devices to access and play music are Amazon's complimentary buffet.

Disruptor and Disrupted

It is the curse of the market incumbent to always buy at the peak. In the Digital Vortex, the inherent disadvantage of incumbency is Moore's Law, which (loosely paraphrased) posits that the cost of technology as a factor of production declines exponentially. Incumbents are on the wrong end of this curve, and disruptive innovators on the right end, enjoying a more competitive cost base.

In short, cost competitiveness is a lagging indicator. This is why, in part, we coined the term "encumbered incumbents" – because they are saddled with cost structures and value chains that were tuned to the competitive dynamics of an earlier era. It is not a truism, however, that younger companies are more competitive than older companies in the Digital Vortex. And as innovators mature and take on the encumbrances of incumbents, they can fall prey to the next generation of disruptive players who benefit from the relentless march of Moore's Law. The challenge for companies is therefore to "reset" their position relative to this cost curve.

As the costs of innovation plummet, disruptors of all stripes – including incumbents – get more "kicks at the can" in creating disruptive offers and business models. As a result, incumbents can pursue exciting new paths to customer value. However, there are also many more rivals vying for that winning formula. Whether this is good or bad for an individual firm boils down to how effectively and efficiently the company creates new value for customers.

SECTION 2

Chapter 5: Digital Business Agility

Agility Is the New Planning

As companies are drawn into the Digital Vortex, the pace of technological change, business model innovation, and the blending of industries accelerate. New competitors are carving out positions of competitive advantage that kneecap or depose market leaders. How should incumbents respond?

Companies must create cost value, experience value, and platform value for customers using the business models we presented in Chapter 2. And they must execute the strategies for fighting value vampires and pursuing value vacancies described in Chapter 4. Doing so requires them to bring successful innovations to market while at the same time maximizing the profitability of existing businesses that are, or will soon be, disrupted. But few companies do either of these things well, much less both of them simultaneously.* In part, this is because companies conflate strategy, which requires speed and flexibility, with *planning*, which is rigid and often ponderous. As a famous boxer once said, "Everybody has a plan until they get punched in the mouth."

Senior executives must set a strategic vision for their companies, but must not fall victim to the siren song of annual and multi-year plans. There is a temptation to view such plans as a protection from digital disruption, but this is a false security. As the University of Toronto's Roger L. Martin has noted, "Virtually every time the word 'strategy' is used, it is paired with some form of the word 'plan,' as in the process of 'strategic planning' or the resulting 'strategic plan.' The subtle slide from strategy to planning occurs because planning is a thoroughly doable and comfortable exercise ... The

---

* For a deeper discussion of balancing the need to "both explore and exploit," see Charles O'Reilly III and Michael Tushman, "Organizational Ambidexterity: Past, Present and Future," *Academy of Management Perspectives* 27, no. 4 (November 2013): 324-338, doi: 10.5465/amp.2013.0025

plan is typically supported with detailed spreadsheets that project costs and revenue quite far into the future. By the end of the process, everyone feels a lot less scared."[1]

Planning then is management's attempt to divine the future, which has always been a fraught undertaking*, and which is now bordering on the nonsensical, given the competitive dynamics and velocity of change we described in Section 1. For while executives are heads-down crafting their plan, they are drawn deeper into the Digital Vortex, where technological change, business model innovation, and industry convergence continue unabated. With growing regularity, digital disruptors effectively negate a company's growth plan even before it is unveiled to employees or shareholders, while the profit pool that was its basis has evaporated.

Too many incumbents are meeting exponential market change with a faith that a distinctly linear approach to strategy (i.e., planning) will rescue them. In a constantly changing world, a long-term plan can act less like a rudder and more like an anchor, tethering a company to a position that no longer makes sense. Woody Allen once said, "If you want to make God laugh, tell him about your plans." In the Digital Vortex, in important ways, planning is the problem.

A New Approach

We believe incumbents must instead build a set of capabilities that will enable them to move with the speed, fluidity, and effectiveness of disruptors.

Creating combinatorial disruption while pursuing both defensive and offensive strategies demands a new approach. We call this set of capabilities† *digital business agility.* Digital business agility is best thought of as a kind of meta-capability that rests upon three underlying

---

* Henry Mintzberg's book, *The Rise and Fall of Strategic Planning,* distinguishes between "deliberate" strategy, which is an attempt to predict the future and plan for it, and "emergent" strategy, based on the ability to respond to unanticipated events. Most executives use a deliberate strategy approach that puts a high premium on anticipating both future events and the right approaches to responding to them. A deliberate strategy encourages companies to stick to a plan amid material changes in the competitive environment. These changes occur constantly in the kaleidoscopic Digital Vortex, making this approach to planning a non-starter. Business agility, which we introduce in this chapter, is a set of capabilities that enables companies to execute emergent strategies as events and opportunities present themselves. See Henry Mintzberg, *The Rise and Fall of Strategic Planning: Reconceiving Roles for Planning, Plans, Planners* (New York: The Free Press, 1994).

† These capabilities are not static "core competencies" that, once built, provide a competitive advantage, such as a strong supply chain or a "center of excellence." While these types of competencies can be advantageous, the point of digital business agility is to help companies anticipate market changes and deliver customer value.

capabilities: hyperawareness, informed decision-making, and fast execution (see Figure 14). With digital business agility, companies can deliver superior cost value, experience value, and platform value by:

- Sensing the changes in a company's environment that matter most by collecting relevant data and insights
- Analyzing data, absorbing learnings, and involving the right people to make good decisions consistently
- Executing quickly and scaling rapidly, while shedding unsuccessful or outdated approaches

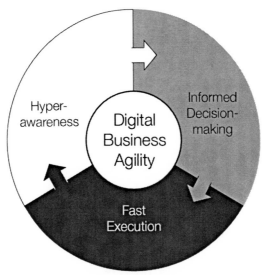

Figure 14: Digital Business Agility
Source: Global Center for Digital Business Transformation, 2015

With digital business agility, companies can anticipate evolving customer needs instead of waiting for disruptors to deliver a more compelling value proposition. They can decide whether to pursue a value vacancy and how to win it based on the best possible information and evidence. And they can move into markets quickly, occupying them for longer, and maximize their margins. This chapter will explore digital business agility in more depth, while Chapters 6, 7, and 8 will delve further into the specifics of how organizations can build hyperawareness, informed decision-making, and fast execution. As we shall see below, these three capabilities work together and reinforce one another.

Companies that possess strong digital business agility respond quickly and effectively to emerging threats, seizing new market opportunities before rivals even notice them (hyperawareness). They use information advantages to dissect sources of value and to formulate winning strategies and value propositions (informed decision-making). And they move quickly to change course, counter threats, and capitalize on opportunities, tapping into platforms to create exponential change (fast execution). These capabilities enable them to:

- Differentiate and bulletproof their core businesses, making it harder for digital disruptors to replicate or supersede the value they provide
- Extract maximum value from declining businesses when value vampires hover
- Move into value vacancies to maintain growth in the wake of disruption

It's no coincidence that the same companies (Amazon, Apple, Google, Netflix, Tesla) keep coming up in discussions about digital disruption. All of them recognize that the struggle for market supremacy in the Digital Vortex is never-ending. All of them have systematic strategies to attack and occupy value vacancies again and again. This is why we see Amazon launching a space venture, Apple moving into payments, Google branching into self-driving vehicles, Netflix undertaking television production, and Tesla entering the energy storage business. These moves are motivated by greed (the growth potential of value vacancies) *and* fear (an understanding that they are vulnerable to attack). Whether these specific investments pay dividends or are later dismissed as hubris is immaterial. All of them depend on a high level of digital business agility.

Consider a sporting analogy and imagine one firm is the best, say, 1,500-meter runner in the world. Then the 1,500-meter "industry" is disrupted, and a new opportunity appears in the shot put. The company is ill-equipped for the new competitive scene because its deep specialization in running a 1,500-meter race (aerobic and anaerobic fitness) is far less important than the strength and explosiveness the shot put requires. Had the company not invested exclusively in the 1,500-meter, but rather trained for a decathlon, which requires well-rounded fitness and skills (flexibility, cardiovascular condition, muscle mass, hand-eye coordination), it wouldn't matter if the new opportunity were the shot put, the pole vault, or the 100-meter sprint. It would be positioned to adapt. Digital business agility therefore equates to the "fitness" of the firm.

Hyperawareness

Hyperawareness is a company's ability to detect and monitor changes in its environment. By "environment" we mean the internal and external factors that impact the company's opportunities and risks. Hyperawareness includes sensing relevant digital trends and changing competitive dynamics, as well as collecting key insights about and from customers, partners, employees, and the company's physical assets (e.g., buildings, machines, vehicles, IT systems).

Thanks to ubiquitous network connectivity, mobile devices, tiny and inexpensive sensors, and the proliferation of data collection tools, companies can understand their environment more fully than ever before. They can gain insight into their operations by embedding sensors in their production equipment, fleets, facilities, and products. They can understand what customers are saying about them on social networks with listening platforms, and know where they are by tapping into data about mobile device usage. Tools that "scrape" the web for data, and "clean" it for analysis, can collect massive amounts of information on nearly anything – competitors, macroeconomic trends, and weather patterns. Companies can also obtain granular detail about their supply-chain partners – not only whether goods are arriving on time, but also whether they are produced ethically and sustainably or have been maintained in a "cold chain" that prevents spoilage. All of these data sources flow continually in the hyperaware company and are monitored in real time.

Hyperawareness provides the lifeblood – data and insights – of the other two pillars of digital business agility. Informed decision-making, in which data is analyzed and distributed to support strategic decisions and automated business rules, depends on the quantity and quality of the data collected in the hyperawareness stage, lest companies find themselves in the predicament of "garbage in / garbage out," where bad data make good decisions hopeless. When it comes to fast execution, these strategic decisions guide the efforts and direction of the entire company. In addition, the conclusions and lessons learned are funneled back into the organization as a "closed loop."

Companies need to understand the insights they want to generate, and then determine what they will monitor, as well as the IT infrastructure and human resources they will need to do so. For example, to detect value vampires before they become obvious (and more dangerous), companies must be attuned to customer dissatisfaction, the emergence of new market needs, and the technologies and business models that could deliver customer value more effectively (including those outside the company's current industry). To identify value vacancies, the first steps include determining a customer need that could be fulfilled, the means of fulfilling it (e.g., by digitizing a link in the value chain), and looking for examples of successful business models in other industries. A strong sensing function can help companies develop sophisticated hyperawareness, with technology as the enabler in support of broader corporate aims.

Hyperaware companies are less likely to be taken by surprise. They are also harder to disrupt because they can sense their own vulnerabilities and adjust their business models and processes accordingly. For example, hyperaware companies understand when their customers are disgruntled and why. They can also zero in on what customers truly value about their products. Likewise, when a company is hyperaware of its competitive landscape, it understands the strengths and weaknesses of traditional rivals and the potential impact of new lines of business or acquisitions. In addition, hyperaware companies anticipate which nontraditional competitors (startups, incumbents from other industries) could threaten their market position and the technology-enabled business models they could use to cause disruption. (We will explore how to build a hyperawareness capability in Chapter 6.)

Hyperawareness in Action: Nestlé

Digital media has rapidly become a critical component of the marketing and communication strategies of consumer goods firms. Most take a very structured approach to managing digital assets, such as social media sites, but this wasn't always the case.

Back in 2010, Nestlé, the world's largest food company in terms of revenue, was just beginning its journey as a social media powerhouse. At that time, it maintained multiple Facebook pages and Twitter feeds across its brands and markets. Each site was maintained independently with some basic oversight from head office. Unbeknownst to Nestlé, the environmental activist group Greenpeace had created a video critical of Nestlé's policies about sourcing palm oil. Greenpeace claimed that Nestlé's demand for palm oil, a key ingredient in chocolate, was leading to deforestation of primary rainforests in tropical countries such as Indonesia, resulting in loss of habitat for orangutans and other wildlife. Greenpeace produced a spoof video of a KitKat commercial in which one of the characters opens a KitKat wrapper to find an orangutan's finger in place of the chocolate bar, and proceeds to eat it with bloody consequences.

Greenpeace uploaded the video to various video-sharing sites, including YouTube and Vimeo. Nestlé became aware of the video only after it had gone viral, and by that point it was too late to remove it (they tried). Worse, on the first night after the video was released, viewers began posting negative comments on Nestlé's corporate Facebook account. At that time, the site was monitored by two interns, who took it upon themselves to respond in an antagonistic way to the commentary. The result was predictable. Nestlé was roundly criticized for its inappropriate response to the incident and its flawed approach to social media management[2]. The company ended up issuing an apology and promising to work with Greenpeace to address the palm oil situation.[3]

Nestlé learned a tough lesson from this experience, and made sweeping changes to its social media and digital engagement policies to prevent a similar situation from occurring in the future. Five years on, Nestlé has an impressive social media presence. There are more than 200 million fans of Nestlé brands on Facebook, and the company publishes more than 1,500 pieces of social media content every day[4]. But reaching this point took a deliberate and highly innovative approach to hyperawareness.

In 2011 Nestlé established sophisticated social media monitoring capabilities through a new program called the Digital Acceleration Team (DAT). The DAT brings together dozens of people from around the world on eight-month assignments to work in digital listening centers. The first DAT Center was established at Nestlé's headquarters in Vevey, Switzerland. Since then, 12 local centers have been set up around the globe.[5] As a possible indication of its perceived importance to the company, the DAT Center in Vevey is located one floor above the executive suites.

The DAT Center at Nestlé headquarters, which resembles a NASA control room, is equipped with rows of flat-panel displays streaming real-time information about social media activities related to Nestlé's brands. Data flows in from all the major social media platforms, including Facebook, LinkedIn, Google+, Twitter, Pinterest, Instagram, and YouTube.[6]

Data visualization applications contextualize incoming data so that the team can efficiently identify salient developments and trends. Staff have access to millions of posts, as well as metrics such as conversation volume, sentiment level, best-performing content, and many others. The team members can track online sentiment about Nestlé's top brands, and how their brands are being discussed online compared with those of competitors. The DAT Center in Switzerland has also deployed a tool called "Pulse" that integrates data on customer service inquiries, effectively pulling in perspectives from beyond the social media realm.

By integrating these many sources of listening, the teams working in the DAT Centers maintain a holistic understanding of their brands' digital and social engagement. But the capabilities of the DAT Center are not limited to listening. Workers can also engage directly with consumers and communities online if they receive an alert about unusual activity. For example, they can answer consumer questions via social networks, and can publish new content based on algorithms that pinpoint ideal posting times to maximize readership. Automated alerts also identify unusual patterns, such as an unexpected spike in post volume on a particular topic.[7] This allows the team to take rapid action in the event of a brand crisis, which is critical in an environment where sentiment can intensify (or reverse course) in a matter of minutes.

The program also helps spread a culture of hyperawareness across Nestlé's worldwide operations. Many of the program's graduates lead digital marketing in their local markets. In fact, while the hyperawareness capabilities of the DAT Center add tremendous value to the company, Nestlé views the investment primarily as a form of leadership development. The company's executives understand that hyperawareness must become a foundational part of the firm's operations to ensure future success in the Digital Vortex.

Informed Decision-making

Informed decision-making is a company's ability to make the best decision possible in a given situation. To excel in informed decision-making, companies must develop mature data analytics capabilities that augment human judgment. Predictive analytics can show how the future may unfold, given past events. Data visualization helps decision-makers understand complex information intuitively. Video and text analytics are transforming knowledge management, making it faster and easier to find the right information.[8] In addition, rapid advances in artificial intelligence, as "personified" by Apple's Siri and Amazon's Echo, are harbingers of future enterprise data access.

Technology that assists in the conversion of data into insight is a prerequisite for informed decision-making. Unfortunately, many companies fail even when they possess all the information needed to make the right moves. Too often, companies make vital strategic decisions by acquiescing to the uninformed opinion of a senior executive, sometimes with disastrous results.[9] There may be some truth in the former British Prime Minister Benjamin Disraeli's adage that there are "lies, damned lies, and statistics," and leaders must not be blindly beholden to data – but in the Digital Vortex the competitive landscape shifts so quickly that what was true yesterday may no longer hold today. One of the clearest lessons we draw from our study of more than 100 successful startups is that they create disruption through a combination of management science and iterative learning, and they place far less emphasis on "past experience" or "gut feel" when it comes to making decisions.

A big part of good decision-making is good data analysis, and ensuring that internal and external experts have access to necessary insights. Such experts should be included in the decision-making process at appropriate stages, regardless of their location, role, or rank. All relevant parties should have the opportunity to participate in the decision-making process and to provide contrary evidence and frank recommendations, even when they contradict the opinions of senior leaders. Diversity of perspective contributes to informed decision-making, but it's just one element of a larger mandate of corporate inclusion.

In addition to maximizing knowledge within the organization, companies can obtain fresh perspectives and challenge received wisdom by collaborating with customers, partners, and third-party experts. Increasingly, companies are turning to crowdsourcing to find answers to difficult questions and to present alternatives when in-house capabilities are insufficient or when decisions need corroboration.

Companies committed to informed decision-making must critique their current strengths and weaknesses. Companies can ask whether they are vulnerable to disruption and how they can improve their position by enhancing the cost value, experience value, and platform value they provide to customers. If they have already been disrupted, companies can make informed decisions about whether they can succeed by taking the fight to the disruptor or by pursuing a different value vacancy. They can also determine whether they have the right skills and business processes to succeed, or if changes need to be made.

Informed decision-making is not applicable only to a company's big strategic decisions. Large enterprises can make thousands of better decisions each day by disseminating business insights broadly throughout their organizations, embedding decision-support tools in their business processes, and automating decision-making through business rules. Digitizing business processes is vital to the "informed" enterprise. (We will explore how to build an informed decision-making capability in Chapter 7.)

Informed Decision-making in Action: DHL

Deutsche Post DHL illustrates how informed decision-making can permeate the individual contributor level of the organization. DHL recognizes that tremendous value can be realized by embedding informed decision-making directly into the business processes and workflows of all workers, whether they are in an office, on a factory floor, or in the field.

DHL is the world's largest courier company with nearly 500,000 employees working across more than 220 countries. The company offers a variety of services, including supply-chain services, freight services, and courier services under the DHL brand.[10]

Most of the company's employees work in warehouses, in vehicles, or in other logistics-related facilities. In one of DHL's three global hubs, 46 million international shipments are processed each year.[11] With operations of this scale, DHL's employees make an astounding number of individual decisions every day across the company's widely distributed footprint.

To help its employees benefit directly from informed decision-making, DHL has piloted innovative digital capabilities. In 2015 the company announced that it had partnered with Ricoh and wearable-computing firm Ubimax to trial so-called "vision picking" in a warehouse in the Netherlands.[12] ("Picking" is the process by which workers collect warehouse inventory items to fill customer orders.)

For three weeks, DHL provided warehouse staff with head-mounted displays, such as Google Glass. Task information about the warehouse picking process was projected onto the displays in a graphical, "augmented reality" format. In their field of vision, workers had direct access to accurate and optimized information about the location and quantity of products to be picked. During the trial, 10 workers picked more than 20,000 items to fulfill 9,000 customer orders.

The solution enabled these workers to perform their tasks without having to look up information manually and make thousands of small, individual decisions about picking items. They had easy-to-understand guidance based on data and analytics that had already been used to make informed decisions about optimal picking patterns.

This freed the workers to focus on more important decisions and other aspects of their jobs. It also generated a 25 percent productivity increase during the picking process.[13]

The DHL pilot is a fascinating example of how analytics, embedded directly into employee workflows, can be transformative. This case does not require individual workers in the warehouse to be data scientists. On the contrary, analytics enable current employees to do the work in which they specialize – only better and faster. Based on the success of the pilot, DHL is considering rolling out this capability more widely.

Fast Execution

Fast execution is a company's ability to carry out its plans quickly and effectively. Unfortunately, it's a rare capability, especially in large companies where execution is slowed by cultural inertia, second-guessing, turf wars, an aversion to failure, and a reluctance to invest in the resources needed to complete tasks. Hence, speed and quality of execution are consistently near the top of CEO concerns.[14]

As we saw in Chapter 1, startups out-execute incumbents in areas such as time to market, experimentation, and risk-taking – areas essential to success in the Digital Vortex, where disruptors appear suddenly and value vacancies are attacked almost as soon as they emerge. To cut through complexity and accelerate execution, incumbents can emulate the strategies of startups. While most large firms struggle to launch innovative new products and services with speed, GE's FastWorks program accelerates the time from concept to a "minimum viable product" that customers can test. Based on customer feedback, GE then refines, redirects, or abandons the idea.[15]

Another area where disruptors excel is using "on-demand" resources to collapse decision-to-execution cycles. The ability to acquire "burstable" expertise using third-party resources that scale rapidly when needed, and quickly contract when the need subsides, is a trademark of fast execution. Incumbents can use an array of applications and cloud services to create more dynamic resource-allocation capabilities. This can be useful when a specific skillset is in short supply internally or is needed intensely during a specific phase of a project. Burstable expertise models also help companies avoid the time-consuming ramp-up normally seen in hiring processes and conventional outsourcing. Eden McCallum, for example, provides on-demand consulting services without the high costs and contractual obligations associated with big professional services firms. Instead of hiring writers, creative designers, and programmers, incumbents can access thousands of freelancers through Upwork and Guru on an as-needed basis, or accelerate software design by tapping into the developer platform of GitHub. As we will see in the case of Starbucks, it is crucial to have an ecosystem that can supply needed capabilities *and is primed to absorb operational changes.*

While people play a huge role in a company's speed of execution, fast execution also includes the automation of workflows. In many circumstances, a machine can execute faster and with more precision than a human being – the very reason automation on manufacturing plant floors has been expanding for decades. In Amazon's fulfillment centers, the activities of employees and machines are so tightly integrated that their model has been termed "human-robot symbiosis."[16] (We will explore building a fast execution capability in Chapter 8.)

Fast Execution in Action: Starbucks

Starbucks, the world's largest coffee retailer,[17] offers an illustrative example of fast execution. In 2014 the company recognized that "line anxiety" represented a major deterrent to sales. Busy consumers tended to forgo purchases if they had to stand in line waiting for their orders. Starbucks, therefore, aggressively pursued new experience value ("Instant Gratification" and "Reduced Friction" business models) through its Mobile Order & Pay (MOP) initiative. With MOP, consumers can order their preferred food or beverage (with the personalized temperatures, levels of foam, and add-ons they have come to expect from Starbucks) directly from the Starbucks mobile app. The customers' payment accounts are automatically debited, and they can pick up orders in the store without waiting in line to order. By integrating the app with in-store analytics and Google Maps, Starbucks also allows consumers to remotely view estimated wait times at nearby stores.[18] In addition, MOP helps speech- and hearing-impaired consumers place customized orders.

MOP allows Starbucks to deepen its return on earlier digital investments, particularly its successful mobile payments scheme. The company has reported that more than one-third of its customers use the app for mobile purchasing, and 21 percent of total purchases occur through the app.[19] Starbucks also makes more money per transaction on app-based purchases, because they contribute to cross-selling as well as impulse buys. The company recently reported a "significant increase in incrementality and transactions" attributable to MOP,[20] and a bump in profits because the system cuts out credit card company fees.

After launching MOP as a pilot in Portland, Oregon, in December 2014, the company scaled the app to 7,400 Starbucks stores by September 2015.[21] It also expanded availability from just Apple iOS mobile devices to include Android devices. In announcing the nationwide availability of MOP, Starbucks Chief Digital Officer Adam Brotman said, "Bringing Mobile Order & Pay to our customers is about meeting their needs of convenience and customization ... The fact that it also represents the fastest technology application rollout we have ever done is indicative of the strength of our digital ecosystem, how well it has been received by both our customers and store partners, and the impact we think it can have on the future of retail."[22]

The following month, the company began a rollout to 150 stores in the United Kingdom and 300 in Canada.[23]

How many incumbents could achieve an operational clock speed like this? How many large enterprises could scale an equivalent innovation with such far-reaching payoffs at such a rate? This is not just an IT issue. It has huge operational impacts in terms of training, staffing, marketing, and physical configuration of workspaces. Brotman said it is "the equivalent of punching a virtual channel into the stores. It's the most cross-functional thing we've ever done."[24]

Putting It All Together

As we explore hyperawareness, informed decision-making, and fast execution in Chapters 6 through 8, we will see that these three phases of digital business agility are a kind of continuum. We can examine them individually to understand their underlying logic and the steps required to create them, but to consider them as completely discrete is an oversimplification. These capabilities are highly interdependent. Let's consider an example of a company we have worked with from the insurance industry to illustrate how hyperawareness, informed decision-making, and fast execution can converge to address a specific business outcome that directly impacts competitiveness: reducing customer churn.

Churn is a big problem for insurance companies, and it's grown considerably with digital disruption as online-only insurers and comparison tools have introduced price transparency (cost value) and reduced the friction (experience value) of switching providers. In the U.S., online-only insurers such as GEICO and Progressive are now two of the top five auto insurers by market share.[25] Recent research from Accenture found that nearly four in ten policyholders would likely switch their auto or home insurance to another carrier within the year.[26] Perhaps more troubling was that two-thirds of consumers would be willing to buy insurance from companies that weren't traditional insurers themselves, including Google and Amazon.[27] Churn is highest in auto insurance, but property, health, life, and other insurance products are not far behind; private capital is flooding into a throng of disruptors targeting the insurance industry.[28]

Amid this disruption – and the threat of worse to come – a reduction in the rate of churn would be a huge win for insurance companies in terms of revenue and profit. And if customers were more satisfied with their service, they would not only stay, but also recommend the insurer to friends. According to research from consultancy Bain and Company, customers who are "promoters" of an insurance brand are worth nearly seven times more in lifetime value than "detractors," and greater retention accounts for three-quarters of that additional value.[29]

How can digital business agility help an incumbent insurer remain competitive in an industry headed toward the center of the Digital Vortex? To illustrate, let's consider the case of a top U.S.-based insurance company we'll call "AgileCo," with more than $15 billion in annual premiums. When we met with their executive team, they told us that customer attrition in their auto insurance business had doubled from 14 percent in 2008 to 28 percent in 2014 – more than a quarter of customers didn't renew their policies, leading to soaring customer acquisition costs and tanking margins. To address the urgent problem of reducing churn, AgileCo took concrete steps and set up a dedicated contact center just to deal with customer attrition. Whenever a policyholder called to complain or to discuss policy cancellation, the unhappy customer was transferred to the contact center, where specially trained agents would try to persuade the person to stay with the company.

AgileCo achieved a 16 percent retention rate at the dedicated contact center. This meant that 84 percent of policyholders who called with the intention to leave *did* leave. AgileCo understood the importance of improving this retention rate and embarked on a program to achieve that.

Like all insurance companies, AgileCo had massive quantities of data. They knew a lot about their customers, including demographic profiles (from the policies themselves), case histories (claims, payouts, etc.), and call histories (e.g., clarifications, complaints). This data was extremely valuable, but AgileCo believed it could be even more valuable if it were combined with data gleaned from external sources. So the company collected as much data as it could from publicly available sources, including vehicle registration databases and social media applications including Facebook and LinkedIn. AgileCo then combined everything into a single data repository.

In addition to specific data about policyholders, AgileCo had millions of records of calls and emails to the contact centers. It had access to interventions that resulted in successful (retention) and unsuccessful (attrition) outcomes. Using advanced analytics, AgileCo analyzed this data, initially restricted to auto insurance policyholders, in search of insights that might help reduce the rate of churn.

For a long time, their analysis came up empty. Although they formulated a number of hypotheses about the likelihood of churn, many of these were refuted by the analysis. They predicted that changes in life situations – e.g., a recent change in marital status or the purchase of a new car or house – would have a big effect on attrition, and while there were significant correlations, the numbers were small. They also hypothesized that length of tenure as a client would play a significant role in the rate of churn, but it didn't. Level of customer satisfaction based on the number of calls and complaints *was* significantly correlated with attrition, but once again, the numbers were much smaller than anticipated.

AgileCo didn't give up. Instead, it widened the search for insights to include more data sources, and one of these additional sources finally provided the answer they were looking for. The answer didn't come from policyholder data, but from another source entirely – a source containing data to which AgileCo had always had access, but hadn't been collecting: the contact center database itself. AgileCo noticed that with certain combinations of callers and agents, retention rates increased dramatically. Something about the connection between particular callers and particular agents produced more successful outcomes. Some agents were naturally better than others at retaining policyholders, but the analysis suggested there was more at play. Certain characteristics of policyholders, when matched with certain characteristics of agents, generated more favorable outcomes, regardless of other factors.

The answer was a very human case of compatibility. Certain customers connected better with certain agents, and when that happened, the outcome was more likely to be successful. And this connection could be statistically predicted. For example, the analysis showed that when female callers in their thirties with young children were connected with female agents in their thirties with young children, the likelihood of retention increased markedly.

For AgileCo, this was a turning-point revelation. Like most contact centers worldwide, AgileCo's followed the "first available operator" rule – meaning an incoming call would be routed to the next available operator in the queue. The reasoning behind the rule is obvious: customers who call contact centers don't want to be kept waiting. It's intuitive that the longer callers wait, the more frustrated they become, and the more likely they are to abandon the call. Therefore, the first available operator rule is premised on an important, unstated assumption – agents are fungible (i.e., one is much the same as any other).

AgileCo's analysis challenged this assumption. They found that the characteristics of the agent were extremely important when matched with the characteristics of the caller in the right way. Hence, AgileCo was faced with a choice: maintain the current policy of caller routing based on the first available operator rule, or change to a new system based on matching callers with compatible agents. It may seem obvious that the right decision was to change the process, but this wasn't the case with AgileCo and is rarely the case in practice. The first available operator rule is deeply ingrained in the operating procedures of contact centers. It's been tried and tested thousands of times over many years. At AgileCo, it had been in place for decades. Not only does the procedure normally work, but it's also a procedure that call center workers, managers, executives, vendors, and other stakeholders know, understand, and trust. What's more, because the procedure is baked into the software systems used by most contact centers, changing to a new procedure is not a trivial matter.

AgileCo decided to conduct a series of live experiments to test the caller-agent compatibility hypothesis, and these experiments confirmed the finding. Today, after implementing the caller-agent compatibility rule across all of its contact centers, AgileCo's retention rates have doubled from 16 percent to 32 percent. Although many callers now wait longer for an operator, the company has calculated that this inconvenience is offset by the improved results. These customers are responding, in part, to superior experience value. They are staying because the customer service they receive is personalized. Customers feel more comfortable sharing their concerns and frustrations with agents who share their characteristics, with whom they are more comfortable speaking, and who may be more empathetic. Digital business agility in this case uncovered a latent opportunity to inject additional experience value into their customer value proposition. *This* is digital business agility in action.

As a first step, AgileCo realized that they needed an expanded view of the churn problem. Their existing data was insufficient, so they sought additional sources of relevant information. This is an example of being hyperaware; they looked beyond their traditional sources for insights – first to public databases, and then to an expanded view of their internal environment.

Hyperawareness involves more than merely sensing shifts in the external environment, such as changes with customers or competitors. It also includes, as we will see in Chapter 6, a more nuanced understanding of the environment *within an organization*, including employee attributes, opinions, and ideas.

This information was critical to the insights of AgileCo during this transition. However, hyperawareness alone did not solve the company's customer retention problem: AgileCo needed to effectively analyze the new data and make decisions based on the resulting analysis. They needed to find the right correlations and translate them into useful insights. But it wasn't enough for AgileCo to just find the key insight about caller-agent compatibility. They also needed to convince very experienced managers to change the way they operated the contact centers – how they executed.

Friend and Foe

We believe digital business agility is the foundation of a new form of competitiveness that rests on adaptability. Digital disruption is the new normal for many industries in the Digital Vortex, and will become so for many others in the near future. However, it's not enough to simply understand this. Hyperawareness, informed decision-making, and fast execution must be actively developed and effectively used. In the next three chapters we will explore each capability, and show some of the digital technologies and processes that organizations can use to build them.

Companies must develop robust digital business agility capabilities to compete against the digital disruptors that are upending their markets, and to move into value vacancies that will soon be contested by disruptors and traditional rivals alike. Without digital business agility, established companies can neither emulate the business models of disruptors, nor successfully execute the strategies for fighting value vampires and occupying value vacancies. These strategies require a level of agility and consistent execution that to date has been beyond the reach of all but a handful of celebrated innovators.

Established companies can use the innovative offerings from digital disruptors *with whom they do not compete* to become more hyperaware, make better decisions, and execute faster.

Digital disruptors are moving aggressively into business functions such as human resources, sales, marketing, and IT. The veritable explosion of new firms offering analytics, artificial intelligence, and connected devices makes it ever-easier for established companies to collect data, analyze that data, and incorporate it into their businesses. These disruptors are bad news for the companies that serve these markets today (e.g., business process outsourcers, IT outsourcers, consulting firms and similar companies), but good news for everyone else – because they can accelerate the path to digital business agility. Simply put, in the Digital Vortex, disruptors that attack your businesses and steal your customers are mortal enemies. Disruptors that help you build the digital business agility you need to defeat these enemies can be staunch allies.

Chapter 6: Hyperawareness

The First Step

Hyperawareness is the ability to sense what's happening throughout the company's operations – among workers and customers, and in the broader environment – and recognize developments and patterns that will impact the organization. Developing the capability of hyperawareness is the first step in building digital business agility. The information captured through hyperawareness is essential to driving informed decisions that will yield the desired business outcomes. Unless the organization collects large quantities of high-quality information at this stage, it cannot make accurate decisions, and the value of its subsequent actions will be diminished. The risk of failure includes more than potentially missed opportunities: in the fast-moving Digital Vortex, time wasted moving in the wrong direction based on inadequate intelligence will give disruptors a chance to seize value vacancies and invade vital profit pools.

OUR METHODOLOGY:
FOLLOW THE MONEY AND ASK THE EXPERTS

To identify the most important enablers of digital business agility, the DBT Center studied the business models of more than 100 disruptive startups. We conducted in-depth interviews with founders and/or CEOs from the most innovative ventures to understand the value propositions of their companies, and how they believe digitization will drive hyperawareness, informed decision-making, and fast execution. We also conducted interviews with senior executives and operational leaders at large global enterprises. These companies represented a range of industries (including retail, manufacturing, and financial services) and geographies (North America, Europe, Latin America, Asia). The goal of the interviews was to understand the drivers and challenges of digitization, the benefits these companies hope to receive, and lessons learned in building digital business agility, especially for large organizations.

In this chapter, we will explore how organizations can build hyperawareness by deploying the optimal mix of technology, labor, and process innovation. In particular, we will examine how organizations can build two types of hyperawareness that are critical for success: Behavioral Awareness and Situational Awareness (see Figure 15).

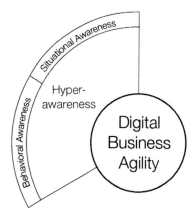

Figure 15: Hyperawareness
Source: Global Center for Digital Business Transformation, 2015

Behavioral Awareness

Given the advances in data collection and analysis, it may seem strange to begin our discussion of hyperawareness with a company's employees. Yet, in an age when technology seemingly reigns supreme, people remain a company's most important asset – and a key source of intelligence about both its customers and operations. When properly channeled, the collective knowledge and skill of a workforce can drive the next multi-billion-dollar market. After all, disruptive business models are fueled by *people* – people who innovate, collaborate, and boldly take chances.*

The value of people, however, is not limited only to an organization's workforce. Ultimately, it's customers who determine whether new ventures will succeed, and for established companies, which ventures will dominate markets and which will cease to exist. This is true for both consumer-focused companies and those serving other businesses. Companies must be hyperaware about customers and their evolving needs and preferences.

Gaining a deep understanding of how workers and customers act (e.g., how they perform their jobs, how they buy and consume), what they think, and what they value is a critical first step in an organization's journey to digital business agility. We call this *behavioral awareness*.

Behavioral Awareness: Employees

Collecting information about the things that matter is at the center of hyperawareness. When it comes to the workforce, a company must be hyperaware *through* its employees. They are the ones closest to customers and partners. They are the ones who execute the decisions made by executives. They also know what customers love and what they complain about. They know when a strategy is not working, and they respond with engagement and enthusiasm when they accomplish tasks that really matter. For these reasons, a company must also be hyperaware *about* its employees. That means answering questions such as "What are they doing, and why?" and "Are they using their time, energy, and intelligence in activities that advance the company's goals and are personally fulfilling?"

When companies are hyperaware *through* and *about* their people, they can mine a rich and extensive source of insights. Indeed, the very relationship between management and employees is changing. To retain talent and optimize productivity and innovation, managers need to know their employees better than ever before, and when possible, customize work experiences to optimize their talents. With hyperawareness in the workforce, executives will know what their people know, and when they

---

* This is supported by Cisco's private-sector Digital Value at Stake research, which projects that people-centric connections will drive 64 percent of future value (2015-2024), while machine-to-machine connections will create 36 percent. Joel Barbier et al., "Where to Begin Your Journey to Digital Value in the Private Sector," Cisco, January 2016, connectedfuturesmag.com/Research_Analysis/docs/Private-Sector-Digital-Value-at-Stake.pdf

know it, as they capture their insights, best ideas, and most important criticisms. Moreover, they will know what their people are doing, when they are doing it, and why. Companies that are oblivious to, or actively ignore, the thousands of "human sensors" on their payrolls will be hard-pressed to make informed decisions or execute quickly or effectively. In the case of the workforce, hyperawareness has two key elements:

- Collecting information from the workforce about the internal and external environment – what we call "insight capture." This includes reaping insights about what customers value from frontline sales associates or account managers; generating ideas for new products from engineers; or capturing frank assessments of corporate strategy and executive decisions from the people who see their effects, both good and ill, on a daily basis. To effectively collect the information from a workforce consisting of thousands (even tens of thousands) of employees and contractors, companies must blend technologies to give employees a voice through business processes that integrate what they say into decision-making and execution.

- Gaining greater visibility into employees' goals and activities while helping them meet their challenges safely and efficiently. Through an approach we call *work-pattern sensing*, companies can gather and analyze data from sensors, business applications, collaborative tools, and other digital sources to understand patterns of how employees perform their work. Such visibility reveals the business processes that generate positive outcomes, and should be spread throughout the organization. These two digital approaches – insight capture and work-pattern sensing – create new forms of intelligence that help companies make better decisions.

Insight Capture: The Real Story in Real Time

There are numerous challenges to creating hyperawareness in a company's workforce. In many firms, one-way communication from senior leadership to the workforce is the norm. Even when companies are receptive to hearing from their employees, frontline staff, individual contributors, and even middle managers often lack access to effective, real-time communications channels, especially those that are integrated into their daily workflows. As a result, companies underutilize their best early-detection mechanisms for spotting growth opportunities and fixing problems. These self-imposed blind spots also present an opportunity for hyperaware competitors to drive new disruption.

It is even more difficult for employees to deliver candid assessments or bad news. When bottom-up communications occur, employees assume that managers welcome only information that reinforces the wisdom of their decisions. Many employees are hesitant to offer candid feedback to their peers, managers, and executive leadership for fear of reprisal. The end result is that, far from being hyperaware (getting the real story in real time), most companies gather little information from their workforce. What they do receive is skewed by the belief that candor is a career-killer, despite the best intentions of some top executives. As Ryan Janssen, CEO of employee feedback startup Memo, told us, "It's not because you have created a hostile workforce or because you are a bad manager. Self-preservation is an extremely strong instinct. You're going to hear exactly what you want to hear. If you continue that process up three or four levels of management, what you ultimately have is managers looking at a mirror of their own creation."

Some firms, however, excel at giving their employees a voice and capturing valuable insights by employing a variety of technologies. Many of these technologies come from digital disruptors. Dropthought and Glint, for example, are pioneering the use of text analytics and natural language processing (NLP) to help companies analyze written feedback and comments from thousands of employees. This enables firms to understand employee sentiment and rapidly identify the most important themes. Speech analytics is another innovative technology for capturing employee insights. This allows companies to gather conversations and verbal input, find common trends, and report them without labor-intensive collection and reporting. Speetra, a speech analytics company, offers a mobile app that lets employees provide feedback by speaking rather than writing. Within five to ten seconds, employees can express their thoughts about corporate policies, operations, customer needs, and strategy.[1] Ryan Janssen of Memo stressed the importance of giving workers a voice in shaping company culture: "People want to like their company. That's actually hard for some company leaders to understand; they don't believe it. But people are essentially good – they just get frustrated when they don't have a voice."

Perhaps most important, companies can use these tools to automate data collection and analysis to gather intelligence from frontline employees. (These workers have the closest relationships and most frequent interactions with customers, but the fewest opportunities to share their insights.) Data visualization technologies can convert their individual insights into trends that are easy to interpret.

Finally, a number of analytics services leverage data and analysis to write succinct reports worthy of a journalist. With automation and analytics, "voice of the employee" can become a real-time sensing engine, instead of a suggestion box that is never checked.

These employee voices will become increasingly important in the Digital Vortex, where companies must identify value vacancies quickly and often. The DBT Center's research suggests that, compared with startups, many incumbents with large organizational hierarchies struggle to unlock the entrepreneurial potential of their workers. Because frontline staff, individual contributors, and junior employees often have the most valuable insights into what customers value, and which processes could be more efficient, companies ignore these voices at their own expense. Michael Papay, co-founder and CEO of digital employee-feedback startup Waggl, told us, "There's a common misunderstanding that leadership needs to have all the answers. But they can't possibly have all the right answers. It's not realistic given the pace of change and the precision of expertise required. Communication, however, is the key to success: clearly, frequently, authentically, transparently communicating with employees and colleagues who can provide additional perspective and knowledge."

Active Listening

One company that excels at insight capture is the Spanish fashion retailer Zara, owned by Inditex. Insights from Zara sales associates and managers are critical to Zara's "fast fashion" business model, which is based on sensing shifting fashion trends and delivering clothes that exemplify these trends before they become passé. Zara trains store managers and sales associates to elicit feedback from customers about what they like, dislike, and would purchase if it were available. They also communicate their own ideas about what will or won't sell. These insights are captured in Zara stores around the world, and reviewed by product designers at corporate headquarters. Zara's vertically integrated structure, in which manufacturing and supply chains are located in Europe for the fastest-moving product lines, gets products to stores in as little as 10 days.[2]

Most important for Zara, the business model encourages customers to visit the stores to get the styles they want, because clothes are produced in limited quantities and stock turns over quickly. For Zara, the quality and timeliness of employee insights help the company identify what merchandise will move, with few misses. In fact, less than 1 percent of Zara's products – versus 10 percent for competitors – despite producing nearly 10 times more kinds of products per year.[3] Zara's store managers and employees are doing more than simply reporting what customers tell them. They are using their knowledge of fashion trends, their professional experience, and their ability to ask the right questions. At a time when most retailers are "de-skilling" frontline jobs and requiring less of their employees, Zara is counting on them to be the company's eyes and ears, and is paying them more for those skills.

Innovation competitions and "hackathons" are another way to give employees a meaningful voice and offer an outlet for their creativity, while encouraging the cross-functional teambuilding that is a hallmark of innovative firms.

Cisco regularly engages its more than 70,000 employees globally through crowdsourcing innovation contests. In 2014 it launched a companywide innovation challenge to identify promising value vacancies related to the Internet of Things. The challenge was open to any employee across the company. In one week, hundreds of submissions arrived from individuals and teams. A high percentage of the submissions involved teaming that crossed geographic boundaries and business units. In the end, six semifinalists were chosen to present their ideas to a panel of senior Cisco executives and subject-matter experts. Three ideas were then selected for inclusion in Cisco's service development pipeline. Many of the submissions showed how Cisco could increase operational efficiency – and break down cross-functional silos – by making incremental process improvements using IoT. Others represented wholesale changes in approach to offer design and business models. Cisco's initial successes with innovation challenges have led the company to launch them with increasing frequency. Teams have developed business models and are competing for "seed money." The winners receive internal resources and executive sponsorship to incubate their ideas via rapid prototyping, with the goal of developing a new Cisco offering.

Companies that adopt these tools must ensure that they have the right internal processes in place to manage competitions, along with support from managers and top executives, to ensure that employees can devote sufficient time to innovation challenges. With such measures in place, any company can see its best ideas rise to the surface, instead of remaining trapped in hierarchies or "pocket-vetoed" by risk-averse departments or uncooperative personalities.

Breaking Down the Barriers

A diverse workforce also improves a company's hyperawareness. Employees from different backgrounds – geographic, educational, religious, gender, ethnic, racial, and age-related – may interpret trends and solve problems in unique and complementary ways. They may also help the company see things through the eyes of its customer base, which in many cases is growing in diversity. We will explore the issue of diversity in more detail in our discussion of informed decision-making.

Companies may not welcome all ideas and feedback. Often, employees have strong opinions about their companies – ranging from strategic direction to the minutiae of policies and procedures – that are not shared by top management. However, differences of opinion between employees and executives, and even harsh criticism, can be healthy when new ideas constructively challenge outdated thinking or cherished fictions. As the expression goes, sunlight is the best disinfectant. Organizations must be hyperaware of disconnects between senior executives and the rest of the company, as well as between middle managers and their direct reports. They need to receive honest assessments from employees while there is still time to make changes. When digital disruptors, investors, or regulators are first to uncover weaknesses, the consequences can be far worse.

Anonymous Feedback Mechanisms

Creating a culture of candor can be especially challenging for organizations with large, geographically dispersed employee bases; those with histories of closed cultures; and those in which layoffs or political infighting has eroded employee trust. In these situations, *anonymous feedback mechanisms** can play an important role in reducing fear of retribution and ensuring the flow of honest communications within companies. These online feedback tools enable employees to submit ideas and constructive criticism to senior executives, their managers, peers, or the entire company – and to do so

---

* When discussing anonymous feedback mechanisms, it is important to distinguish between confidential feedback and truly anonymous feedback. Many companies provide confidential feedback mechanisms. Using confidentiality statements, these companies promise employees that responses will not be attributed to them, often by establishing a minimum threshold for data aggregation (e.g., aggregating responses of at least five employees). However, an employer could conceivably use various means, such as attribute data and network data, to identify employees. This is why simple confidentiality statements often do not convince employees to provide candid feedback. With truly anonymous feedback mechanisms, employers cannot attribute responses to individual employees because of the technical or process measures in place, such as automatic deletion of all personally identifiable information, or the use of a third-party platform to manage feedback, data storage, and analysis. Increasingly, employers will need to prove to employees that their feedback is truly anonymous, such as by explaining the technical or security mechanisms in place to guarantee anonymity.

securely. Many companies may be unnerved at the prospect of giving employees a megaphone for voicing their ideas and concerns. However, there are a variety of ways they can elicit honest feedback to maximize positive impact while minimizing antagonism.

New anonymous feedback mechanisms are built with high ease of use, and in some cases, use gamification to make feedback fun. One example is Officevibe, a highly automated anonymous feedback platform that lets companies poll their employees weekly to capture their ideas and assess their satisfaction. Officevibe's "FaceGame" is designed to help everyone in an office remember colleagues' faces and names, while "PraiseGame" makes the process of providing peer feedback a positive and enjoyable experience. Such features can encourage honest feedback while dulling the sharp-edged criticism that often leads to defensiveness. Officevibe reports that the response rates for its surveys are more than three times the industry average.[4]

Some anonymous feedback mechanisms allow individual employees to not only submit feedback, but also to anonymously "up-vote" or "down-vote" the feedback given by their peers. This lets organizations tap into the collective sentiment of their workforces in a transparent and efficient manner, and then determine whether an idea or criticism has broad support. Early in its history, Google recognized the importance of creating a culture of open communication. As part of his "20 percent time" for creative thinking,[5] Google employee Taliver Heath built an online platform called Dory* that allowed individual employees to anonymously submit questions at meetings. Other employees voted on these questions, and those that received the most responses rose to the top of the list in real time. Dory was quickly adopted for use during Google's weekly "all hands" meetings so the moderator could identify and address the most pressing issues on employees' minds. Dory is an example of an anonymous feedback tool that addresses a key challenge to candor: the fear of speaking up about sensitive topics in front of a large group. The widespread nature of this challenge is supported by research we recently conducted with more than 800 companies. It revealed that only 33 percent of employees feel comfortable sharing their ideas during such company meetings.[6]

Anonymous feedback mechanisms can also provide an avenue for bringing contrary viewpoints or complaints about behavior to the surface. Although such information can benefit the company and its stakeholders, many employees fear embarrassment or being identified as whistleblowers

---

* Named after the curious fish in the movie *Finding Nemo*.

– a label that can result in career stagnation (or worse). However, when employees know that their identities are protected, they are far more inclined to help their employers avoid failed product launches, expensive lawsuits, and even loss of life. As MIT's Edgar Schein writes, "In airplane crashes and chemical industry accidents, in the infrequent but serious nuclear plant accidents, in the NASA *Challenger* and *Columbia* disasters, and in the British Petroleum gulf spill, a common finding is that lower-ranking employees had information that would have prevented or lessened the consequences of the accident, but either it was not passed up to higher levels, or it was ignored, or it was overridden."[7] Anonymous feedback mechanisms have the potential to prevent such devastating losses.

Work-pattern Sensing: Measuring How Workers Work

Hyperawareness reveals what employees do, in addition to what they know. Only by understanding how and with whom their employees work, which tools they use, and what they produce can a firm make the changes necessary to ensure that each employee is helping accomplish an important collective goal. The growth in knowledge work* has made understanding how workers perform their jobs much more complex. Rather than physical labor that can be observed and measured directly, knowledge work – as well as its outputs – is often intangible. As a result, companies often have little or no visibility into how workers perform their jobs. "Work" is a black box of activity for many organizations. As a consequence, it is difficult for employers to uncover ways that employees can do their jobs more effectively and to drive improved results for the organization. Indeed, management consultant, educator, and author Peter Drucker called knowledge work "grotesquely unproductive."[8]

---

* The term "knowledge worker" was coined by Peter Drucker in 1957 when he observed: "The most valuable asset of a 21st-century institution, whether business or nonbusiness, will be its knowledge workers and their productivity." Over time, this segment of the workforce has grown, and it is estimated that in 2015, knowledge workers accounted for 44 percent of the U.S. workforce. Non-routine problem solving, the use of tacit knowledge, information seeking, collaboration, and other cognitive tasks characterize knowledge work. This does not mean that all knowledge workers sit behind a desk all day. In fact, many jobs that were once defined by physical labor have become much more aligned to knowledge work. For example, in some manufacturing industries, production workers on the factory floor often must be highly trained, and must use their experience and skills to address non-routine problems. See Peter Drucker, *Management Challenges for the 21st Century*, (Oxford: Butterworth-Heinemann, 1999), p. 116, and William G. Castellano, *Practices for Engaging the 21st Century Workforce: Challenges of Talent Management in a Changing Workforce* (Upper Saddle River, New Jersey: Financial Times/Prentice Hall, 2014), p. 22.

The convergence of several digital technologies, including IoT, analytics, and collaboration platforms, is throwing new light on knowledge work through *work-pattern sensing*. This analyzes data from sensors, business applications, collaboration tools, and other digital sources. The result is a clearer picture of how employees communicate and collaborate with one another, as well as their physical movements and how they perform specific job tasks. Once these patterns are sensed and understood, organizations can take steps to improve how employees perform their jobs.

Cisco projects that by 2020, 50 billion objects will be connected to the internet.[9] These billions of connected devices will enable the capture of data in previously unimaginable ways. By applying analytics to this data, companies can become aware of how employees collaborate and perform their work – for example, through employees' "smart" badges.

Humanyze offers employee smart badges, each about the size of a deck of cards, which are embedded with four types of sensors: a Bluetooth sensor, an accelerometer, an infrared scanner, and two microphones. The badges capture 40 types of information, or about 4GB of data per day, allowing companies to identify patterns of work and communication in detail. For example, the badges can sense if two people are conversing, as well as detailed dynamics of the conversation such as speaking time, interruption patterns, and tone. They can also track movement patterns, such as when employees lean forward during conversations – a sign they are engaged in the discussion.

Data from the badges can be aggregated with other information sources, such as collaboration system data or performance data. It can then be analyzed and presented to both management and employees via data reporting dashboards. This innovative approach to work-pattern sensing has led to some interesting and useful results. Bank of America has used the badges to understand the relationship between productivity and social engagement for its call-center employees. By making changes to the way BofA schedules teams (and even by rescheduling lunch breaks to encourage greater interaction), the bank increased productivity by 10 percent and reduced staff turnover by 70 percent.[10]

As the variety and power of sensors grow, and as the cost continues to decrease, we expect to see increased use of work-pattern sensing. Manufacturers such as Steelcase are embedding sensors in office furniture and buildings to understand how workers interact.[11] Furniture maker Herman Miller and property management firm Jones Lang LaSalle (JLL) are both experimenting with space-use sensors to understand how workers use conference rooms. This will help optimize designs for the workplace of the future.[12]

Collaboration systems such as email, telepresence, and social platforms offer a wealth of data that can be used to drive work-pattern sensing. VoloMetrix, an application provider, enables companies to analyze data from company communication systems to drive outcomes such as organizational simplification and employee productivity. For example, through data visualization, company leaders can pinpoint which groups are communicating with one another, and how often. Employees can receive confidential weekly dashboards to understand how much time they spend on email and in meetings compared with their peers. Companies can use this information to benchmark best practices and identify employees (and groups) that need to improve their collaboration skills and overall effectiveness. Most important, this data can reveal *specific* best-practice behaviors and work-patterns instead of merely providing general feedback.

Companies using work-pattern sensing software have uncovered some surprising patterns of employee time-wasting activities. For example, Seagate Technology, one of the world's largest computer storage manufacturers, found that some of its groups were spending more than 20 hours a week in meetings, and wasting thousands of hours on unneeded emails. As a result, the company refined its collaboration practices.[13]

To compete more effectively in the Digital Vortex, companies must ensure that employees are engaged in work that ultimately contributes to customer value. In fact, companies can improve the cost value they provide simply by reducing time-wasting activities and redirecting employees toward more fruitful pursuits aligned to organizational goals. Given the noted difficulty of measuring the productivity of knowledge workers, work-pattern sensing that helps quantify the value of employee activities – ensuring that talented (and often highly paid) people are doing valuable and rewarding work – can give incumbents a competitive advantage.

Work-pattern sensing has the potential to improve both employee performance and engagement. However, leaders must consider some important issues; privacy concerns are the greatest challenge to adoption cited by entrepreneurs and senior executives we've interviewed. Given employees' legitimate concerns, innovators in this space are experimenting with different approaches to address privacy. Humanyze relies on opt-in participation and presents a contract guaranteeing that no individual's data is shared with another party, *including the employer*. VoloMetrix removes individually identifiable info from its analysis, showing employers only data aggregated at the group or company level. Companies must be extremely clear with employees – and with government regulators – about privacy protection measures when deploying work-pattern sensing capabilities.

Behavioral Awareness: Customers

Historically, many of the decisions about marketing and selling to customers have been based on demographic and psychographic research, such as customer surveys, focus groups, and ethnographic studies. These sources of information are increasingly ill-suited to the Digital Vortex. A customer survey that takes three to six months to conduct may provide an organization with customer insights that are outdated, leading to product or service development decisions that are out of step with the current wants and needs of customers.

Traditional sources of knowledge about consumers, moreover, such as demographic information, are declining in value. Demographic data increasingly represents an incomplete picture of the modern consumer resulting from changing patterns of behavior that no longer fit typical customer segments. Such "post-demographic consumerism" reveals results that can puzzle firms that cling to yesterday's customer personas. In the United Kingdom, for example, women account for the majority of video game players, and between 2012 and 2013 the fastest-growing demographic segment on Twitter was the 55-64 year age group.[*]

Uncovering Hidden Patterns

Digital technologies, in particular mobile phones and sensors, are expanding the horizons of what organizations can sense about how their customers communicate and consume. This new hyperawareness is redefining the underlying nature of what organizations can feasibly know about their customers' behaviors. Rather than being limited to behaviors observable during "snapshots in time" (e.g., during focus groups), companies now have access to an always-open window into how customers act. This hyperawareness creates unprecedented opportunities to understand the mix of cost value, experience value, and platform value that customers want, and then to deliver it through new and improved offerings.

Today's smartphones pack a proliferation of sensors, including accelerometers and gyroscopes used to measure movement and orientation; magnetometers and GPS chips for location services; environmental sensors for temperature and light intensity; and

---

[*] According to research and consulting firm Trend Watching, "People – of all ages and in all markets – are constructing their own identities more freely than ever. As a result, consumption patterns are no longer defined by 'traditional' demographic segments such as age, gender, location, income, family status, and more." "Post-Demographic Consumerism," Trend Watching, accessed April 6, 2016, trendwatching.com/trends/post-demographic-consumerism/

increasingly, fitness sensors such as heart rate monitors and pedometers.[14] Companies are even exploring ways to go beyond the sensor data to derive insights based on phone usage. Researchers at Samsung have found that by monitoring certain phone usage patterns, such as typing speed, and how often the "backspace" and "special symbol" buttons are used, they can predict a person's emotional state with 68 percent accuracy using machine learning algorithms.[15]

Several disruptive startups, including Branch.co and inVenture, are reinventing financial lending in developing nations by offering mobile apps that assess consumers' creditworthiness based on their mobile phone usage patterns. This type of hyperawareness meets a critical need in countries where hundreds of millions of consumers lack access to banking services, and where a dearth of reliable data means that many individuals don't have credit scores. The apps offered by these startups track up to 10,000 data points per consumer to assess creditworthiness. Users of the apps agree to share their mobile phone data in exchange for the ability to secure loans. If they are judged to be a good risk, they can receive immediate approval and access to funds directly from their mobile phones. Many borrowers are small business owners who use the loans to buy things such as fuel and inventory. In this sense, the apps expand not only individual opportunities, but also the growth potential of local business markets.

New methods of capturing and analyzing data on mobile phone usage have generated interesting, and sometimes counterintuitive, results. For example, these apps have found that the faster consumers drain the batteries on their mobile phones, the less creditworthy they are. Another finding is that those who take the effort to enter the last names of their contacts on their phones are *more* creditworthy. These apps are a great example of how hyperaware disruptors use digital technologies and processes to target a value vacancy. Without the capability to gather data from a non-traditional source (a mobile phone), these companies would be unable to address the needs of this sizable yet underserved market. According to the philanthropic investment firm Omidyar Network, such apps could enable 325 million to 580 million people in emerging economies to access consumer loans.[16] The apps can also accelerate the loan generation process in developed countries such as the U.S., where it takes an average of 46 days to close a mortgage (we touched on the ideas of credit scoring and loan processing using mobile devices in the example of WeChat in Chapter 3).[17] Such apps can also help prevent bad lending practices by accurately assessing the creditworthiness of borrowers who use "low-documentation" mortgages to gain approval for loans they cannot repay, a factor that played a role in the 2008 financial crisis.*

Combining Digital with Physical Sources of Data

Some companies are exploring options to combine the hyperawareness enabled by mobile devices with physical assets and offerings to deliver new forms of value. In February 2016, Clear Channel Outdoor Americas, which deploys and manages tens of thousands of billboards in the U.S., announced it would be partnering with AT&T and several other technology providers to roll out a service called Radar to 11 markets, including Los Angeles and New York.[18] Radar tracks and aggregates mobile phone usage data to identify the travel and behavior patterns of people near billboards. This data can be linked to store visit data to provide advertisers with detailed information about the viewers of billboards, such as their average age and gender, and whether they subsequently visit the advertised stores. According to Clear Channel and its partners, all data is aggregated and anonymized so that individual consumers cannot be identified.

Radar converges technologies including mobile, cloud, and analytics with the physical environment (e.g., roadside billboards) to enable marketers to gain a level of hyperawareness about consumers that was once impossible. Initial tests of Radar with shoe company Toms have shown that the service can drive advertising decisions that improve brand awareness and purchases.[19]

The growth of the Internet of Things also opens up new possibilities for building hyperawareness of customer behavior – e.g., through wearable devices such as connected wristbands. According to research firm International Data Corporation (IDC), manufacturers shipped 78 million wearable devices in 2015, an increase of 172 percent from the previous year.[20]

In 2013, Disney launched its MagicBand system, the result of a $1 billion investment, at its Disney World theme park in Orlando, Florida. MagicBands are electronic bracelets embedded with a Radio-Frequency Identification (RFID) chip and radio, among other technologies, which allow guests to accomplish almost all visit-related tasks in an automated, seamless manner. Before they even arrive at the park, guests can plan which

---

* These mortgage practices are making a comeback as banks look to increase their loan portfolios. While our analysis in this book focuses on the private sector, we can see the potential for hyperawareness to help public sector organizations, such as regulatory agencies, detect and prevent fraud. Kirsten Grind, "Remember 'Liar Loans'? Wall Street Pushes a Twist on the Crisis-Era Mortgage," *Wall Street Journal*, February 1, 2016, wsj.com/articles/crisis-era-mortgage-attempts-a-comeback-1454372551

rides and attractions they want to visit, and the system will provide them with an optimized itinerary that minimizes travel and maximizes time spent having fun. Guests can use the MagicBands to do everything from entering the park without tickets to paying for food and merchandise. They can check in at rides and obtain services simply by touching their MagicBands to kiosks located throughout the park. The overarching goal of the system is to eliminate all sources of friction so guests can focus on enjoying their experience instead of standing in lines or paying at the register.

Disney's MagicBand system has helped the company with hyperawareness of many guest behaviors – behaviors Disney once knew little about. For example, MagicBands can track the routes that guests take through the park, what they purchase, which rides they visit, and even the restaurant tables where they sit. This hyperawareness is the first step in enabling informed decision-making and fast execution. In turn, it enables the transformation of the guest experience at Disney World.[21] And Disney's use of digital to increase awareness of its customers' behavior will continue to evolve. The company announced that upon opening its $5.5 billion Shanghai Disney Resort in the spring of 2016, it will not deploy its MagicBand platform. Instead, it will enable visitors to use their own mobile phones to accomplish many of the same functions, such as gaining entry to the park, purchasing merchandise, and accessing rides.[22]

Knowing Customers Like Never Before

Beyond understanding consumer behavior, such as travel and mobile phone usage patterns, companies are now building hyperawareness capabilities that will enable them to pinpoint their customers' emotions. Imagine stepping into your car for your morning commute, and your car already knows whether you are cheerful, anxious, or angry. It could then adjust its environment, such as music, interior temperature, or commute route – to optimize your commute experience (an example of "Customization" experience value). Forward-thinking companies are now building the hyperawareness capabilities to allow them to recognize their customers' emotions – much as a friend, spouse, partner, or family member might. Companies can then use this understanding to create customer experiences tailored to the customer's unique needs and wants in a given context, and to monetize these insights for sale (e.g., to brand marketers).

The ability to use hyperawareness to build a context-based emotional connection with customers can allow companies to change behaviors at critical moments in the customer journey. Affectiva, spun out of the Massachusetts Institute of Technology, has built the world's largest "emotion database" of more than 40 billion data points by analyzing more than 3.9 million facial images.[23] The company enables its customers to deploy emotion-sensing capabilities through a cloud-based "Emotion-as-a-Service" model – a model that includes programming tools that developers can use to embed the functionality into mobile apps and other digital solutions. Affectiva's service uses a camera (e.g., webcam, mobile phone camera) to recognize facial patterns that reveal an individual's emotional state. This presents myriad opportunities for retailers, healthcare providers, government agencies, entertainment firms, and others to acquire in-depth knowledge of their customers so they can custom-tailor the experiences they offer.

The Hershey Company, the largest chocolate manufacturer in North America, has embedded Affectiva's emotion-sensing capabilities into a kiosk known as the Smile Sampler. The Smile Sampler invites customers into a less traveled aisle (usually where the candy is located) in a grocery store, and asks them to smile in return for a free sample of chocolate. An iPad on the kiosk uses facial recognition software to detect the smile – and then dispenses the sample. Because the software recognizes faces, it will dispense only one sample per person, and the facial mapping data is deleted from the machine within 24 hours, ensuring consumer privacy.[24]

Hershey piloted the in-store device after its research identified samples are the number-one thing that consumers want while shopping for chocolates. Hershey hopes to use the kiosk to encourage shoppers to travel down the aisles where its chocolate products are shelved and to build an emotional connection while customers are there. The company hopes to scale the approach to other types of products, with four large retailers already expressing interest in deploying the system.[25]

Building Deeper Insights

Digital technologies and processes can help create hyperawareness that allows customers and employees to interact in ways that build stronger relationships. Cogito, another company that originated at MIT, has developed voice analytics software for call centers. The software analyzes the voice patterns of both the customer and call-center agent in real time as they converse. Based on unique characteristics of speech, such as speed of talking, pauses, interruption patterns, and vocal tone, the software can determine the emotional state of callers, including whether they are annoyed or confused. Meanwhile, the software analyzes the speech patterns of call-center agents to alert them whether they are communicating effectively or displaying empathy and confidence. Call-center agents are provided with an on-screen visual guide that displays real-time recommendations. This helps them dynamically adapt their style of speaking to improve customer satisfaction or close a sale.

One large healthcare insurance provider piloted Cogito's software to analyze interactions of 300,000 members who used the company's call center. The software identified conversational patterns that made it less likely that members would sign up for new services, allowing the agents to adjust their speaking styles in real time. Customer enrollments increased by 4 percent, generating millions in additional profits.[26] Consider the potential for such analysis to augment the call center approach of AgileCo, described in Chapter 5, where the critical factor in retaining customers was found to be the "personal connection" between the agent and the policyholder.

The digital technologies and processes we have described for building behavioral awareness rely on new ways of gathering information about workers and customers, including mobile phone tracking, facial recognition technologies, and speech analytics. These approaches were not widely available even 10 years ago, but they are now. It is unlikely that the pace of technology evolution and personal data collection will slow. (Facebook alone collects more than 600 terabytes of personal data provided by its users every day.)[27] Of course, the ability to track an individual's movements, emotional states, and social connections raises genuine privacy concerns, but an in-depth exploration of this important topic is beyond the scope of this book. But this issue must be addressed by companies, technology providers, and governments in the not-too-distant future.

Situational Awareness

Thus far we have focused on the capability of hyperawareness as it pertains to the people who drive value for an organization – its workers and its customers. However, as important as people are to success, for many companies, managing their physical resources and infrastructure is an even greater challenge. Moreover, all firms must navigate the challenges caused by macroeconomic forces, regulatory regimes, competitive change, and technology trends. In short, companies must develop situational awareness,* which we define as the ability to identify changes in an organization's *business environment*, and its *operating environment*, and to understand which changes matter.

---

* In its original military context of aerial "dogfights," Situational Awareness is the ability to observe and understand enemies, in order to anticipate their next move and act first.

Situational Awareness: Business Environment

Situational awareness of the *business environment* involves sensing changes in the marketplace – including the company's customer base, competitors, and partner ecosystem – that are relevant to an organization's mission. This includes the ability to capture insights about customer sentiment, macroeconomic and sector trends, competitor moves, partner activities, as well as (and perhaps especially) new digital technologies and business models. *

As a master of product pricing, Amazon depends on robust situational awareness. Using software agents to continually scan competitors' sites, the company gathers competitive pricing data on millions of products. It then uses this intelligence to dynamically lower or raise prices to lure customers from competing retailers or to maximize profits. According to Boomerang Commerce, a provider of e-commerce pricing software, during the 2014 holiday season, Amazon made an estimated *10 billion* pricing changes.[28]

Without hyperawareness of competitors' pricing on an immense scale, this dynamic pricing strategy would not be possible (we will discuss dynamic pricing in more detail in Chapter 8). Amazon has even extended this hyperawareness beyond automated online price checking to the physical world through the launch of its Price Check app (now Amazon Shopping app). Launched in 2011, the app allowed consumers to use the cameras on their mobile phones to scan the bar codes of products while shopping in stores. They then received information about the pricing of the same products at Amazon. This feature let customers quickly check whether they were indeed getting the best price in stores, and gave them the option of immediately purchasing from Amazon at the lower price. It also turned users of the price-scanning feature into enablers of Amazon's hyperawareness capabilities. Every time a consumer used the app to scan the price of an item in a store, Amazon captured that data to help make pricing decisions.[29]

Recorded Future is a digital disruptor that has raised nearly $30 million from investors, including Google Ventures and In-Q-Tel, the venture arm of the U.S. Central Intelligence Agency. Recorded Future has built a platform that constantly mines online public data to identify

---

* *Behavioral* awareness of customers and *Situational* Awareness of the "business environment" can in some cases bleed into one another. The former is focused primarily on understanding an *individual* customer's behavior, whereas the latter addresses "bigger picture" trends and learnings from larger *populations* of customers. Possessing behavioral awareness of all individual customers can play a role in making a company situationally aware of its business environment by rolling up micro-level data to generate macro-level insights.

potential cyber-security attacks. Sources of data include news, blogs, company filings, social media, and even conversations between hackers on "underground" forums. Recorded Future applies sophisticated analytics including natural language processing (NLP) and machine learning to this data to isolate signals that may indicate potential security threats. Recorded Future's clients, which include some of the world's largest companies, can append these alerts with security data collected from their own systems (e.g., firewalls) so they can take proactive steps to prevent future attacks.[30] In the case of Recorded Future, hyperawareness plays an important role not just in sensing and understanding competitive change, but in detecting physical or financial danger.

In Chapter 5, we described how Nestlé has established its Digital Acceleration Team (DAT) to gather actionable intelligence about its brands from a range of social media services. Social media listening has, in fact, become a critical competitive tool for companies worldwide looking to capture insights about different aspects of their business environments. In 2013 General Motors created a global Social Media Center of Expertise (CoE), with a staff of approximately 600 distributed across five regions. The goal of this new organization was to support "market-based decision-making" at the company by establishing hyperawareness in the area of social media.

The CoE located at GM's headquarters in Detroit, Michigan, occupies a 6,200-square-foot building, and is enabled by a range of digital technologies including collaboration and analytics. The staff actively monitor hundreds of GM-owned and third-party social sites and vehicle owner forums, racking up, on average, more than 6,000 customer interactions each month.[31] The action-orientation of GM's social listening efforts illustrates that capturing information is not the destination, but the beginning of the journey. The company uses the hyperawareness generated by the CoE to build relationships with its customers, whether it's through promoting its brand, engaging customers in online discussions, or addressing specific problems that customers submit through social platforms.[32]

Hyperawareness is also crucial to another area of growing import in the Digital Vortex: the partner ecosystem. This is especially so for organizations that depend on complex supply chains. Digital disruptors are pioneering new ways of using technology to provide greater visibility of their partners' operations.

Segura Systems is a London-based provider of supply chain visibility applications that enable retailers and manufacturers to track every part of their supply chains, including those of their trading partners. By increasing supply chain visibility, Segura Systems' applications can reduce human rights abuses such as child labor and human slavery. Major retailers such as Debenhams, the British department store operator, require that their suppliers document every component of their own supply chains within the software platform. [33] Because the system is cloud-based, a company's suppliers can easily access the system, no matter their size or location. This allows an organization to create a fully transparent, real-time audit trail of its supply chain partner interactions. It also helps the retailer ensure that the goods it sells are sourced only from manufacturers and subcontractors that have been previously approved, based on their demonstrated compliance with relevant labor laws and standards.[34] Subcontractors that might be less expensive, but do not adhere to established codes of operation, will not be able to access the software platform, making them ineligible to participate in commerce. In addition to helping Debenhams and other retailers monitor and manage their corporate social responsibility (CSR) practices, the system puts upward pressure on labor conditions and worker safety.

Situational Awareness: Operating Environment

Even as organizations face pressures in their business environments, it is often their *operating environments* that present the greatest management challenges. Operating environments include physical assets such as oil rigs, manufacturing plants, vehicle fleets, buildings, and facilities that companies use to deliver the products or services they sell. The complexity of operating environments has been rapidly increasing. Supply chains are global, and the number of suppliers in many industries is proliferating. At many global enterprises, their portfolios of physical assets have reached an unprecedented scale. For example, global logistics company FedEx has 43,000 delivery vans in its fleet, which its couriers use to travel 2.5 million collective miles each day.[35] BP, the energy firm, operates in more than 70 countries, produces 3.3 million barrels of oil per day, and operates 17,200 retail sites. [36] These operating footprints create a daunting challenge for organizations looking to track the condition or status of their assets and drive operational efficiency.

As we shall see, IoT is a key digital enabler of hyperawareness in the Digital Vortex. The ability to maintain hyperawareness of operating conditions across a vast footprint of production assets can drive significant results in asset-intensive industries such as manufacturing, especially those that operate on a global scale. Cisco and Japanese industrial robot manufacturer FANUC have partnered to develop an IoT solution called

"Zero Downtime," which offers manufacturers real-time awareness of the state of every robot on a factory floor. A range of operational and maintenance data is captured from the robots, then analyzed on the plant floor. The data is then transmitted to a cloud-based analytics platform so proactive maintenance can be initiated before any problems arise. For example, the need for a replacement part can be identified in advance, so it can be shipped to a plant and ready for the next planned maintenance window. FANUC and Cisco have tested the solution with General Motors in a pilot involving about 1,800 robots. The test has saved roughly $38 million, and based on its success there are plans to deploy the solution more widely.[37] FANUC Zero Downtime is an example of the "Data Orchestrator" business model we explained in Chapter 2.

Let's now look at situational awareness in the context of an industry that doesn't leap to mind in conversations about digital change: mining. As we noted in Chapter 1, in the Digital Vortex, everything that *can* be digitized *is* digitized as industries move toward the center. In mining, some elements are (and will remain) physical. However, there is tremendous potential for using digital technologies to improve the efficiency and safety of physical "digging and moving," thereby improving competitiveness. For example, although there may be hundreds of personnel underground at a given time, in many operations, not much information comes out of a mine. The information that *does* emerge tends to be paper-based and issued episodically, after miners and supervisors come off shift every eight hours. This creates serious inefficiency in terms of how mines are run. Worse: operating "blind" can compromise worker safety.

Digital disruption is enabling players such as Dundee Precious Metals (DPM) to separate themselves from inefficient competitors through hyperawareness. DPM is a Canadian mining company that owns Europe's largest gold mine (located near Chelopech, Bulgaria). The company has connected the entire mine, including assets such as conveyer systems, haulers, lights, fans, the blasting system, and even the miners themselves. The mine's wireless network – along with collaboration tools, analytics, and mobile devices – makes the DPM site a case study in hyperawareness of the operating environment. Miners, drivers, and supervisors can communicate by voice from anywhere, above ground or below, including areas of the mine where voice communications have been historically limited by a lack of radio or cellular signals, and they can exchange instant messages on mobile devices.

As DPM's director of corporate IT Mark Gelsomini explained, DPM's goal was to "take the lid off the mine. We wanted to see exactly what was going on, as it was happening, rather than waiting for the shift change."[38]

This is hyperawareness at work – complete situational awareness of an extremely complex and harsh environment, one that happens to be located deep underground.

DPM supervisors can direct drivers where to go in real time, monitor production and equipment status, and make adjustments to operations to improve efficiency. In the event of an equipment problem, employees can share video from iOS and Android mobile devices with engineers and mechanics elsewhere on the site in real-time, or can perform preventive maintenance instead of shutting down valuable production machinery or having it repaired off-site.

This kind of hyperawareness impacts production. Since connecting its physical assets and adding collaboration and analytics capabilities, the mine's production has quadrupled – from a half million tons to 2 million tons per year.[39] Video collaboration capabilities also connect the Chelopech mine staff to DPM executives, geologists, and metallurgists in Canada. Finally, the mine's blasting system is integrated with location-tracking applications to ensure that no personnel or equipment are in the area, improving on-site safety for miners.

Evaluating Hyperawareness

As we have seen, organizations have the opportunity to be more hyperaware of their workforces, customers, business environments, and operating environments. How can companies assess their level of hyperawareness? Answering the following four questions will help.

Do we have the ability to capture insights about our workers? Innovative companies are deploying insight capture tools to gather honest feedback and the best ideas from their employees. In an effort to uncover hidden value, they are also implementing work-pattern sensing to better understand how workers perform their jobs.

Do we have the ability to capture insights about our customers in a given context? By employing digital enablers such as sensor-embedded mobile devices, wearables, and emotion-sensing analytics, companies such as inVenture, Disney, and Hershey are gathering information that will help them understand their customers in ways that have never before been possible.

Do we have the ability to capture insights about our business environment (competitors, macroeconomic trends, and

partners)? Amazon, Recorded Future, and other disruptors are using automation, analytics, and the cloud to drive hyperawareness on a massive scale, enabling them to detect the many complex changes in their markets.

Do we have the ability to capture insights about our operating environment? As we have seen, FANUC has gained situational awareness of its fleet of industrial robots, and is using this awareness to help its customers prevent unplanned stoppages on the plant floor.

Hyperawareness provides an organization with a wealth of information about its workers, customers, business environment, and operating environment. Until now, much of this information has been "invisible" because there were no ways to capture it. But with the emergence of new digital capabilities, many of them offered by disruptors, is it now possible to benefit from this information. In Chapter 7, we will explore how organizations can use this information to compete in the Digital Vortex by taking the next step in the journey toward building digital business agility, by developing the capability of informed decision-making.

Chapter 7: Informed Decision-making

Millions of Better Decisions

As the phrase suggests, informed decision-making involves using information captured through hyperawareness to make sound decisions. In the Digital Vortex, these decisions arise more frequently than ever before, with higher stakes attached to each one. As we have seen, senior executives must navigate a competitive environment in which rivals can emerge seemingly from nowhere, creating value for customers in new and startling ways. As Google Executive Chairman Eric Schmidt said, "Someone, somewhere in a garage is gunning for us ... the next Google won't do what Google does, just as Google didn't do what AOL did."[1]

Informed decision-making is the linchpin of digital business agility. If a company fails to make consistently good strategic and daily decisions, hyperawareness (and fast execution) is for naught. All the data and insights collected will be squandered, and the ability to execute quickly will be transformed from a critical advantage to a stark disadvantage as activities sprint in the wrong direction.

When it comes to decision-making, we are talking about both strategic decisions and "daily" decisions that range from executives directing the business to employees doing their jobs.* In the Digital Vortex, companies must get both types of decisions right. Making good strategic decisions has become more difficult because digital disruptors move faster than traditional rivals, emerging from the proverbial garage or from an adjacent industry. This makes threats trickier to spot and plan for. And because rivals claim value vacancies nearly as fast as they emerge, speed is invaluable. Hence, companies must ensure that when strategic decisions are made, they are based on the right information; the right decision-

---

* In this chapter, we will use the terms "workforce" and "employee" to include traditional full-time and part-time employees, contract staff, and talent brought in through staffing agencies, consulting firms, and related companies. The term "partner" includes supply chain partners, channel partners, and other companies that have contracts or affiliations with a company.

makers are at the table; the criteria are data-driven; and the decisions are clear and executable.

Companies – and those who advise them – tend to give less consideration to the millions of decisions that managers and employees make every day, perhaps because senior executives don't make them. Yet these decisions play a huge part in the success of every company. From figuring out when to offer a discount to a loyal customer on the brink of defection, to determining the fastest way to load a delivery truck, to deciding whether to comply with orders that are contrary to company policy, the impact of daily decisions made by frontline managers and employees adds up quickly. Their sheer volume implies enormous economic and competitive value. Companies must look for ways to improve those many daily decisions and to identify resources employees need to improve decisions.

Most important, companies need to make excellent strategic decisions and daily decisions to deliver the cost value, experience value, and platform value their customers demand. Without *timely* strategic decisions, firms will miss short-lived opportunities to fight value vampires before they seize profitable chunks of the business. Without *good* strategic decisions, companies will find it harder to disrupt rivals and move into new markets. Recent history is littered with the corpses of companies that missed warning signs that their businesses were under attack by new forces. Most companies are left to marvel from the sidelines at the swiftness with which agile firms seize one value vacancy after another.

Unfortunately, decision-making excellence is elusive. In the DBT Center's research, established companies acknowledged their inferior innovation and agility compared with startups. We found that only 8 percent of companies excel in all three areas of digital business agility: hyperawareness, informed decision-making, and fast execution. Our analysis reveals that companies are most challenged by informed decision-making. To address this shortcoming, firms must focus on two areas: inclusive decision-making and augmented decision-making (see Figure 16).

Inclusive decision-making: Too often, companies exclude individuals with critical skills and perspectives from decision-making because of their roles in the company (junior managers and individual contributors), the organizational structure (siloed decision-making), their geographic location, or other attributes (conscious or unconscious discrimination based on religion, gender, race, sexual orientation, age, disability, or other factors). Moreover, companies often exclude partners and suppliers from the decision-making process even if their participation is vital to executing the decisions.

In this chapter, we will explore several technologies that improve coordination in decision-making. These technologies ensure that people with the right expertise, diverse points of view, and organizational interests have a seat at the table. Inclusive decision-making is not about collaboration for its own sake, nor is it simply about expanding "diversity." Rather, inclusive decision-making is about picking the brains of the people who are best positioned to evaluate alternatives, provide expert advice, and represent important stakeholders and viewpoints.

Augmented decision-making: Decision-making capabilities must be "augmented" by incorporating data and analytics into the process. The incredible advances in predictive analytics, artificial intelligence, and data visualization enable decision-makers to actually see into the future (or multiple potential futures) before making a strategic decision. Companies can also mitigate human error and decision-by-fiat through the quantification of alternatives. Augmented decision-making puts a premium on how – and to whom – data and analysis are presented. This augmentation must include tailoring the data and analysis to the role and workflow of the decision-maker, whether this is an executive committee or a frontline employee. Decisions can also be fully automated, based on the application of analytics to business rules. In this case, the company's decision-making as a whole is augmented by analytics rather than the decisions of an individual. Sometimes the best decisions are made by systems autonomously, using machine learning and algorithms.

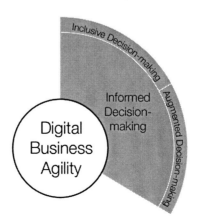

Figure 16: Informed Decision-making
Source: Global Center for Digital Business Transformation, 2015

When decisions are inclusive *and* augmented – meaning the right people are involved (if people *are* involved), the decisions are based on the best available data and analysis, and are distributed throughout the organization based on role and function – then companies are properly equipped to make fast and consistently good decisions. As we discuss inclusive decision-making and augmented decision-making in more detail, we shall see that in several instances, analytics helps initiatives become more inclusive, and inclusion is central to the success of augmented decisions. Of course, context will govern how companies blend inclusive and augmented decision-making, and how they balance automated decision-making with decision-making that involves human judgment. But to succeed, companies must ensure that decision-making processes contain both elements whenever possible. Although no company will get every decision right, getting decisions wrong can have swift and lamentable consequences in the Digital Vortex. That's why many companies are enlisting digital disruptors to accelerate and scale their own informed decision-making capacity. As noted in Chapter 5, disruptors can be allies as well as adversaries.

Inclusive Decision-making

As we have seen in our discussion of hyperawareness, the starting point for innovation is the ability to tap into the expertise and best ideas of the workforce. Because every worker brings a unique blend of education, experience, and skill set, diversity is essential in spotting trends and suggesting solutions to problems. Diversity – whether through gender, race, religion, culture, age, or other factors – is equally important for informed decision-making. A diverse workforce possesses tremendous latent value. However, unless these individuals are brought together in an environment in which they can efficiently share ideas and perspectives, that value will remain unrealized.

Inclusive decision-making – shared intelligence that springs from the collaboration of disparate individuals and teams* – can ensure that diverse viewpoints and relevant expertise are considered when decisions are made. Inclusive decision-making does not require consensus or that executives

---

* Though the concept of "inclusive decision-making" shares similarities with the concept of "collective intelligence," the emphasis is on the participation of individuals with diverse viewpoints or backgrounds, rather than on reaching consensus. See Wikipedia for more on collective intelligence: Wikipedia contributors, "Collective intelligence," *Wikipedia, The Free Encyclopedia*, accessed April 11, 2016, en.wikipedia.org/w/index.php?title=Collective_intelligence&oldid=714619437

cede control over decision-making by yielding to the "crowd." However, companies that routinely consider diverse viewpoints are less likely to make mistakes stemming from the myopia of powerful executives. Emerging digital technologies and business models enable employees to work together to drive inclusive decision-making.

Three Goals

Corporate silos are the nemesis of inclusive decision-making.* A recent study analyzed more than 100 million emails and 60 million calendar entries over a three-month period from a company with 100,000 employees.[2] Two people who were in the same business unit, function, and office interacted *1000 times more frequently* than two people who were in otherwise similar roles, but in different business units, functions, and offices. Analysts also found that communication silos were caused by hierarchy, and that interactions across pay grades were practically nonexistent.[3] Inclusive decision-making allows companies to accomplish three goals of informed decision-making:

1. Involve the right mix of employees in the decision-making and problem-solving process
2. Provide the environment for these employees to efficiently and effectively share their ideas and perspectives
3. Offer the means to make informed decisions based on the diverse perspectives and "mental toolbox" of the group

Finding the Right Mix

Inclusive decision-making depends on enabling workers to identify the right individual or group to arrive at a decision. To make decisions today, most executives do not seek expertise outside their organization (or outside a handful of direct reports) when people with valuable knowledge or experience are available elsewhere in the company. This hurts a company in two ways. First, the decision is less likely to produce a successful outcome. Second, it underutilizes the expertise that companies painstakingly accumulate and pay for. In the future, we expect to see software that enables executives to identify employees who should be part

---

* The term was originally coined in 1988 as "functional silo syndrome" by Phil Ensor, an organizational development practitioner for Goodyear Tire and Rubber. The isolated communications channels in many organizations reminded Ensor, who was from rural Illinois, of the many grain silos dispersed across the countryside.

of specific decisions. Algorithms will match individuals and assemble teams based on a spectrum of relevant characteristics that optimize diversity, experience, skill set, location, and many other factors to maximize the chances of an initiative's success.

Such technology is being developed by startups such as Ranktab, a visual, collaborative decision-making platform that identifies employees whose skills and dispositions will help them make effective decisions as a team. As Francisco Ruiz, Ranktab's co-founder and CEO, told us in our interview, "We're working on artificial intelligence in order to foresee within any organization or group of individuals who are the best people to work together. We're able to visualize which clusters aren't being effective in their decision-making because they have a very high tendency to always agree on everything, and those clusters which disagree on everything, which is not necessarily bad."

Seamless Collaboration

Once members of the group have been identified, leading companies are deploying new collaboration platforms that enable a seamless flow of ideas from all contributors. The technologies primarily used to collaborate today, such as email, are often aligned to the traditional organizational structure, communication dynamics, and decision-making processes. As such, they are ill-suited to creating digital business agility.

New collaboration platforms, such as Slack and Cisco Spark, replace email communications with online "room-based" chat that integrates document sharing, video calling, and other capabilities. Individuals create rooms or collaboration spaces where they can communicate via text, voice, or video; post searchable content; and maintain historical communications. This new approach unlocks institutional knowledge from individual email inboxes and hard drives, making communications and deliverables available to all team members. It also bypasses traditional chains of communication and reporting, providing greater transparency and promoting assessment of contributions based on merit. Team participants have direct access to the contributions of other members: there is no need for "filtering" results to senior management. Finally, these tools scale the number of people working on a collaborative team by integrating synchronous and asynchronous communications. New members can join and come up to speed quickly.

The Wisdom of the Right Crowd

A final, crucial step in inclusive decision-making is capturing shared wisdom and using it to drive informed decisions. New tools promise to bring order and inclusion to the decision-making process. In addition to helping companies build strong decision-making teams, Ranktab uses algorithms to improve inclusive decision-making through multi-criteria voting. The tool helps users understand the evaluation of different options by others in the group, discuss decisions, and view consensus decisions in a graphical format.[4] Organizations can use the platform to make hiring decisions, expedite the approval of leasing applications, or identify the most promising startups for venture funding.

Our experts noted that companies are facing information overload as the volume and diversity of data mount. In addition, companies face a proliferation of workforce-related data, owing to new sources such as collaboration data, wellness monitoring, and sensors in office furniture. For unstructured data in particular, user-friendly analysis techniques are sorely lacking. Therefore, when deploying digital technologies to improve informed decision-making, it is important to keep the end results in mind. Leaders should think about the business outcomes they want to achieve in a given function or area, develop an in-depth understanding of the process involved, and then work backward to identify the data sources and analytics techniques required to produce these outcomes.

To ensure that decision-makers represent diverse perspectives, companies must hire people who are different from most executives and managers, who in some incumbents may be a relatively homogeneous group. As the demographics of countries and regions shift, new groups emerge as vital customer segments – and potential sources of talent.*

Eliminating Unconscious Bias

To take advantage, companies must set aside biases about what ideal candidates look, sound, and act like. This can be very difficult. When it comes to talent acquisition (i.e., recruiting), companies have difficulty eliminating unconscious bias, which exists beyond people's awareness, but nonetheless affects their decision-making. Research studies have found

---

* For example, in the U.S. there were 9.6 million Hispanic people in 1970. By 2014, the number had increased to 55.4 million, or 17 percent of the total population. This is a large but gradual change. In contrast, Germany expects to receive 1.5 million immigrants from the Middle East from 2015 to 2016. These populations are both potential customers and potential employees.

that people tend to favor others who look like them, come from similar backgrounds (e.g., schools or cultures), and have similar interests.[5]

Unconscious bias is a barrier to building diverse workforces, which research shows are important in driving overall competitiveness. When unconscious bias is removed from decision-making, results can change dramatically. A Stanford University study found that the share of female musicians in orchestras has increased fivefold since the 1970s (from 5 percent to 25 percent), an increase brought about by having musicians audition behind screens.[6]

Technology from digital disruptors is emerging as one solution for eliminating unconscious bias in people management. Unitive, a software company, created a digital platform that embeds analytics based on psychological studies directly into a company's hiring workflow to make informed decision-making an integral part of the business process. For example, the software's résumé-review function first assesses which characteristics a hiring company seeks in potential candidates. Only *then* does it present recruiters with objective information about candidates, separating out non-relevant information such as the candidate's name, educational background and hobbies, all factors that can influence unconscious bias.[7] This analytics-fueled approach stands in sharp contrast to the usual process of scanning résumés and attributes all at once before making subjective decisions about suitability. By embedding analytics and an informed decision-making process directly into the hiring workflow, the software eliminates opportunities for unconscious bias before it occurs.

When they tap into the expertise and counsel of their workforces, senior executives can make informed decisions that integrate relevant knowledge, experience, quantitative data, and contrary views. Unfortunately, companies tend to neglect the considerable expertise they have amassed – and paid for – because it is scattered across multiple departments or is considered too "junior." Inclusive decision-making helps companies maximize the expertise and diverse views of their workforces, as well as those of the partners and contractors in their extended ecosystems, to make better decisions. Collaboration can help companies hear from more employees, and bring them into the decision-making process when and where they will have the greatest impact.

Collaboration in Real Time

As we noted in Chapter 4, one of the greatest challenges facing an organization is the ability to innovate and scale operations at the speed of disruptors, especially when the core business involves physical products.

Sub-Zero, a U.S.-based high-end appliance manufacturer, is using collaboration technology to bring decision-makers together across locations and supply chains to accelerate its innovation program while scaling production. Sub-Zero recently combined the biggest product launch in its history with the opening of a new production facility. The company needed to simultaneously design the product line at their Wisconsin headquarters, build the manufacturing plant in Arizona, and work with its supply chain and installation partners.[8]

This required senior executives and designers in all these locations to continually collaborate when making decisions about final designs, production-line issues, training installers and service technicians, and minimizing travel time for engineers, experts, and others. To do this, Sub-Zero used immersive collaboration tools including high-definition video conferencing, mobile conferencing, and ruggedized cameras that worked in plant-floor settings. These tools allowed teams to share videos and images from the plant floor with design teams and top executives in Wisconsin. It also allowed Sub-Zero to communicate more effectively with globally dispersed supply chain partners through secure live-video sessions in which they could share and mark up designs. The tools improved overall communication and made collaborative decisions faster. Sub-Zero estimates it cut design cycle times 10-20 percent by connecting teams and speeding decisions.[9]

Augmented Decision-making

Ideally, companies will combine inclusive decision-making with augmented decision-making to empower the right people to make both strategic and daily decisions. Below, we will provide examples of how digital technology is making inclusive, augmented decision-making a reality.

Beating the Odds by Learning from the Past

The process of acquiring the right partner, quickly closing a merger or acquisition, and – most important – generating value once a deal closes is fraught with difficulty and uncertainty. Only 30 percent of mergers succeed; the 70 percent that fail cost companies not just the purchase price, but also time, effort, and lost talent.[10]

For IBM, the need for successful mergers is particularly acute. IBM spent over $20 billion in acquisitions from 2010 to 2015 in its pursuit of growth. Sales have declined in recent years, driven in part by digital disruption.[11] IBM's hardware, storage, and enterprise software businesses are being shaken up as companies accelerate the move to inexpensive cloud-based services,[12] where Google, Amazon, and Microsoft are engaged in a bare-knuckle price war to dominate the low-cost "public cloud" value vacancy. As a result, IBM is using acquisitions to move into other value vacancies such as big data analytics and healthcare technology. In 2015 alone, IBM spent $4 billion on healthcare technology firms such as Truven Health.[13]

To ensure its acquisition strategies pay off, IBM is using an analytics system that it developed: M&A Pro. The system uses a due diligence algorithm that employs machine learning to identify risks in IBM's potential acquisition targets. M&A Pro also helps accelerate decision-making by completing due diligence faster, allowing IBM to close deals that pass muster before its rivals can pounce. The system uses data on over 100 past acquisitions, and distills hundreds of variables into 28 success factors that are presented in easy-to-consume formats for executives, including data visualization and scorecards that highlight risks and integration concerns. It can also make predictions about the deal's financial impact based on the performance of past acquisitions.[14]

IBM executives can then make an informed, data-driven decision about whether to move forward. This helps the company avoid both human error in assessing risk and the influence of executives pushing for a deal based on opinion, relationships, or other factors. Many digital disruptors have developed technology-driven capabilities for their internal uses and converted them into monetized services. One of these, Amazon Web Services, is among the biggest disruptors of IBM's business. IBM is copying this approach by monetizing its internal systems and offering M&A Pro as a service to its customers.[15] This case is a fascinating example of how an incumbent can leverage *existing* assets (created for internal use) to pursue a value vacancy in a new market.

Ubiquitous Analytics

To be agile, companies must make strategic decisions about managing their operations as issues arise and events unfold. For big global firms, the complexity and scale of their business footprint can make this challenging. Procter & Gamble, the global consumer goods company, sells its products in more than 180 countries.[16] The company markets more than 70 brands ranging from diapers to detergent. Given the vast scope of its operations, P&G needs accurate data about its business environment, and this data must be analyzed and presented in a way that accelerates decision-making.

P&G has built more than 50 connected meeting spaces it calls "Business Spheres."[17] These immersive meeting rooms are equipped with large screens on the walls that display visualizations of a range of business data, such as company results, forecasts, and competitive intelligence.[18] Executives and managers meet periodically in these rooms to monitor real-time business indicators they can use to make strategic decisions. The system provides access to hundreds of terabytes of data, eliminating the process of manual collection and aggregation of data.[19]

P&G then uses analytical models that allow executives to dive deeply into different parts of the business. For example, P&G has an analytical model that helps the company gauge the performance of its 40 largest product categories[20] and see the market share by geography using "heat map" data visualization.[21] These rooms serve as a single source of "truth" across the company: no matter where they are, executives can make decisions based on actual business conditions. Most important, executives can then use this data to create "what if" scenarios that will predict the outcomes of potential business strategies.[22] The company also sees the value of providing analytics to its rank-and-file managers and employees. Decision-support cockpits deliver customized analytics to over 50,000 employees, giving them visibility into the key performance indicators that apply to their business units.[23] In so doing, Procter & Gamble is at the forefront of a growing trend: democratizing data and analytics throughout the organization.

Although companies must get the big strategic decisions right, the decisions their employees make every day are also essential for success. Every employee is a decision-maker. When they have access to high-quality information tailored to their roles and requirements, they can do their jobs better. And by giving every employee access to real-time information and analytics, companies can increase productivity and lay the groundwork to transform their business models.

Ubiquitous analytics can help employees make better, faster decisions that improve both individual and company performance. Sophisticated analytics and decision-making tools have proliferated in recent years, but they are often concentrated in the hands of two principal constituencies: senior executives and business analysts. As noted, in a large enterprise, frontline employees – those in the field, in customer-facing roles, and in individual-contributor positions – are collectively making millions of individual decisions every day. A small number of specialized analysts crunching numbers from a massive company database can offer only so much insight, while having limited influence on these decisions. The real value of analytics occurs when all employees, regardless of rank or location, are equipped with the best possible information to make decisions and perform tasks.

This analysis is important for not only improving the quality of decisions, but also for developing and maintaining a productive and engaged workforce. A 2015 study by the American Psychological Association found that senior leaders within U.S. companies reported more frequently that they had sufficient opportunities for involvement in decision-making than frontline employees reported that they did (78 percent versus 48 percent). Not surprisingly, senior managers viewed their workplaces more positively than frontline employees did – 70 percent of managers said they felt valued by their employers, compared with just 51 percent of frontline employees who did. [24] Employees who have little autonomy or believe their opinions don't count tend to be disengaged,[25] and this lack of engagement costs companies an estimated $450 billion to $550 billion per year in lost productivity in the United States alone.[26]

Being involved in decisions helps employees stay engaged and direct their energies in positive ways, instead of feeling overlooked and undervalued. Ryan Janssen, CEO of Memo, a startup that helps companies capture the latent knowledge* of their employees, told us, "Employees get meaning out of work by being invested in what is happening. That's what all this transformation is about. It's about empowering your people to make the decisions that matter. Our belief is that an organization that creates a more engaged workforce is going to make better decisions, and do better executing on decisions."

Most organizations believe that the average employee is not a candidate for using analytical tools. Perceptions regarding employee skill sets and attitudes usually inform such thinking.

Analytics are by definition highly technical. As such, they are considered unsuitable for a large percentage of workers or irrelevant to their jobs as benefits managers, food service personnel, salespeople, or facilities managers. However, we are now seeing a true paradigm shift in how analytics are used within a business. Individual contributors are beginning to use analytics tailored to their roles and integrated into their workflows. Complexity disappears when decision rules and contextual analytics are embedded in frontline applications.

---

* Memo is also used to collect anonymous feedback from employees. See Chapter 6 for a discussion of anonymous feedback mechanisms.

Analytics at the "Point of Work"

In short, analytics are not just for analysts. Several technologies are converging to allow the insertion of analytics at the "point of work" to improve performance. Data collected with work-pattern sensing can be analyzed to optimize a range of work decisions – from tactical decisions such as which box to pick within a warehouse to the highest-level strategic decisions. Cloud platforms and wireless connectivity make this data, the algorithms, and the resulting outputs available anytime, anywhere. Finally, augmented-reality capabilities, such as augmented visual display technology, enable workers to access detailed information to do their jobs more effectively without disrupting the work process. Such intuitive data visualization brings critical insights to those who may need them most, whether at a desk or in the field with a customer.

The DHL pilot project described in Chapter 5 provides an example of ubiquitous analytics – embedding analytics and informed decisions directly in the work process while freeing employees from decisions that can be made more effectively by automation and algorithms. As a result, employees spend more time on other aspects of the job, including those they may find more rewarding.

Ubiquitous analytics applies to a broad range of industries and business processes. These processes could be based in an office setting, but also reside in factories, hospitals, research labs, or even vehicles. Therefore, organizations are making ubiquitous analytics accessible through tablets, mobile devices, kiosks, telematics, and other digital channels available at the point of work.

United Parcel Service (UPS), one of DHL's main competitors, is deploying a computer platform called Orion, which it has spent a decade and hundreds of millions of dollars building in-house. Orion extends ubiquitous analytics into the field, enabling employees to access analytics at the point of work while supporting informed decisions that benefit workers, customers, and the company.[27]

There are 55,000 UPS routes in the United States, and each driver makes an average of 120 stops per day. As the percentage of deliveries generated by e-commerce sales has risen, so has the complexity of routes. Drivers and planners must try to optimize delivery routes based on a host of factors including roadwork, traffic, special-delivery requirements, and package volume. This has been further complicated by the rapid growth in UPS's "My Choice" self-service platform. With 13 million current users, this service allows customers to change the time or location of their deliveries.[28]

When they begin their shifts, UPS drivers use their tablets to access routes suggested by Orion. To determine a route, Orion computes hundreds or thousands of route alternatives and makes adjustments as new factors (such as special-request delivery times) arise. Orion also accounts for the behavioral preferences of drivers and customers, including predictable driving routes and delivery windows. To date, Orion has been used on more than 40 percent of UPS's routes, reducing distances by an average of seven to eight miles per trip. UPS CEO David Abney said that by 2017 Orion could save the company $300 million to $400 million per year.[29]

The pioneering use of ubiquitous analytics is by no means limited to route optimization. Los Angeles-based startup DAQRI is bringing ubiquitous analytics to industrial environments such as manufacturing plant floors and oil rigs. The company has developed a "smart helmet" and the software to support it. The smart helmet features an augmented-reality display and integrates thermal imaging, head tracking, motion sensing, and pattern-recognition technologies. Workers using the helmet perform their jobs with analytics-driven information overlaid on their field of vision. In one pilot, DAQRI partnered with Kazakhstan Seamless Pipe (KSP Steel), outfitting workers in a pipe production line with smart helmets to test a "decentralized control room" model of operation.[30] The production line can produce 110 tons of pipe per hour, and generates more than 23,000 data points, ranging from production data to safety parameters. Normally, plant workers would need to access this data in a control room, necessitating trips between the control room and plant floor. Using the smart helmets, plant workers access this critical data on the plant floor, reducing trips and interruptions. According to DAQRI, the pilot delivered a 40 percent increase in worker productivity.

Analytics Across the Sales Cycle

For years, companies have sought to increase the effectiveness of their sales forces by making it easier to track and target the best opportunities, spending $234 billion on customer relationship management (CRM) solutions alone.[31] Business procurement has followed consumer trends as companies conduct their own research and purchase through online and mobile channels, bypassing sales forces and shortening traditional sales cycles. As a result, B2B sales teams are increasingly out-of-step with the buying behaviors of their customers.

To compete in this shifting environment, companies are equipping their sales teams with analytics and artificial intelligence tools to help them decide which customers to target, when, and how. Startups are leading this digitization of the sales cycle with tools that predict likely buyers by analyzing internal data such as staff emails, calendars, and customer databases, as well as external data such as business articles and social media.[32] The result is a combination of prediction, automation, and intelligent scripting that helps sales people increase their conversion rates, and ensures that customers are contacted when they are most receptive.

For example, ClearSlide automatically alerts account managers when a potential customer opens an email, even telling them how much time the customer spent reading it. The account manager can then call, knowing that their company's product is top-of-mind at that moment and the customer may be receptive. Other startups such as 6Sense can provide granular detail on prospects who visit the company's website, including their job titles, and tell a salesperson the best time to call, down to the exact hour of the day, based on predictive analytics.[33] These analytics are not only integrated into the workflow of the sales force, but also prompt them to act at the right time.

Helping Customers Make Better Decisions

Although much of informed decision-making involves internal processes that allow a company to make the right decisions, companies also realize that helping their customers make better decisions can be a major differentiator. (This is the basis of the Data Orchestrator business model described in Chapter 2.) To accomplish this, many companies are building informed decision-making into their products and services using a combination of IoT and autonomous analytics systems.

For example, French cosmetics firm L'Oréal has developed a small, transparent adhesive strip called My UV Patch that monitors exposure to ultraviolet rays. After placing the patch on his or her skin, the customer can photograph the patch with a smartphone, or scan it using near field communication (NFC). The app analyzes the level of UV exposure the person has received throughout the day and over time. It then offers users tips about how they can manage UV exposure safely, including the use of products that provide UV protection. L'Oréal, through its skincare brand La Roche-Posay, plans to offer the patch for free so consumers (especially those concerned about UV exposure because of health or aging) can take precautions before their skin is damaged.[34]

Health insurance startup Oscar Health is taking a similar approach with wearable devices. Customers who opt in receive a wristband, which is connected to an app that measures their activity levels. They are then provided with cash incentives to reach their daily exercise goals of walking or running a certain number of steps. For every day they reach their goal, they receive one dollar, which they can redeem in the form of an Amazon gift card once they've done it 20 times, to a maximum of $240 per year. Oscar Health's customers receive cost value in the form of cash incentives, experience value from a personalized, frictionless method of measuring their exercise goals, and the health benefits associated with a more active lifestyle. In essence, they are offered information to make better decisions about their health with real-time data about the status of their health goals, as well as a monetary incentive for reaching goals.[35]

Oscar Health benefits from the platform value of an IoT and analytics-based solution that allows it to scale the service exponentially. Most important, active customers tend to be physically and mentally healthier, and less likely to require costly healthcare and acute interventions. In addition, Oscar Health can use the data collected and analyzed from customers to improve its actuarial analysis, potentially to personalize its policies for each customer based on level of fitness and overall health. As the sophistication of wearable devices improves and costs diminish, Oscar and other health insurers will be able to offer real-time coaching on cardiovascular health, blood pressure maintenance, nutrition, and stress reduction.[36]

Evaluating Informed Decision-making

How can companies know they are in a position to make informed decisions? When companies can answer the following seven questions affirmatively, and have the right digital technologies in place to assist them, they have a strong capability for informed decision-making.

Do we make fast decisions? IBM is making faster decisions about whether to acquire companies by using predictive analytics that can tell them whether the targets will deliver financial returns.

Do we make unbiased decisions? Unitive helps firms make unbiased decisions about hires, ensuring they select the best employees from a variety of backgrounds.

Do we make distributed decisions (empowered at the appropriate level)? Frontline workers at DHL and KSP Steel are making augmented decisions with the help of augmented-reality headsets that let them visualize data on the shop floor.

Do we make inclusive decisions (merit, not rank or proximity)? Collaboration tools such as Slack and Cisco Spark enable individuals to contribute to decision-making by removing "gatekeepers" and giving senior team members visibility into such contributions. Ranktab helps ideas rise to the top based on collective interest, rather than the seniority of individual decision-makers.

Do we make coordinated decisions (not isolated or siloed)? Sub-Zero uses collaboration to make coordinated decisions among far-flung executives, design teams, and the factory floor – decisions that have accelerated time-to-market and boosted innovation.

Do we make predictive decisions? Procter & Gamble managers are using the company's Business Spheres data analytics rooms to predict the impact of potential business strategies and to visualize how key performance indicators could change as a result.

Do we make decisions that are executable? UPS helps its drivers make executable decisions – literally turn by turn. Meanwhile, analytics can identify the most promising potential customers to sales teams, and prompt them to call at an ideal time.

Clearly, it takes more than technology to improve decision-making at any company. If a small cadre of senior executives holds sway, or if business instincts are valued over business intelligence, technology will have little effect on the quality of decision-making. We contend that companies with closed decision-making cultures will find the going increasingly tough in the Digital Vortex as more firms use technology and decision science to uncover new opportunities and avert problems before they grow too big.

Although future DBT Center work will address the steps a company can take to improve its culture, the technology-enabled business processes we've discussed above can play an important role – if companies want to change. For example, Ranktab's analytics can help companies compose cross-functional teams that make better decisions based on the characteristics of individual employees. Improved performance begets shared success, which begets organizational acceptance, which begets improved performance in a virtuous circle of change.

When companies have the information they need about their business and operating environment through hyperawareness, and are making good strategic and daily decisions, they are well positioned to compete against digital disruptors and other fast-moving firms. But just as having good information was not previously enough, the same now holds true for good decision-making. Companies need to capture the value of digital business agility by acting on decisions.

Chapter 8: Fast Execution

Reimagining Work

Digital technologies are not only spurring disruptions in markets or between organizations. They are also leading to new disruptions *within* organizations. The technology-led upheaval we see in the competitive landscape of the Digital Vortex is playing out inside the walls of the business as well.

As with most things in the digital arena, perspectives on the "future of work" are not in short supply. These perspectives, however, frequently revolve around topics such as prospects for different job functions, expectations of millennials, or telecommuting and other flexible work arrangements.* Few examine how a company can *enable a disruptive approach to work* and how this can translate into improved competitiveness. To that end, this chapter on fast execution focuses on the "next practices" uncovered in the DBT Center's research, so companies can reimagine work (and how they compete) and leverage disruptive execution models that depend on analytics, collaboration, automation, and the power of platforms.

Digital business agility really boils down to one thing: the capacity to change. In a recent interview, Ryan Armbruster, then chief innovation officer at UnitedHealth Group, the largest health insurance provider in the U.S., told us, "A culture of innovation is not about finding and generating the best ideas, actually. It's about being ready for change."

In a company with strong digital business agility, how work is done and by whom (or what) changes a great deal. The company is constantly sensing,

---

* See, for example, "The Future of Jobs: Employment, Skills, and Workforce Strategy for the Fourth Industrial Revolution," *World Economic Forum*, January 2016, reports.weforum.org/future-of-jobs-2016/ or "The Future of Work: A Journey to 2022," *PwC*, 2014, pwc.com/gx/en/managing-tomorrows-people/future-of-work/assets/pdf/future-of-rork-report-v16-web.pdf

analyzing, and acting in response to changes in its environment. In Chapter 5 we defined fast execution as a company's ability to carry out its plans quickly and effectively. It is a response capability that converts informed decisions into action. But where does a fast execution capability come from?

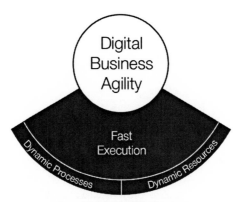

Figure 17: Fast Execution
Source: Global Center for Digital Business Transformation, 2015

Disruption on Two Fronts

To create fast execution, work must be reimagined on two fronts: resources and processes (see Figure 17). Resources represent the human, financial, and technological capital at the organization's disposal. Processes are the structured activities by which organizational goals are accomplished. In most firms, both resources and processes are highly static. There is a fixed pool of resources on which the organization can draw – the employees and systems of the company. You do your work and compete with rivals with these resources. The pool of resources can be increased or altered only on a sporadic basis, usually after a protracted negotiation with HR and finance departments.

Processes in large organizations are notoriously rigid – the result of a complex cocktail of organizational dysfunction with ingredients including bureaucracy, institutional inertia, and risk aversion. As a consequence, execution is governed by circumscribed resources and entrenched processes that make changing hard, if not impossible.

At a recent conference on digital business at the University of California, Irvine, GE's Chief Digital Officer Bill Ruh put it concisely: "The hardest thing to change is speed." Let's look then at how an organization can foster fast execution by taking a disruptive approach to both resources and processes.

Dynamic Resources

To drive fast execution, companies need to treat resources as dynamic. Dynamic resources are acquired, deployed, managed, and shifted rapidly, as business conditions dictate. Dynamic resources can be divided into two stocks of organizational capital: 1) agile talent and 2) agile technology, which we will examine in sequence.

Agile Talent

In the U.S., paralleling the growth of the so-called "gig" economy, 34 percent of workers in 2015 were classified as freelance, temporary, or contingent workers,* and that number is predicted to rise to 40 percent by 2020.[1] Setting aside whether that's a good or bad thing for healthcare costs, income inequality, the balance between innovation and worker protections, and other real public policy concerns (themes we will revisit in the conclusion of this book), this is a reality that will shape companies' workforce planning. So what does this herald in terms of how work gets done?

Talent Clouds

The human resources function is witnessing an evolution similar to cloud computing and other on-demand services. Thanks to an approach we call *"talent clouds,"* companies can assemble their teams with much greater speed and precision. They can also decide which human resources they want to invest in long-term, and which they want to access without committing to a traditional hire. In short, companies can now decide which capabilities should reside in-house and which should be accessed dynamically from outside.

Essentially, talent clouds represent people ecosystems of near infinite diversity. They provide a pipeline to expertise and skills the company lacks, or requires for only a short period, coupled with enabling applications that make finding, engaging, managing, and then relinquishing talent faster and easier. Constructing an agile pipeline to talent involves developing

---

* Estimates vary. See, for example, "How Far Reaching is the 'Gig Economy?" Wells Fargo Securities, February 29, 2016,
https://www08.wellsfargomedia.com/assets/pdf/commercial/insights/economics/special-reports/gig-economy-20160229.pdf

mechanisms to access the right sources of talent, and to attract candidates with needed skills.

Cost Value $	**Free / Ultra-low Cost:** Lower cost to hire, lower wages, no requirement to provide benefits
	Consumption-based Pricing: Pay only when labor is needed, variabilizes costs
	Reverse Auctions: Employers provide "specs" for jobs, employees compete to provide service
	Price Transparency: Employers can view competing sources of labor, "comparison shop" for cheaper providers / wage arbitrage
Experience Value	**Customer Empowerment:** Employers can "go direct" to hiring pools, eliminating expensive contracting agencies and outsourcers
	Customization: Employers can locate highly specialized expertise, secure resources when and where needed, for unique projects
	Instant Gratification: Faster time to hire
	Reduced Friction: Elimination of costly and time-consuming HR processes for recruiting and onboarding
	Automation: Reliance on cheaper human resources (e.g., offshore)
Platform Value	**Crowdsourcing:** Access to scarce know-how and skills, greater diversity of hiring
	Communities: More effective publicizing of job openings, expanded reach to candidates
	Digital Marketplace: Connecting employers with job seekers in new ways
	Data Orchestrator: Analytics on candidates, workforce trends
	Ecosystem: Gamification of work projects

Table 6: The Value of Talent Clouds
Source: Global Center for Digital Business Transformation, 2015

Out-tasking and "virtual enterprise" concepts have been discussed and implemented for decades. Still, the process of sourcing talent from traditional staffing agencies and independent contractors is cumbersome in most large incumbents, requiring preferred vendor status, purchase orders, and lengthy approvals. Worse: it often fails to deliver greater agility – an agility that is especially important when companies are seeking employees with skills or know-how in high demand. For example, the rapid growth of the tech sector and the increasing importance of technology to all aspects of business have heightened competition for software development skills and data scientists. According to the Boston Consulting Group, demand for software developers is expected to increase more than six-fold through 2022.[2] Recruiters are finding that traditional means of accessing talent no longer function in a market with such scarcity. When a value vacancy appears, companies must act fast – or miss an opportunity. Immediate access to the right skills is critical.

A number of digital platforms have emerged to help companies access valuable talent pools quickly and effectively. Drafted, a Boston-based startup, offers a mobile service that enables companies to offer a monetary reward or bounty (as high as $15,000) to users who "draft" or refer their friends for job openings. As of April 2016, $919,000 in rewards was available for positions across 70 startups. [3] Drafted takes a different approach to the talent pipeline by relying on candidates' social networks and peer referrals. It is also a mobile platform, which makes sense for the technology-savvy candidates it wants to attract. Other startups, such as Jopwell and WayUp, are building marketplaces focused on specific communities (minorities and students, respectively) to enable employers to access a diverse pipeline of talent using new digital platforms.

Finding the Needle in the Talent Haystack

In the Digital Vortex, the skills companies need are increasingly specific, yet the traditional means of advertising for job openings has become more of a liability than an asset. In talent acquisition, a focus on headcount, rather than a richer view of candidates' abilities, has led to companies being inundated with résumés, most of which do not fit their requirements. For example, Procter & Gamble recently received nearly a million applications for 2,000 positions.[4]

Largely in response to résumé overload, some companies are shifting to data and analytics in their candidate search – aided by the wealth of data now available about candidates. Beyond traditional résumé data, employers can access a range of available social data through sites such as LinkedIn and Facebook. However, it is not only the amount of data that has changed. Algorithms that identify the most promising candidates are also advancing rapidly, multiplying the ways that employers can target prospective employees. Startups such as Entelo and TalentBin offer platforms that search databases of millions of candidates based on data crawled from social sites such as LinkedIn, Quora, and GitHub. Beyond identifying candidates, such services use predictive analytics to filter talent by gender, ethnicity, or military experience. This data-driven approach to hiring identifies the best candidates and maximizes chances of job acceptance.

Talent cloud approaches must also integrate with the increasingly powerful external talent platforms that are emerging for all types of work. According to a McKinsey study, by 2025 up to 540 million people could use online talent platforms to find jobs, become more fully employed, or land positions that better match their skills.[5] Kaggle, Upwork, and HourlyNerd are platforms that let companies tap highly skilled talent on demand.

These platforms provide for new modalities of work that are more virtual and more social, and include P2P interactions that can transform execution. As organizations are becoming more physically distributed, with more employees around the globe, and with customers, partnering structures, and sourcing processes that span multiple countries, work inevitably becomes more collaborative and more virtual. As renowned computer scientist Bill Joy is said to have remarked, "Most smart people don't work here" (that is, at any given firm or location). The ability to connect workers with smart people who do not work proximate to them – or at the same company, for that matter – is one of the most compelling benefits of platforms in terms of reimagining work.

Once firms have created their shortlists, they face the most critical step: making the final selection. Digital technologies are driving fundamental changes in how candidates are tested, auditioned, and assessed.

Companies such as GapJumpers, HackerRank, and HireVue enable companies to present coding challenges to candidates to demonstrate software development skills.[6] These tools let employers assess capabilities directly rather than relying on the information presented in a candidate's résumé. Digital testing platforms have been shown to demonstrate hiring success, sometimes exceeding that of human-originated decisions.[*]

Intelligent Talent Allocation

Beyond talent acquisition, most companies do a poor job of allocating labor and forming teams. There is a strong need for new practices that enable employees across the organization to come together based on the best combination of skill sets, experience, perspectives, and other factors. Large

---

[*] A recent National Bureau of Economic Research study of 300,000 hires at 15 companies found that job testing improved job tenure by 15 percent; human intervention to override test findings significantly worsened results. In addition, there was no difference between test-driven and human-driven hiring in terms of job performance. See Lydia DePillis, "Computers Are Now Really Good at Hiring People – but HR Keeps Getting in the Way," *Washington Post*, November 23, 2015, washingtonpost.com/news/wonk/wp/2015/11/23/computers-are-now-really-good-at-hiring-people-but-hr-keeps-getting-in-the-way/

companies face the daunting task of determining which employees across multiple departments and geographies possess the right capabilities to maximize value creation. These employees could be "buried" in organizations that do not appreciate their value or understand how their knowledge could be applied more effectively.

While talent acquisition is essential for meeting the challenges of digital disruption, companies should first determine whether current employees have the capabilities most critical to success. In short, companies need a way of conducting "talent audits" that find the right employees within the company. Employees with the right skills must then be moved into teams and roles that maximize the impact of those skills. *Intelligent talent allocation* can help companies do both.

Current talent allocation mechanisms within firms often do not make effective use of the data available to identify each employee's skill set, or recommend where in the organization a worker can be most successful. Teaming, collaboration, and talent allocation tend to occur within a narrow functional context, and rarely in a way that traverses multiple functions or contemplates third-party resources.*

Teaming assignments, who is directed to work with whom, and decisions about where and how talent is used are overwhelmingly governed by the power of the managers involved, rather than any semblance of management science. With so many talent allocation decisions being made in an uninformed manner, internal talent is underutilized, and teams are poorly constructed. As a result, companies can't execute fast enough. One executive we interviewed stressed that in many companies, the biggest "people" challenge in becoming a digital business is "not a skills gap, but a talent allocation gap."

The rising importance of teaming presents a huge opportunity to use intelligent talent allocation to create a more agile approach to talent and drive value within organizations. Getting the right resources in place helps a company execute more *effectively*, not just more quickly. Improved speed comes with better quality, too. When teams are composed of individuals with the required expertise, rather than people who happen to be in the

---

* See Deborah Ancona, Elaine Backman, and Henrik Bresman, "X-teams: New Ways of Leading in a New World," for a discussion of the limitations of traditional teaming models and how organizations must move beyond inward-facing teaming structures. The authors define X-teams as "teams that enable companies to practice distributed leadership and to reach beyond internal and external boundaries to accelerate the process of innovation and change." Deborah Ancona, Elaine Backman, and Henrik Bresman, "X-teams: New Ways of Leading in a New World," *Ivey Business Journal*, September / October 2008, iveybusinessjournal.com/publication/x-teams-new-ways-of-leading-in-a-new-world/

same department, they will hasten execution by avoiding missteps and inertia. As Ray Gillenwater, co-founder and CEO of SpeakUp, told us: "For the companies of the future, their success will be defined by how well they can extract the best thinking from their teams, and how well they can turn that intelligence into actual work, into product changes, process changes, customer enhancements, and everything in between."

Getting the Best out of Your Talent

The increasing power of artificial intelligence and analytics tools, combined with the widespread availability of employee data, can transform how talent is allocated. Workforce innovators are beginning to incorporate advanced analytics into their offerings to make talent allocation smarter and more efficient. Visier, a provider of workforce management software, has launched what it calls "interactive talent flow visualization," which lets companies obtain a real-time analysis of how employees have progressed in their careers and roles in order to improve talent allocation.[7]

We spoke with Belinda Rodman, vice president of global services at SOASTA, a disruptor in the performance analytics space, and she said most employees have skills that transfer across many different areas. "But they're only known for the skills for which they were hired," she added. "A new understanding of an employee's value in the organization, how to allocate them to best leverage that value to the organization, is on the horizon." Similarly, Samar Birwadker, founder and CEO of Good&Co., a social analytics platform that links job seekers with employers that are a cultural fit, succinctly described the value of applying analytical rigor to team formation when we spoke in late 2015: "Based on the collective culture and personality of the people on a team, you can quantify what types of people and what combination of strengths and skills have a much higher likelihood of thriving in this particular team. We're adding more analytics and quantified data around likelihood of success; how you can improve things based on people analytics that are both about themselves and each other."

Firms face two problems when they underutilize their most valuable employees: they get less value from them, and the employees are more likely to quit.[8] Companies can leverage internal HR data and external data sources to identify employees at risk of attrition, find more fulfilling roles for them, and place them on teams with others who will complement their skills. Using technology originally developed for the Netflix movie recommendation engine, Workday is a platform that uses HR and market information to identify workers likely to quit. The platform can offer prescriptive recommendations for job role changes that are best suited to the employee.[9] Approaches to talent allocation that leverage such digital technologies hold the promise of greater employee engagement, lower turnover, and faster, more effective execution.

Agile Technology

IT goes to the very heart of fast execution. Let's look at the role of IT in driving digital business agility, and the benefits of an "agile technology" approach.

In the introduction to this book, we defined "digital" as the convergence of multiple technology innovations enabled by connectivity. This convergence is the seed of the exponential change and turbulence we are witnessing throughout markets in the Digital Vortex. The complexity that results, however, has huge implications for how IT is run and how it can contribute to increased agility and competitiveness.

Beyond the "Department of No"

Within enterprises, IT departments tend to be among the entities most resistant to change, which actually serves to *slow* execution in many cases. In part, this is because IT leaders are generally judged by the absence of problems. A common metric (or "service level agreement" in IT-speak) is uptime, a measure of the percentage of time during which there are no problems. Change, by its very nature, implies less certainty, increased risk, and the potential for new problems, which are anathema to IT leaders. This spawns cultural resistance that makes IT known as the "Department of No."[10]

Even so, IT leaders acknowledge that the business expects more of them today. In fact, Cisco's research shows the number-one area in which IT leaders concede they must do more to meet the expectations of their stakeholders is in driving innovation.[11] In this regard, not enough IT shops are making the leap from a perceived "cost center" to a true business partner. Therefore, the lines of business (the internal clients of IT such as sales and finance) are circumventing the IT organization and buying directly from technology companies to obtain greater speed and flexibility, usually in the cloud. One might say that a large number of IT organizations are failing to deliver the cost value, experience value, or platform value that would secure their continued relevance to the business, and are consequently being disrupted. The growing trends of bring-your-own-device (BYOD) and software-as-a-service (SaaS) are symptomatic of this. Cisco's research suggests that nearly half of all IT spending – 46 percent – already comes from the lines of business, rather than the IT organization.[12] This should be a signal to IT "leopards" that it's time to change their spots.

Cisco's research reveals that more than 80 percent of IT budgets are dedicated to existing technology environments – to maintaining and securing the multitude of applications, hardware infrastructure, legacy systems and the rest – where complexity is rife. The complexity of existing IT environments has only worsened in the wake of an unprecedented proliferation of digital devices, applications, and services.

Enterprise IT environments are characterized by both heterogeneity (a lot of different stuff must be maintained) and flat or declining budgets. This means IT spending on business outcomes the organization truly cares about (e.g., time to market, enabling new business models) is pushed to the margins of the IT portfolio. It's very difficult to compete with nimble, well-capitalized disruptors when more than 80 cents of every IT dollar at a typical incumbent is devoted to merely "keeping the lights on." What makes matters worse is that many IT leaders are also effectively *blocked* from driving innovation: they must first bring down costs and then divert the freed-up cash to doing new things (sometimes referred to as "save-to-invest").

A Single Pane of Glass

Given all this, how can IT help the business with the speed, agility, and risk-taking that are needed in the Digital Vortex? In most organizations, IT is managed as a series of discrete silos: storage, compute, network, security, and applications. Going forward, however, an agile technology approach can bridge those silos, treating all IT components as a dynamic, on-demand resource pool that spans all aspects of IT service creation. This enables the company to "orchestrate" end-to-end IT capabilities at speed, so that each time the business has a new requirement, there is a repeatable process by which functionality, security, bandwidth, computing resources, and integration services – all the IT resources needed in one fell swoop – can be immediately brought to bear. This means IT can automate how resources are stood up to support a request from the business, dramatically shortening cycle times.

A dynamic resource-based approach to IT lowers the total cost of ownership (TCO) for a company's infrastructure and applications, and frees up resources for more value-adding activities – in effect, "saving" in order to invest. [13] More important, this enables IT to be dramatically more responsive to the needs of the business and create faster execution in how IT resources are provisioned and managed.

In an agile technology model, rather than managing IT resources as a series of individual technologies, the company's entire IT portfolio can be managed by setting top-level policies and automating business rules for service and security levels, traffic prioritization, user privileges, and other expensive, error-prone, and time-intensive manual tasks normally performed by IT staff. Instead of managing islands of IT, and manually configuring servers or switches or other devices, leading IT organizations are working toward the Holy Grail of IT management: a so-called "single pane of glass," meaning a centralized console through which IT leaders can monitor and manage their environment. This "programmability" means IT leaders can set operational policies, automate workflows, improve quality, and accelerate service delivery to business users. Thus, IT becomes a dynamic resource that is integral to enabling fast execution.

Coca-Cola's CTO and chief innovation officer Alan Boehme has talked about a concept he has advanced in his operation, memorably called "throw-away IT," which "encourages developers to create inexpensive, quickly-deployed applications and services to meet emerging business needs."[14] This kind of accelerated resource deployment can be critical to helping the business adapt to its evolving competitive pressures and priorities. A note of caution, however: adding many new applications and IT services in response to business demands, especially in a short window, may actually exacerbate IT complexity and ironically lead to slower execution. Recent research from the Corporate Executive Board found that for a typical $100 million technology portfolio, the number of individual IT projects rose 38 percent from 2012 to 2014.[15] This results in the overhead costs and preoccupation with maintenance that we described above. In some cases, this proliferation in IT initiatives is an earnest attempt at greater agility, and a signpost of the desire to try new things; in others, it's merely sloppy IT portfolio management. Being "responsive to the needs of the business" must, therefore, be balanced by governance and direction from management to ensure that pilots and skunkworks-style programs deliver the desired business outcomes or are killed quickly.

The Future of Dynamic Resources

The cloud is clearly a core element of how disruptors move with such speed. We have touched on the idea of "talent clouds" that enable companies to quickly and efficiently activate the right human resources for a given business opportunity. In technology, cloud computing has become a mainstay of company IT strategies, enabling organizations to consume IT resources in an on-demand fashion.[16]

But cloud can also help companies more dynamically leverage *physical* assets and processes. This capability is particularly promising for firms that compete in asset-intensive industries such as healthcare, oil and gas, and utilities – those that are located on the outer edges of the Digital Vortex. In these sectors, market leaders have invested immense sums in the physical assets required to run their operations. For example, it was estimated that the global oil and gas industry spent over $1 *trillion* on capital investments in 2012 alone, during an era when oil prices were particularly high.[17] Digital enablers that promise to drive higher asset utilization (i.e., to "sweat the assets") in these industries are very compelling. This is especially true in the Digital Vortex, where incumbents face the prospect of competing with disruptors who may completely sidestep the traditional value chain and the corresponding investments in physical assets.

Cohealo is a disruptor that has launched a cloud-based platform to enable health systems to track and share non-emergency hospital equipment among the multiple hospitals within a system. It is estimated that in the United States, $100 billion is spent on medical equipment annually, and much of this spending is wasteful because the equipment sits unused most of the time.[18] Furthermore, in health systems comprising multiple hospitals, each facility may lack visibility into what equipment the other hospitals in the system own. The result: member hospitals each purchase, store, and maintain the same equipment, resulting in massive redundancy. A cloud-sharing platform such as Cohealo can enable hospitals within a system to "see" all of the equipment in all the facilities and coordinate the sharing of these valuable resources. This reduces the investment an individual hospital must make while allowing it to access a much larger pool of equipment when needed. Here the focus is on effective execution, more so than speed.

In the future, we expect to see this model of cloud-based dynamic resource allocation expand to industries such as manufacturing. Industry experts are already exploring the development of "cloud manufacturing" business models which, while still in their infancy, give producers on-demand access to shared manufacturing resources and production lines so that assets such as production machinery can be acquired, used, and redeployed among organizations.[19] In technology circles, this sharing of the same resource among multiple organizations is referred to as "multi-tenancy." 3D Hubs, a 3D printing service platform headquartered in Amsterdam, is an example of such a disruptive model. The platform connects parties in need of 3D printing services with owners of 3D printers (Hubs). According to the company, the platform supports a network of 3D printers across more than 20,000 locations.[20]

Dynamic Processes

Incumbents' business processes are often seen as dumb, slow, and immutable. By contrast, dynamic processes are intelligent and fast, and look different every time. They adapt to circumstances and customize what occurs in order to maximize value to the company. It is easy to imagine dynamic processes in a host of situations, such as a clinical setting (e.g., detecting and fixing a dosage error) or a manufacturing plant (e.g., predictive maintenance on factory floor equipment). Dynamic processes involve rapid enablement and rapid intervention. Let's look at each of these and how they contribute to faster, better execution.

Rapid Enablement

During the DBT Center's research to disentangle the occurrence of disruption, we found again and again that speed is one of the most effective arrows in the disruptor's quiver. Let's consider an under-explored area in which disruptors use speed as a primary weapon: *rapid enablement*.

Rapid enablement is the accelerated introduction of new organizational capabilities across a broad spectrum of value-creating activities, including marketing, customer support, commerce, application development, and channels.* As discussed in Chapter 1, disruptors focus on the value, not the value chain; and whatever *can* be digitized *is* digitized.

What this means in terms of capability enablement is that disruptors digitize both "primary activities" and "support activities" (in the classical description of a value chain used by Michael Porter) on which incumbents have relied.[21] Primary activities include logistics, operations, marketing, sales, and service. Support activities include human resources, finance, procurement, and IT. These are the parts of industry value chains that are being unbundled and recombined to create new competitive forms. For disruptors, rapid enablement isn't just old-fashioned outsourcing of "context" or overhead activities to outside vendors that support the business. Instead, these functions may be core to the firm and how it creates value, whether it is supply chain, sales, R&D, HR, or services.

---

* In their book *The Only Sustainable Edge*, John Hagel III and John Seely Brown urge leaders to move beyond the orthodoxy of "core competencies" and contemplate "accelerated capability building" as the source of durable advantage. In this framework, capabilities are the "recurring mobilization of resources for the delivery of distinctive value in excess of cost." This provides a beginning for companies to imagine competitive positioning that depends upon rapid creation of capabilities. To achieve competitive success in the Digital Vortex, a company must hone its ability to mobilize resources – tangible and intangible – across an ecosystem of partners (rather than just inside the four walls of a lone firm) to speed innovation and create new customer value.

Fast-tracking to Customer Value

Disruptors' approaches to creating new organizational capabilities across the value chain are utterly different from those of incumbents. They begin with customer value, purpose-building organizational capabilities that maximize it – ideally in a way that clearly differentiates the disruptor from incumbents. In most instances, of course, disruptors also build organizational capabilities from scratch. As digital natives, their environment for capability enablement is a "greenfield" that can be digitized from the ground up. Not so for most incumbents. For a large, established organization, the complexity and expense associated with the people, processes, and systems used in these activities are enormous.

Earlier, we cited the example of Adyen, the Netherlands-based payments processor. It's instructive that Adyen counts among its clients Netflix, Airbnb, Uber, Spotify, and Facebook.[22] What these disruptors ask themselves is, "Why do I need to create a billing and payments system when I enter a new market?" They know Adyen has already digitized this component of their industry's value chain. They don't need to hire anyone, buy any facilities, or create a multi-million-dollar IT system to address this link in the value chain. The disruptors get cost value, experience value, and platform value from other disruptors that help them accelerate their own execution and create new value for *their* customers. They know that with a rapid enablement approach they can piece together virtualized organizational capabilities that give them faster execution, and the agility to create the new forms of customer value that disrupt markets. This is a key point worth underscoring: disruptors not only *deliver* but also *seek* cost value, experience value, and platform value when building organizational capabilities. They then use the benefits they derive to *create* combinatorial disruption themselves.

It's not just billing and payments; it's everything. To set up benefits for employees, you can use Zenefits. For customer relationship management and a contact center-in-a-box, use Freshdesk or Salesforce.com or SugarCRM. For an e-commerce site in minutes, use Shopify.

Many disruptive innovations rely on mobile apps. Disruptors don't use expensive interactive agencies and IT services companies to custom-code apps. They practice rapid enablement, using open-source tools and "container" technology such as Docker to simplify app creation and shrink time from development to production. To quickly add mapping and geospatial analytics functions to their app, they might use data from HERE or OpenStreetMap. For transactional emails, they could turn to SendGrid; for electronic signatures, DocuSign. And they might use Twilio to enable two-factor authentication or to send dispatch notifications and estimated times of arrival.

Connection Speed

Platforms involve network effects and "exponentiality," making them major sources of disruption in how execution occurs. In Chapter 4, we pointed out that platform formation is mysterious to many incumbents. A cross-section of digital disruptors is seizing on this fact, creating a new market in helping companies rapidly enable platforms. (They found a value vacancy.) In essence, they *use* platforms to *sell* platforms to companies that want to *be* platforms. Platform creation, in short, is being demystified. Sharetribe enables all manner of multi-sided digital marketplaces. Zuora can help you create a subscription-based business model, replete with billing and metering. Platform giants such as Facebook and Google extend their robust user-authentication capabilities as a credentialing mechanism to other digital disruptors (e.g., "log in with your Facebook account"). This creates convenience for users and also positions these companies as "platforms for platforms," marketing their ability to create information-transmission efficiencies to other entities.

Rapid enablement can be a critical mechanism to drive faster execution, for both startups and incumbents. As noted in Chapter 4, there is no single way to pursue Disrupt strategies. Companies will use a variety of spin-offs or spin-ins, joint ventures, innovation incubators, or acquisitions. These are all instances ripe for rapid enablement approaches.

Rapid Intervention

Fast execution is not limited to how an organization can supercharge its innovation engine and "behave" like a disruptor. It also occurs in the more operational sense of "execution," helping the company create greater customer value by speeding up the day-to-day running of the business. It's not just about producing prototypes faster, or shaving deployment times for enterprise applications, but also about being fast enough to capitalize on opportunities on a more mundane level – in individual customer interactions, during momentary events in the supply chain, or any opportunity in which value is time-bound. We call this *rapid intervention*. Fast execution is vital to creating operational efficiencies, which can play a huge role in digital disruption strategies, particularly defensive strategies (Harvest, Retreat) where cost control and quality of experience increase in importance.

Connecting Dark Assets

Like many aspects of the organization, business processes will encounter incredible levels of disruption in the Digital Vortex. That disruption, however, is coming from an unlikely source, one that may surprise many executives: the Internet of Things.

What does IoT have to do with business processes? We call the "things" that have historically not been connected in the physical business environment "dark assets." When we connect these dark assets – in factories, bank branches, retail stores, hospitals, schools, airports, warehouses, oil rigs – we unleash vast troves of information about them, and lay the groundwork for designing dynamic processes. This intelligence underpins an element of the fast execution model that we call *"rapid intervention"*: taking immediate action to capitalize on opportunities or neutralize threats, whether it's capturing sales, optimizing operations, or preventing accidents.

Rapid intervention can be done through machine learning and automation *or through human action* enabled by digital technologies. In this respect, dynamic processes don't necessarily imply replacing people with machines. Dynamic processes can also enhance and optimize work performed by people, though the intervention can be made by a machine, or a person supported by a machine, depending on the circumstance.

Let's consider an example of rapid intervention in a retailing scenario.

Imagine that a "big box" retailer, a large mass merchandiser, has instrumented its store with low-cost sensors. Bluetooth beacons and other sensors have been placed on previously "dark" assets: store shelves, shopping carts, doors to the parking lot, the POS, even individual stocked products (Moore's Law is driving down the cost of beacons and other IP sensors so they will soon be disposable from a cost standpoint).

Two customers, Rohan and Maria, are each out to do some shopping. Rohan plans to pick up some items for dinner, while Maria is seeking a high-definition television. Real-time analysis of data obtained from in-store sensors, the store's wireless network, and video feeds from IP cameras tell the retailer the following: Rohan is pushing his shopping cart at twice the average speed of all the other customers. Meanwhile, Maria is "showrooming," examining the televisions on display in the electronics department, but comparing prices from other sellers with her smartphone, connecting over the store's guest Wi-Fi network.

What would a dynamic process model look like here? First, the retailer can intelligently interpret Rohan's and Maria's behaviors in their actual contexts. The speed of Rohan's shopping cart likely indicates he is in a hurry. This is not the time to push on him an extraneous, out-of-context offer for a sale on winter tires, even though he's purchased items from the automotive department in the past. Instead, the retailer uses a digital display (or Rohan's phone) to provide wayfinding to departments or "go-with" products relevant to what he wants to accomplish. This is based not on his past purchasing history but on machine intelligence about what he has in his shopping cart (food items). This experience value – including Customization, Instant Gratification, and Reduced Friction – is delivered *automatically, in real time,* as Rohan moves through the store. This is a key form of fast execution.

In Maria's case, analytics tell the retailer that she's considering a big-ticket purchase: a television. She has spent seven minutes of dwell time in the television aisle, and has been checking competitors' prices on her phone. The accelerometer on Maria's smartphone detects she's mostly been facing an "endcap" (the end of an aisle) where a particular brand of television is displayed. The sensor-based store network, combined with decision analytics, alerts a store associate to approach Maria, offer her some help selecting a television or accessories, and extend a modest discount to entice her to buy a television then and there, rather than risking that she'll head home to complete an e-commerce transaction with another merchant.

"Maria's price" for the television is determined by algorithm – subtracting the minimum discount that predictive analytics suggests will offset her intention to shop elsewhere – and this dynamic pricing, along with intelligent recommendations on up-selling (e.g., speakers, cables, a warranty) is transmitted to a connected mobile device held by a store associate. The employee can glance at the device as he makes his way over to Maria with the offer of assistance.

In this case, analytics, applied to sensor and network data, informed the employee of the need to take action, and how it could be optimally done. This is an example of dynamic processes that empower intelligent human intervention, rather than pure automation. With prompting from analytical tools that contextualize what is occurring, the store associate could move quickly to intercept a potentially lost sale – fast execution. Maria enjoys an improved experience and a potentially lower price. The retailer benefits by making the sale, satisfying the customer, and boosting basket size by including up-sold merchandise.

This execution must be fast because the value "up for grabs" is temporary. Rohan and Maria will be in the store for just a few minutes, and during that time, there may be only a brief moment when their purchase decisions can be influenced. Information about these customers and their context at that instant must be processed on the spot. It's no good for the retailer if, hours or weeks later, business analysts crunching numbers about store footfall data notice opportunities to sell to Rohan and Maria. By then, dinner has been served and TV shows have been watched!

Finally, Rohan and Maria head to the front of the store to pay for their purchases, but both find long waits at the checkout. Queues at the point of sale are among shoppers' greatest frustrations, and often lead to lost sales.[23] With dynamic processes, the retailer can mitigate this problem. It can use sensor-based analytics to post wait times at different checkouts and (even better) notify store associates that long queues are forming at the checkout, recommending that they head to the front of the store with mobile "line-busting" POS devices. Again, this shows how both automation and intelligent human interventions can allow company operations to adapt on the fly. In fact, this scenario provides a good example of how a retailer creates hyperawareness (they know what's happening in the store in real time), informed decision-making (they can offer a discount or move labor to where it's most valuably utilized), and fast execution (they can provide wayfinding or estimated wait times automatically using digital signage, or have employees offer assistance to customers before they exit the store).

Is this kind of execution the stuff of science fiction? Whether this scenario thrills or alarms, managers would be wise not to dismiss it as implausible. In fact, it represents a competitive reality for retailers today, one that is mirrored in many other industries in the Digital Vortex.

We met in early 2016 with RetailNext, one of the leading providers of in-store analytics, to understand the maturity of these technologies and their potential impacts. RetailNext boasts hundreds of the largest global retailers as its clients, and analyzes the in-store behaviors of more than 800 million shoppers every year, collecting more than a trillion data points.[24] In our interview, RetailNext CEO Alexei Agratchev said, "The need is for systems that allow you to treat every store as a different store, every day as a different day, and at some point every customer as a different customer. That's where retail overall is heading. It's a very difficult transformation, but that's where technology plays a huge role."

Test, Learn, Repeat

Recall that executives in our survey found a culture of experimentation and risk-taking one of the biggest differentiators for startups. This finding wasn't surprising: one of the most frequently asked questions we hear is,

"How can companies innovate faster?" One answer: rapid intervention can play an integral role in accelerating innovation.*

Tencent, the Chinese incumbent provider of online services, including mobile messaging platform WeChat, relies on an approach of iteration and fast failure to bring new services to market. An example of this approach is the company's use of internal competition to spur the development of innovative new offerings. In fact, the original WeChat platform was developed through an internal competition. Two different product teams in different locations were given the same instructions for developing a new platform, and positioned to compete against one another. After two months, the winning group had developed a new mobile platform for text messaging and group chat that would eventually become WeChat.[25]

Tencent has also pioneered new forms of quick iteration that help them quickly launch and improve their online services. The company follows a "launch-test-improve" model through which it releases new platforms with limited features to its user base. [26] Within hours of a launch, Tencent observes how the new services are used, and captures user suggestions about improvements and additional features they would like to see. In this way, the company can launch and improve its offerings within a few weeks, a much shorter timeframe than the traditional "beta testing" process.[27]

Unlike online services, physical products typically require more time and investment in the early stages of development as companies create working prototypes, test them, and iterate until the product is ready for mass production. Industries such as manufacturing, oil and gas, and pharmaceuticals, which are currently on the outer edge of the Digital Vortex, struggle to innovate quickly because the products they create (or require) are highly complex and often highly regulated. Bringing them to market requires multiple phase-gates, and companies can find themselves years and millions of dollars into a development cycle only to discover that the product(s) cannot be brought to market.

A concept called the "digital twin," which combines multiple technology and operational innovations, is helping these industries develop products faster and adapt them to changing circumstances in a rapid intervention model. A "digital twin" is a virtual representation of a physical

---

* Rapid *enablement* also lends itself to better, faster innovation. When disruptors can switch on and off particular organizational capabilities at high speed (and low cost), they are positioned for more experimentation, design iterations, testing of business models, and continuous learning. In this sense, rapid enablement and rapid intervention can have compounding effects on speed of innovation.

object that exists in the real world, such as a car, a wind turbine, or a building. Digital twins go beyond computer-aided design (CAD), which can simulate a product and physical conditions. Instead, digital twins use sensors and analytics to create a one-to-one mapping of the physical object and its digital *doppelgänger*.

The digital twin can then be used to create extremely accurate simulations to see how the physical object would perform in a variety of circumstances. The data from these simulations can be used to show how changing conditions or design alterations would affect performance, to create new virtual prototypes, and to accelerate design iterations. Digital twins can also be used to improve the accuracy of predictive maintenance, because simulations can be run on specific machines, rather than on a generic model, to identify areas of vulnerability or wear. Thus, they enable *business model* innovation for manufacturers, namely the move from selling capex-based physical products to higher-margin, services-based offerings.[28]

Manufacturers such as GE and Siemens are using digital twins to customize product development and deliver predictive maintenance services. GE, for example, uses them to design wind farms for specific sites and adapt turbines to changing conditions. This can increase the efficiency of power generation by 20 percent.[29] Siemens is partnering with Boeing to simulate the entire development and engineering process for new airplanes, including flight tests.[30] In Formula One auto racing, cars can undergo up to 1,000 design changes in a single week, all of which can be simulated using a digital twin approach that can gives teams a competitive edge on the track.[31]

In addition, digital twins can dramatically improve the integration of suppliers and partners, which is vital to producing complex products in automotive, aerospace, and other industries. Miscommunication and imprecision in the design of components can lead to costly delays and product recalls. Digital twins allow manufacturers and their supply chain partners to co-innovate, interact with the digital representation, test it, and ensure that their components will integrate with the product. Software firms that specialize in product lifecycle management such as PTC have been acquiring digital disruptors in predictive analytics to build their own digital twin capabilities. This allows them to create a collaborative product design network (incorporating platform-based business models such as Ecosystem and Crowdsourcing).[32]

Finally, digital twins are being applied to the human body to improve the efficacy of medical treatment. Dassault Systèmes has created a digital twin of the human heart that can be adapted to simulate the heart function of an individual.[33] For example, by creating a virtual copy of a heart with congenital abnormalities or blockages, doctors can predict how treatments such as surgery or the insertion of a pacemaker will affect the performance of the heart – and the patient's health. The digital twin approach also holds promise for improving drug discovery.

The Future of Dynamic Processes

Process change is a tough nut to crack. What does a dynamic process model imply for how processes will run in the coming years? Let's address this question by looking at history.

The digitization of business processes that's already occurred – all the way back to the dawn of "e-business" two decades ago, and business process re-engineering before that – gave rise to a key improvement: standardization. Standardization meant efficiency, consistency, and productivity. Although dynamic processes means there is no monolithic notion of "process," this does not contradict the logic of process standardization. On the contrary, *routinization,* driven by business rules, is indispensable in dynamic processes and fast execution. As those business rules grow in number and intelligence, the value of dynamic processes will increase.

Finally, in the future, "real time" will actually be too slow. Instead, the Digital Vortex will demand that companies anticipate new business processes. Instead of merely sensing, deciding, and responding to the current situation, firms will need to sense, decide, and proactively adapt their processes *based on what is likely to unfold.* In 2014 Amazon patented a technology it calls "anticipatory shipping," sending merchandise before customers actually purchase it. Amazon says it may box and ship products it expects customers in a specific area will want – based on previous orders and other factors – but haven't yet ordered. According to the patent, the packages could wait at the shippers' hubs or on trucks until an order arrives.[34]

Thinking, Fast and Secure

As we consider processes and fast execution in general, we must pay heed to security considerations. Security plays a crucial role in agility, particularly in efforts to accelerate innovation, but companies are rightly concerned that digital technologies and business models may leave them more vulnerable to attacks from hackers. With tens of billions of new IoT connections coming online in the next five years, there will be many new points of ingress for those who wish to do harm. In other words, the "attack surface" of the company is expanding.

Many incumbents have sprawling IT systems that combine decades-old legacy technologies, which were not designed to be exposed beyond corporate firewalls, with digital technologies that require extensive connectivity – to customers, partners, the cloud, etc. The complexity of these systems, and the inherent vulnerability of some legacy IT, makes cybersecurity an imposing challenge.

As a result, companies are torn between the imperative to pursue digital business models and the disaster that security breaches can cause. This conflict is causing companies to slow the pace of innovation. In a recent Cisco study of senior business executives, [35] 71 percent indicated that cybersecurity risks are hindering innovation. Another 60 percent admit they are reluctant to develop the very digital offerings on which growth, and even survival, depends in the Digital Vortex. Inadequate security means less appetite and capacity for experimentation and risk-taking, which can undermine a company's ability to pursue offensive strategies (Disrupt, Occupy).

Evaluating Fast Execution

Is your company building a foundation to enable fast execution? As a test, answer the following questions:

How have we changed our approach to acquiring talent? For many incumbents, the ways they hire employees or engage outside services are an anachronism. They look like something created for the television program *Mad Men*, rather than the Digital Vortex. Even receiving electronic résumés and posting employment openings to third-party job portals are a far cry from the dynamic approach to talent acquisition and team formation represented by Entelo, TalentBin, and other social media analytics players.

How do teams form at our company? Most companies create well-defined divisions (more commonly called "business units" today) that are intended to align resources to similarly well-defined market opportunities. Of course, market opportunities are less and less well-defined in the Digital Vortex. The tendency to create organizational silos and hierarchy to match a market opportunity is a common trait of incumbents that most disruptors disdain. Most disruptors take an agile approach to talent that should be adopted by incumbents as well. Companies such as Visier enable organizations to visualize their talent holistically so they can allocate it in a way that maximizes value to the worker and the firm.

Could someone else provide a (digitized) piece of the value chain to enable faster execution? Too few incumbents are focused here, even though this is a key ingredient – a kind of "secret sauce" – of some of the global economy's most disruptive players. Owning the value chain is undesirable in many instances, especially those frequent situations in the Digital Vortex in which "what is required" often changes. A diverse set of capability "arms merchants" including Adyen, Zenefits, and Zuora can help incumbents quicken their pursuit of value vacancies.

How often do business processes actually change? For most incumbents, business processes follow a predictable path. Deviations from that path are unwelcome, even if they may represent opportunities to create more customer value or could benefit the organization. Disruptors embrace the need to adapt business processes on the fly. In fact, they *count on* the inability of incumbents to adapt at the same speed when designing their business models. Disruptors such as RetailNext illuminate a new path – one in which business processes adapt dynamically and drive continuous learning based on the current context of the business.

The Lean Incumbent

In Chapter 1, we introduced the term "encumbered incumbent" to explain how large, market-leading enterprises are saddled with assets, value chains, processes, and organizational behaviors that make them uncompetitive in an age in which disruption is everywhere. We pointed out that incumbents tend to lack advantages characteristic of startups, such as speed, agility, and a culture of experimentation and risk-taking. Replicating these startup advantages in the context of large, complex organizations is, in many ways, the purpose of this book.

With so much money and mindshare directed at digital disruptors in recent years, the philosophy known as "Lean Startup" has taken off, popularized by the work of serial entrepreneurs and authors Eric Ries and

Steve Blank.* Lean Startup methodologies stress extensive customer listening and iterative design to raise the intelligence of innovation and support learning, and to increase the likelihood that a startup will succeed. Rather than plowing resources up-front into expensive design and development, lean startups produce a cheap "minimum viable product" (MVP) that can be socialized with customers to uncover shortcomings, identify what is valued (and what is not), and discover opportunities for rethinking the company's offering. This "validated learning" enables the startup to "pivot," re-conceiving its product or service so it more closely matches the needs of the market.

As the name suggests, Lean Startup is primarily focused on smaller, less mature companies. However, this has not stopped leaders with large market incumbents from trying to import this approach into their own innovation processes.† Although commendable, incumbent attempts to employ Lean Startup doctrine have mostly fallen flat. At best, they have produced what Steve Blank has called "innovation theater" – the trappings of innovation and lots of hype, but no substantive change.[36]

Imagine an organization that could accomplish validated learning, not just in the realm of new product introduction, but in *everything* it does – in all aspects of its operation. After learning through hyperawareness, and making a sound choice with informed decision-making, the company could pivot (do something differently) that would result in the creation of new or greater value for customers. Finally, imagine the organization could do this on a pervasive and continuous basis, and at speed.

Is a "lean incumbent" (versus an "encumbered incumbent") so far-fetched? Not at all. In fact, creating the capacity to carry out "pivots" in large, complex organizations is precisely what the DBT Center's core construct – digital business agility – is intended to do. Behavioral and situational awareness, inclusive and augmented decision-making, and dynamic resources and processes collectively manifest as *intelligent change*, going beyond how the company innovates to encompass how the company executes as a whole.

---

* See Eric Ries, *The Lean Startup: How Today's Entrepreneurs Use Continuous Innovation to Create Radically Successful Businesses* (New York: Crowne Business, 2011), and Steve Blank, *Four Steps to the Epiphany: Successful Strategies for Products That Win* (California: Steve Blank, 2013).

† Several worthwhile efforts have addressed this issue. See, for example, Vijay Govindarajan and Chris Trimble, *The Other Side of Innovation: Solving the Execution Challenge* (Boston: Harvard Business Review Press, 2010), and Nathan Furr and Jeff Dyer, *The Innovator's Method: Bringing the Lean Startup into Your Organization* (Boston: Harvard Business Review Press, 2014).

Conclusion

Key Themes in This Book

As we conclude, let's review a few of the main ideas in this book, their roles in spurring organizational renewal, and how they can be applied in your company. In addition, let's examine some of the longer-term implications of the Digital Vortex, and appraise both digital disruption and its effects in a wider sense.

In the introduction, we defined digital business transformation as "organizational change through the use of digital technologies and business models to improve performance." We noted that *Digital Vortex* is not a book about transformation per se, but a manual on how to compete. The organizational change that is the basis of transformation is a broader undertaking that dominates our future research agenda – how companies can implement and absorb agility-oriented innovations, in particular.

Through extensive original research, this book has decomposed how digital disruption occurs, outlined the organizational attributes and capabilities of digital disruptors, and charted some of the compelling "next practices" that incumbents can adopt to increase their competitiveness.

Our discussion of these practices should not be interpreted as endorsements of specific applications or as taking a tactical "point solution" approach to transformation. Transformation is more than a summation of digital solutions in use. As Richard Nixon, perhaps apocryphally, remarked, "Solutions are not the answer." Many of the startups described in this book will flame out. Nonetheless, we can learn from their models.

It would also be accurate to say that our aim has been to move beyond generic principles of transformation – leading from the top down, focusing on change management – that permeate the management literature. Failure to apply such principles is surely a good predictor of a corresponding failure in transformation efforts, but applying them does little to create competitive separation from those companies that do likewise. In the Digital Vortex, application of these maxims amounts to table stakes.

We have shown how digital disruptors ignore traditional value chains and focus on creating cost value, experience value, and platform value, and then merging them to produce combinatorial disruption. We have introduced a taxonomy of 15 business models that describe most of the value-creation and value-capture activities occurring in the Digital Vortex. These take place across industries, straddling both B2C and B2B segments, and can be employed by incumbents as part of their strategy to deal with the new competitive forms confronting them.

We have looked at the emergence of value vampires that are irrevocably changing markets and profit pools, but also at the upside of disruption – value vacancies – the rapidly evolving, highly contested market opportunities that will be the source of future growth for many incumbents. Our task has been to identify cross-cutting capabilities commonly found in companies that succeed at disruption – in select incumbents, but more frequently in startups – and how they can drive competitive differentiation in the Digital Vortex.

Understanding how customer value is created, the business models used to produce it, the competitive dynamics in play, and the strategic response options available to companies creates a "North Star" for the journey of digital business transformation. There is no one-size-fits-all approach to transformation, no universal course of action, and executives should view with suspicion any such claims from consultancies or "digital" advisors. Far too many digital transformation efforts are nothing more than strategic shams – transformation for transformation's sake – that sap organizational resources and ultimately lead to cynicism and lost competitive standing. Our research and experience working with executives tell us that one of the biggest factors in failed transformation programs is a poor understanding of the end game – the value created for the customer and the right business model(s) – that a company needs to win. This is our point of departure.

The Transformation-Ready Enterprise

Digital business agility is not just another factor to keep an eye on, or an issue to be considered, among a raft of competing priorities. It is, we believe, the single most important organizational capability required to compete and win in an increasingly disruptive world. Digital business agility is, quite simply, the core foundational capability in the Digital Vortex.

Digital technologies underpin each of the three agility elements. Although these technologies are necessary, they are not sufficient to create digital business agility, which is rooted in people and processes. Digital technologies, and the companies that offer them, change constantly. Organizations that are able to identify the appropriate tools, technologies, and business models, and leverage them to build hyperawareness, informed decision-making, and fast execution, are the organizations that will sustain their agility over time. Put another way, digital technologies are just one of the means to an agile end.

Digital business agility is the cornerstone for all of the frameworks described in this book. We see it as the basis for understanding, building, and delivering cost value, experience value, and platform value. Identifying value vacancies depends on hyperawareness. Exploiting them requires informed decision-making and fast execution. The cycle of "sense, decide, and act" that drives digital business agility is a common characteristic of successful digital disruptors, including value vampires.

We have further laid out six sub-capabilities that underpin hyperawareness, informed decision-making, and fast execution: behavioral awareness and situational awareness; inclusive decision-making and augmented decision-making; and dynamic resources and dynamic processes, respectively (see Figure 18). These must act as an integrated whole that drives closed-loop learning and operations.

We believe that all organizations need to become digital business agility experts. Its importance to continued success is not restricted to just digital giants and their immediate competitors. It is relevant to companies and industries across the Digital Vortex. This book offers many examples of disruptive threats in traditionally slow-moving sectors such as healthcare, energy, and manufacturing.

The strategies we introduced to respond to digital disruption – Harvest, Retreat, Disrupt, and Occupy – also rely on digital business agility. Of course, determining the appropriate strategy means hitting a moving target. As circumstances change, so does the most suitable strategic response. For example, identifying the right time to block and the right time to retreat is critical. Perfecting the correct approach to disrupting an existing business, or occupying a new value vacancy, requires constant adjustment.

Digital business agility is as relevant for B2B companies as it is for B2C companies. As we have repeatedly stated, digital disruptors focus on the value, not the value chain, and B2B companies must therefore be cognizant of where value is created. Unfortunately, many of the B2B companies we work with lack a heightened sense of hyperawareness, perhaps because they tend to be a few steps removed from how the value created is ultimately consumed (i.e., by their customers' customers). As we have seen, forward-looking B2B companies, such as GE and elevator company KONE, are

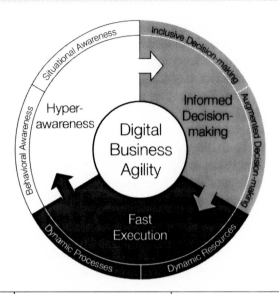

Hyper-awareness	**Behavioral Awareness:** The ability to understand how workers and customers act, what they think, and what they value	**Situational Awareness:** The ability to identify changes in an organization's internal and external environments, and to understand which changes matter
Informed Decision-making	**Inclusive Decision-making:** The ability to make decisions based on the shared intelligence that emerges from the collaboration of disparate individuals and teams	**Augmented Decision-making:** The ability to incorporate data and analytics into the decision-making processes across an organization
Fast Execution	**Dynamic Resources:** The ability to acquire, deploy, manage, and re-allocate resources (e.g., talent, technology) as business conditions dictate	**Dynamic Processes:** The ability to rapidly introduce new business processes and adapt existing business processes to changing business conditions

Figure 18: A Holistic Approach to Digital Business Agility
Source: Global Center for Digital Business Transformation, 2015

taking active steps to build a backbone of digital business agility into their operating models.

Digital business agility is as relevant for service companies as it is for product companies. Services tend to be relatively static and not particularly innovative. Think of the inefficiencies and customer experience deficits that plague sectors such as banking, telecommunications, tourism, and professional services including law and accounting. Because customers in service sectors tend to be highly responsive to improvements in experience value, they present huge opportunities for digital disruptors. Agile competitors can identify the many value vacancies that exist in service industries, and conduct dynamic experiments to find new and better forms of customer value.

We believe that digital business agility must be built into the very fabric of organizations. It must be explicitly recognized, practiced, incentivized, and improved. Digital business agility – the "fitness" of the firm – is about readying the organization for transformation, becoming a company that is adept at adapting, changing when things change. This does not mean everything is a priority, but rather that digital business agility must be your top priority.

Applying the Concepts

How can you begin to put some of these constructs into your own company context? To guide you on the journey to digital business transformation, we provide (in Appendix B and Appendix C) two frameworks to map out your destination and route. (We use these frameworks in interactive exercises with executives at the DBT Center.) The first framework, the Digital Disruption Diagnostic, spans much of the content covered in Section 1 of this book: forms of customer value, business models, and strategic responses. It begins by asking you which form (or forms) of value your company creates: cost value, experience value, or platform value. You should assess this in terms of today and four to five years' time. This allows you to consider your company's current and aspirational business models, and the kinds of value and relationship you intend to provide to your customers.

Next, we ask you to consider all 15 business models in our taxonomy, and to rate them on a scale of 0-10, where 10 represents a "severe and imminent threat." You should then list some current and potential disruptions that could threaten your business. This part of the exercise often works best in a small group setting in which different perspectives can be used to brainstorm potential vulnerabilities, especially from non-traditional competitors. This process always results in considerable debate in the workshops we manage.

Finally, you must determine which defensive strategies (Harvest, Retreat) and offensive strategies (Disrupt, Occupy) you might employ as a result. Again, this often works best in a group setting in which you and your colleagues can consider different approaches, fleshing out what each

181

strategy might entail. The entire diagnostic process can be used repeatedly for each of your company's business lines (this is a good practice because disruptions will not normally affect all aspects of your business in the same way).

The second framework is the Digital Business Agility Diagnostic, which contains the content from Section 2. It examines the specifics underlying digital business agility capabilities. For hyperawareness, you rate your company's abilities on a 0-10 scale (where 10 represents "very strong") in both behavioral awareness and situational awareness, considering workers and customers, the business environment, and the operating environment. The process is repeated for informed decision-making and fast execution, and for their respective sub-capabilities.

Many companies do not score well in these areas. Although these cutting-edge practices are a high bar, it's eye-opening to learn just how little many companies really understand about what their employees do or know, how their customers are behaving, or the status of their physical assets. It can be discouraging when we consider how little is done in most big companies to ensure that good decisions are made, or how far from concepts such as "dynamic processes" the average incumbent is today. The good (and bad) news is that, at this stage in our research, we have found scant evidence of digital business agility in most large incumbents.

This exercise, therefore, will often focus on a desired future state rather than current capability. We ask you to identify areas you would like to change, as well as some potential "digital enablers" – people, processes, and technology – and then prioritize them. Once you have thought through this, you have taken a first critical step on the path to digital business transformation.

The Road Ahead

Digital disruption presents many more intriguing questions than we can hope to address in this book, but let's consider a few of the weightiest issues, including the longer-term implications for managers and the companies they lead. We have seen how digital disruptors are unseating incumbents with breakthrough technologies and business models that reimagine, on many fronts, the value created for customers. We have pointed out that disruption is not occurring merely at the market level, but inside companies themselves, in terms of how work is performed.

But what about "management"? After years of relatively low levels of innovation, management structure is now receiving renewed scrutiny and an infusion of new thinking. Companies are stepping back to consider the broader question of what it means to be a manager.

In a world where work is reimagined, where talent is allocated dynamically through market mechanisms on an opportunity-by-opportunity basis, the role of a manager changes dramatically. Rather than overseeing the work of individual employees over an extended period, a manager must orchestrate a changing mix of contributors who regularly join and leave projects for which the manager is responsible. This requires managing more people and different types of contributors, including contractors and vendors from the company's "talent cloud," for shorter durations.

Digital disruptors are at the forefront of managerial innovation, largely because they must find ways of scaling their operations without a large number of permanent employees or byzantine processes, both of which are viewed as millstones by the entrepreneurs who run disruptive companies. They have thus become laboratories of innovative staffing and management strategies.

Zappos, one of the leading e-commerce retailers of footwear and accessories, recently transitioned its entire organization to a management model known as "Holacracy." In the Holacratic model, authority and decision-making are distributed through self-organizing teams rather than through a traditional management hierarchy.[1] There are no titles and no managers. Zappos CEO Tony Hsieh believed in this approach to such an extent that he offered a severance package to employees who didn't want to work under such a management model – and 14 percent of the workforce took the offer and quit.[2] According to recent reports, turmoil resulted in the company, and the success of this experiment very much remains to be seen.[3] Hsieh is willing to try, however, because if Holacracy is a success, Zappos will gain competitive advantage by simultaneously increasing agility and eliminating the need for expensive management talent.

Other firms, such as software company Basecamp, tomato producer Morning Star, and textile manufacturer Gore-Tex, have implemented new management structures such as lattice organizations, flat organizational charts, and self-management.[4] Next-generation management structures and leadership models will be a focus of the DBT Center's future research.

As companies shift to more dynamic resource and process approaches, reporting chains, largely static and top-down, become more network-like, supporting more flexible resource configurations and platform effects among contributors. We also expect to see a significant upswing in support of executives and middle managers via ubiquitous analytics. In short, we expect more "management science" in management itself.

And the companies that employ these managers? What about them? Digital disruption is not merely disaggregating industries, but also unbundling the corporation, calling into question the rationale for the very existence of companies. In 1937 Ronald Coase's famous essay, "The Nature of the Firm," established a cornerstone of management theory. He wrote that the reason firms came into being was that they were highly transaction cost-efficient.[5] Entrepreneurs and managers didn't want to set up a new process every time they created a new widget or sold it to a customer. In the Digital Vortex, however, transaction costs are in steep decline. There is more transparency between buyers and sellers, lower switching costs, fewer barriers to entry for innovators, and less friction in conducting commerce.

We have also established the precept that, for companies aspiring to harness disruption, it's the value that matters, not the value chain. This suggests that a focus on value chains is misplaced, and that organizations should instead develop and select capabilities to create, as directly as possible, cost value, experience value, and platform value. Moreover, as the importance of value chains dwindles, ownership of the assets that comprise traditional value chains (factories, warehouses, call centers, vehicle fleets) actually becomes a competitive disadvantage. What if a company could grow on a near-limitless basis, but without getting big? As the digital is separated from the physical, firms that don't own assets, but can *wield scale*, are primed to create disruption.

How far can this evolve? Ethereum, a Switzerland-based disruptor, offers a platform, virtual currency, and programming language that have the potential to automate transactions between counterparties (buyers and sellers) by creating "programmable money."[6] Sometimes described as "Bitcoin 2.0," the technology takes blockchain to new heights, enabling the creation of "smart contracts" – programmable transaction rules that can function autonomously, without the need for intermediaries such as banks.[7] Some believe this approach could one day result in the "decentralized autonomous organization" (DAO), which eliminates practically all the manual processes inherent in today's businesses (i.e., the company runs itself). According to Ethereum spokesman Stephan Tual, "You can have a machine that negotiates all its financial contracts, for instance. It could make money for you, if you chose so. You could also decide to step down after setting off the contract, and it will keep operating on its own. Then you'll have a machine making money for itself. Just a machine becoming richer. It might even become an employer and hire humans."[8] Ethereum co-founder Vitalik Buterin says his goal is to establish the technology as "the foundational platform for everything."[9]

Following this to a logical extreme, one can imagine not just a corporation run by robots or mutually-policing algorithms *à la* blockchain, but a pervasive form of extreme decentralization of economic activity, a world with no corporations at all, whether physical and human-led, or even virtual – a post-corporate era. As Ethereum's then chief technology officer explained in a 2015 blog post on the evolution of open-source models and their broader economic application, "Software writing was just the first thing to go fundamentally decentral ... [With Ethereum] all aspects of services will follow the same route. The idea of a rigid organization or corporation will evaporate."[10]

This reality remains a distant and uncertain prospect. But one recurring lesson of studying the dynamics of the Digital Vortex is that the rate of market change is exponential, and uncertainty should not be confused with impossibility. The landscape envisioned by Ethereum (and others, including like-minded venture capitalists, technology industry juggernauts, and multi-national financial institutions, all of whom are investing millions in this technology) represents the mother of all combinatorial disruptions, attaining truly revolutionary levels of cost value, experience value, and platform value. Such a future is difficult to reconcile with any familiar notions of commercial exchange and competition – an economy that runs on automation, analytics, and connection.

The Good, the Bad, and the Ugly

We have not shied away from the reality of digital disruption and the wrenching change it represents for how business has always worked. We have also adopted a fairly neutral stance on some fairly controversial topics, including the effects of digital disruption on the overall economy, implications for labor, and the potential for eroding privacy as work and commerce are digitized. This is because our focus is on the competitiveness of individual firms, rather than the ramifications for society writ large. However, this neutrality should not be interpreted as ambivalence toward those ramifications, particularly for the typical worker.* When a software program can "write" a newspaper article about a sporting event that is nearly indistinguishable from an article composed by a human journalist,[11] or a 3D printer can construct an entire apartment building without the aid

---

* For an overview of how digital disruption is affecting workers in multiple countries, see the *Financial Times'* series "New World of Work," accessed April 25, 2016, ft.com/indepth/new-world-of-work

of skilled tradespeople,[12] there are real risks to employment that should not be minimized.

We have asked you to accept that digital disruption is real and unlikely to be rolled back any time soon, even if the disruptors now dominating the business press implode.* This is because, as we have stressed, it's the disruption that matters, not any one disruptor.

What can we make, though, of the seemingly conflicting trends of market-share consolidation and wealth concentration on the one hand, and disruption and displacement on the other? How can there be not enough competition[13] and an unprecedented level of competition at the same time?

Many of the biggest incumbents have the best defenses (having what JP Morgan Chase CEO Jamie Dimon has called a "fortress" balance sheet,[14] for example) and are using these to good effect. Incumbents are hoarding cash†, deploying their armies of lawyers and lobbyists, and squeezing suppliers and customers to delay or avert being knocked off their pedestals. These defenses may prove more porous than in the past as we have suggested, however. Squeezing customers with price increases or poor service is an invitation to disruption. And while it is standard to speculate about the prospects of startups in a scenario where cheap money dries up, incumbents too are enjoying easy access to capital that allows many under-performing players to mask or stave off competitive decline.

Big companies can adapt to the Digital Vortex, and some will flourish. Those that occupy value vacancies by sustaining combinatorial disruptions may be extremely successful and remain market leaders. What best predicts displacement, based on the DBT Center's research, is not the size of the company or its market share, but rather the level of customer value created, and the organizational agility that delivers it.

---

* There are cracks in the dam for many of today's high-profile disruptors. See, for example: Farhad Manjoo, "The Uber Model, It Turns Out, Doesn't Translate," *New York Times*, March 23, 2016, nytimes.com/2016/03/24/technology/the-uber-model-it-turns-out-doesnt-translate.html and Ted Schadler et al., "What Comes After the Unicorn Carnage? Smart CMOs Will Exploit the Slowdown to Catch Up With and Serve Customers," *Forrester Research*, March 30, 2016, blogs.forrester.com/ted_schadler/16-03-30-what_comes_after_the_unicorn_carnage

† Some observers attribute the rise of corporate cash holdings directly to the increasing prominence of technology in the economy. Recent analysis from the Federal Reserve Bank of St. Louis notes, "The rise in cash holdings of U.S. corporations [is partially a function of] the increasing predominance of research and development (R&D). Because R&D is an activity intrinsically connected with uncertainty, the association of R&D and cash holdings is a natural one. The rising importance of R&D in the overall economy is a long-term phenomenon that is due to the rapid growth of information technology firms." Juan M. Sánchez and Emircan Yurdagul, "Why Are Corporations Holding So Much Cash?" Federal Reserve Bank of St. Louis, January 2013, stlouisfed.org/Publications/Regional-Economist/January-2013/Why-Are-Corporations-Holding-So-Much-Cash

What makes the Digital Vortex spin? In other words, why is this disruption occurring, and whom is it for? The answer, on all counts, is that unmet needs in the market and in our societies can be addressed through digital means. While maximizing profits, delivering convenience, and furnishing users with new sources of amusement play a big role in attracting private equity and venture capital, these don't fully explain why we are experiencing an emergence of digital disruptors.

Many of the forces driving this change are more fundamental – for consumers, getting more value on less income; for institutions, making public goods such as healthcare, energy, or education more affordable and effective. Human ingenuity and a pervasive desire to "make life better" are powering the Digital Vortex.

While clearly not without its downsides, digital has "delivered" in many ways. Economists may debate the productivity gains associated with digital technologies,[15] but this debate obscures the fact that individual and business customers are realizing enormous value through learning, connecting, and selling or buying, particularly when digital *business models* are considered as well.

There is a legitimate argument to be made that digital disruption is our best hope for combating climate change, for example. Where traditional market mechanisms, political leaders, and entreaties to change behaviors have failed, digital disruption presents an opportunity to create scale and move with great speed on our climate crisis in areas including alternative energy, intelligent transportation, and consumption efficiencies. This basket of beneficial outcomes is perhaps why executives in our survey believe that the effects of disruption are, by and large, positive (see Figure 19): 75 percent said digital disruption is a form of progress, that it's moving us in the right direction. Nearly as many say the customer ultimately benefits, and two-thirds believe the individual is empowered – not merely as a consumer, but as a human being.

Although negative for some companies, and perhaps entire industries as currently constituted, digital disruption may be positive for the whole, in a utilitarian sense. This view of digital disruption among surveyed executives may be simply a contemporary vindication of economist Joseph Schumpeter's well-worn observation that capitalism is "creative destruction" in which the old economic order is perpetually cast off to make room for new sources of wealth creation.[16] It is also worth noting that respondents to our survey are executives in large and mid-sized private-sector companies, not government officials, labor leaders, or the unemployed.

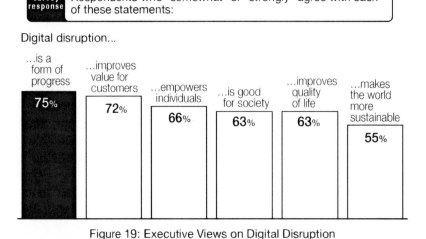

Figure 19: Executive Views on Digital Disruption
Source: Global Center for Digital Business Transformation, 2015

It would be naïve to assert that digital disruption does not result in economic dislocations. Stalwarts of industry are being displaced, forced to limp along, or consigned to the dustbin of history. Entire professions are sideswiped by automation, artificial intelligence, and disintermediation. The stature of countries on the global stage waxes and wanes as their fortunes respond to digital change. It is up to all of us – businesses, governments, and civil society – to mitigate these negative impacts and give a helping hand to those who are affected.

These dislocations must be considered from a balanced viewpoint, however, accounting for the unprecedented new sources of cost value, experience value, and platform value in the digital age. Pocketbook savings, convenience, more opportunities to learn and share ideas, improving sustainability – these are just a few sources of value we are collectively realizing. When combined, these values can yield outsized benefits. This likely explains why business leaders generally view digital disruption in an optimistic light, despite recognizing that their own firms may get the short end of the stick.

Choose Your Own Future

The Digital Vortex contains a logic that might be considered fatalistic – we are all swept up in it, and are bound by its sovereign laws of change and competition. The only thing that is actually inexorable, however, is that digitization in business and in our lives will increase. There are almost no scenarios in which this trend is reversed. What is *not* inevitable is what this digitization means to us as businesspeople, employees, and citizens.

The future presented by the Digital Vortex is neither inherently utopian nor inherently dystopian. We are seeing signs of a "winner-takes-all" dynamic in competition that is leading to market share and wealth consolidation. The growing digitization of commerce and human interaction has the potential to threaten our privacy and security. However, the larger narrative of the Digital Vortex is not one of control, but one of choice and empowerment. For companies, digital business agility helps them to choose and navigate their own path in the Digital Vortex. For citizens, digital disruption means we can dispense with many of the economic and social patterns that have governed capitalism for millennia, connecting peer-to-peer, and throwing off constraints of access to information, location, socio-economic status, and pressure to conform.

Khan Academy is a nonprofit organization that provides free educational content (cost value) to students worldwide. Their stated mission is to provide "a free, world-class education to anyone, anywhere."[17] The company's students number more than 30 million, and their lessons, which have been viewed upwards of 580 million times, on many typical K-12 topics and beyond, have been translated into nearly 40 languages (experience value).[18] Khan Academy uses YouTube videos to reach an under-served, previously disconnected constituency – students who don't have access to education and those who need tutoring (platform value). Khan Academy also provides online tools and resources via Creative Commons licensing and open-source applications to more than a million registered educators, many of whom work in cash-strapped school systems.

The Khan Academy model represents a global combinatorial disruption – one with no downsides, only winners. Khan Academy has chosen to harness digital disruption in support of a future they want. We all must follow suit.

Afterword

Publishing a Book in the Digital Vortex

"We should write a book." This was a widely shared sentiment when teams from IMD and Cisco first convened in Lausanne in late 2014 to discuss what was then just an exciting partnership idea. At the time, however, this was seen as a worthy but long-term goal.

The DBT Center was officially launched at IMD in June 2015, at which point we released the first wave of our original research. Over the course of the next several months, we were able to conduct a sizable volume of additional new research and engage with hundreds of executives on the topics of digital disruption and transformation.

In November 2015 the DBT Center team – composed of both IMD and Cisco employees – had a routine telepresence meeting during which the idea of a book re-surfaced. The more we discussed it, the more we realized that we possessed a lot of valuable new information on a subject that is (or should be) increasingly top-of-mind for executives – enough data, in fact, to justify a book-length piece.

Although there was a high level of interest from different imprints – that is, big-name publishers of business books – about the possibility of working with us, we quickly reached a consensus, in part because it would be a book *about digital disruption*, that we would follow a disruptive approach to creating our product. A cursory comparison of traditional publishers' offerings and those of disruptive players (Amazon CreateSpace and IngramSpark were our top two choices) revealed some telling insights. Chief among these was that the disruptive publishers were creating a clear combinatorial disruption benefiting book authors. We found that the disruptors charged a much lower margin than traditional publishers, increasing author royalties and thereby creating cost value for us. We also realized cost value through their print-on-demand model, which is a manifestation of the business model we call "Consumption-based Pricing." There was no printing, buying, and holding physical copies in inventory, and no carrying costs (either for us or for booksellers who might stock the product). Instead, books are printed on a dynamic basis when a customer clicks "buy."

The disruptors also created experience value in multiple ways. The first was Customer Empowerment. Disruptive publishers allow authors to treat their books as a "perpetual beta"; the possible number of versions of a book is limitless. Because of their print-on-demand model, there is little in the way of "sunk costs," and authors can update their books as often as they wish, simply by uploading a new source file of their manuscript. The book you are now reading may or may not, in fact, be a first edition.

Customer Empowerment-based value was also delivered by virtue of the fact that we did not have to choose a single publisher/printer – we actually selected two. How many traditional book publishers would countenance this? For us this was hugely beneficial because one had a global reach, while the other had more flexibility in form factors (e.g., hardcover, e-reader), giving us the best of both worlds. The essence of the Customer Empowerment business model is enabling self-service and eliminating middlemen, and that is precisely what we were able to do.

The second form of experience value was Instant Gratification. In fact, this was the biggest factor in our decision to go with a disruptive publishing platform (once we had confirmed basics such as the comparable quality of paper and printing in an independent publishing* approach). Quite simply, the disruptors were dramatically faster than traditional publishers, who unofficially told us we were looking at a year or more to have our book readied, printed, and shipped. We were able to cut that by more than half: from the time we agreed we would move forward with a book to the time we first held a physical copy in our hands, the process took about six months.

Experience value was also created through Customization, as we could choose the format for our book, with a variety of options for creating e-reader and audiobook versions; Reduced Friction, in that we could manage the process of creating and uploading content for publishing directly; and Automation, as key steps in the process – printing, e-commerce transactions, payment, and fulfillment are handled almost completely online.

These publishers also introduced a measure of platform value. Amazon is one of the top Digital Marketplace examples in the world, connecting a multi-sided market of authors, booksellers, book buyers, and other parties. Amazon also created platform value via a Communities dynamic, by

---

* What used to be called self-publishing, with its attendant (and deserved) negative connotations, is now more accurately called independent publishing – and the two terms (and activities) are quite different.

offering the book through their vast sales channels. IngramSpark, part of the Ingram Content Group, one of the world's largest distributors of books, gave us access to thousands of bookselling entities across hundreds of countries. These platforms promoted efficiency in the transmission of our information and a high level of reach.

In designing the book's cover, we found platform value (Crowdsourcing) through the services of 99designs, a firm with an agile talent pipeline for those in need of design services. The company, headquartered in San Francisco, offers a crowdsourcing platform on which customers can hold "contests" in which designers from around the world submit designs to win a cash prize, ranging from $200 to $2,500 depending on the project. After receiving dozens of submitted designs *within a few days*, we iterated on designs with a shortlist of submissions, and then picked the one we liked best. Using this service, we were able to obtain a book cover that matched our specifications in a fraction of the time and for a fraction of the cost of traditional full-service design agencies. We liked the process so much that we then had 99designs run two more competitions, one to crowdsource our website design (digitalvortex.com) and another for our marketing materials. Thus, the publishing process for our book looked quite different from what we had initially imagined, thanks to the power of combinatorial disruption.

What about the research that went into the book, and the content creation itself? Let's examine these elements from the standpoint of another key construct contained in this book: digital business agility.

Hyperawareness – gaining a comprehensive understanding of what's happening in the environment – is actually a close cousin of research. We wanted to follow multiple vectors to get a full picture of how disruption is occurring, and to ensure we weren't missing key ideas or bending our learnings to fit with any preconceived notions we might have had. In particular, we wanted a mix of quantitative and qualitative insights. For the former, we partnered with Global Market Insite (GMI), a division of LightSpeed Research, to survey some 941 executives in 13 countries via an online questionnaire. We worked with GMI to put in place a cross-section of quality control measures we expected in terms of recruiting respondents and completing the actual fieldwork. Because of the scale of GMI's network, and its global ecosystem of research partners, we were able to collect nearly 1,000 respondents from a list of pre-vetted participants in less than 30 days. We also engaged Lionbridge, a company offering an agile talent approach for low-cost translation, to convert our survey instrument into nine languages in less than a week.

For the latter, we conducted qualitative interviews with dozens of senior executives using an online membership-based platform for expertise sharing from the Gerson Lehrman Group (GLG). This platform enabled us to identify, recruit, and communicate with these experts. To conduct the interviews, our team relied on collaboration technologies, including telepresence and cloud-based conferencing tools, provided by Cisco and disruptive startups. Without all these capabilities, we would not have been able to obtain such a detailed and evidence-based global understanding of how disruptors are reshaping industries and markets and about what market leaders are doing in response. In other words, we couldn't have been as hyperaware.

To analyze our data, we used a range of analytical and collaboration tools to foster informed decision-making. These included cloud-based data analysis and sharing platforms to exchange and make sense of the large data sets and insights we'd collected. For example, we used MarketSight and R, two low-cost, cloud-based data analysis software tools, to obtain different views of our primary research data and to run statistical analysis. We used the online file-sharing service Box.net to exchange large volumes of content, including video and audio files, across the team; we obtained written transcripts of our many interviews with entrepreneurs and executives through a cloud-based transcription service called Rev.com, which turns around a finished transcript for $1 per audio minute, within 24 hours. Rev.com itself functions as a talent marketplace that assembles a virtual network of transcriptionists and translators located around the world.

When creating a book with four principal authors and more than a dozen other key contributors (project managers, researchers, designers, editors, reviewers), and especially in a working team spanning four countries (Canada, India, Switzerland, and the U.S.), effective collaboration was paramount. The authors and our extended team relied heavily on collaboration tools such as Cisco TelePresence, Jabber, WebEx, and Spark to discuss concepts, visualize information, co-create content, obtain feedback from reviewers, and to iterate and refine the numerous versions of the book. We practiced inclusive decision-making, enabled by digital technology.

Finally, in the marketplace of ideas, much of the value that a reader or learner derives from content is a function of the currency of the information – is it fresh? This is especially true when covering a topic as dynamic as ours. Getting to market quickly is critical. Although we had our share of the inevitable delays and frustrations (competing work priorities, writer's block, differing viewpoints) that come with producing a coherent piece of content of roughly 70,000 words, we were able to take a disruptive approach that permitted fast execution.

For example, distressingly late in the editing process, we realized we had neglected to budget either time or funding in our project plan for construction of the book's index. Solution: we used an Automation business model from Upwork, a "gig" and micro-job marketplace, to engage an indexer who specializes in crafting indices for books, following a highly industrialized process. This was rapid enablement in practice, and allowed us to maintain our deadline, which was IMD's annual conference, "Orchestrating Winning Performance," in June 2016.

As we saw in Chapter 1, the media and entertainment industry, of which publishing is a part, is second only to technology products and services in its proximity to the center of the Digital Vortex. Disruptors from within the industry, and from adjacent industries (e.g., retail, wholesale), are busy innovating new forms of value and digitizing anything that can be digitized. This book is a simple but real example of how customers of this industry (us), are using the offerings of digital disruptors to obtain higher value, bypassing the traditional value chain in the process. We hope that you, our customer, have benefited from this approach as well.

Acknowledgments

In the afterword, we outlined the "disruptive" approach we took in creating *Digital Vortex*. This book represents a collaboration of literally dozens of contributors. The core team of four geographically-dispersed authors has benefited enormously from the coming together of two very different organizations, IMD and Cisco, each a world leader in its own sphere. It has been our distinct privilege to learn from the assembled minds, experiences, and customers of both organizations.

Thousands of executives pass through IMD's doors each year, and few realize the value they have contributed to the development of this book. A good number of the examples and insights contained in these pages came from conversations with executives struggling with digital disruption within their own organizations and industries. As we were teaching them, we were also learning from them. As our ideas and frameworks were taking shape, we were testing them in real time during training programs and workshops at IMD and elsewhere. Our sincere thanks go out to all of these executives for their willingness to share and listen. Your insights are the centerpiece of this book.

The DBT Center is physically located in Lausanne, Switzerland. Without it, this book would not have been possible. Setting up the Center required a great deal of collaboration among multiple stakeholder groups. We would like to extend our deepest thanks to IMD President Dominique Turpin, Chairman Peter Wuffli, and other members of the Management Team for agreeing to support the formation of a completely new model of thought leadership, deeply rooted in practice. In particular, we would like to single out Anand Narasimhan, James Henderson, Sandra Bouscal, Marlène Borcard, John Evans, Michael Boulianne, Aurora Barras, and Marco Mancesti for their support. Thanks also to Christian Bucheli, executive director and head of strategic ventures at SIX, in his capacity as DBT Center advisory board member. Finally, we need to extend a very special thank you to Remy El Assir, DBT Center associate manager, who kept everything working with the efficiency and precision of a Swiss watch, while we frequently disappeared into the book-writing vortex.

Sincere thanks to the many Cisco executives who have lent their unflagging support to the DBT Center, including Chuck Robbins, John Chambers, Kelly Kramer, Hilton Romanski, Karen Walker, Fran Katsoudas, Michael Ganser, and Maciej Kranz. Very special thanks to Thierry Maupilé, who has been the driving force in the creation and running of the DBT Center from the get-go. As an executive in residence at IMD and vice president of strategic partnerships at Cisco, it was Thierry's foresight and determination as much as anything that led to the founding of the DBT Center and ultimately created the conditions for this book, as well as all the research and engagement with companies yet to come.

Thank you to Kevin Bandy, Cisco's chief digital officer, for his thought leadership and guidance, and for encouraging us at every turn to work on the big, thorny unknowns – the peculiarities, pitfalls, and promise – of digital business transformation. Under Kevin's direction, the Cisco contributors to this project have been able to assume a dual role of researcher and change practitioner. These two vantages have been of immense value to our work. It has been an incredible education to work alongside Kevin to help shape Cisco's own digitization roadmap, and we look forward with excitement to the next steps in the journey. Colleagues within Kevin's organization, including Michael Adams, Joel Barbier, Donna Cox, Clare Markovits, and Marivell Quinonez, have provided invaluable support to our team over the months it took to write this book.

Heartfelt thanks to Kathy O'Connell and her team in Cisco Marketing – Caroline Ahlquist, Kevin Delaney, Nicole France, Cheri Goodman, Lisa Lahde, Stefanie McCann, Melissa Mines, Bob Moriarty, Bill Radtke, Rick Ripplinger, and Virgil Vidal. You have been not just marketing partners but true thought partners throughout this process. Your collaborative spirit, intellect, and execution-oriented mindset are nothing short of world class. We are in fact indebted to many others from Cisco, particularly Inbar Lasser-Raab, Jim Grubb, Stephan Monterde, Christian Kuun, Andrea Duffy, and Alan Stern. We would also like to extend our deep thanks to Joseph Bradley, a long-time friend and mentor whose acumen in all things Internet of Things is without peer, as are his vision and professionalism.

On content creation, thanks to our development editor Pete Gerardo and production editor Kelly Andersson. We also extend our gratitude to our graphic design wizard, Scott Fields. It is rare to find someone who works as hard as Scott, yet is so easygoing – a true pro. On research and analysis, thanks are due to Divya Kapoor, Sierra Parker, Isabel Redondo Gomez, Hiten Sethi, Jialu Shan, Gaurav Singh, and Andrew Tarling. Your assistance in investigating the models of more than 100 digital disruptors, unearthing all kinds of strange creatures – unicorns, vampires, shapeshifters, and goliaths – and your skill in flat-out crunching of data have played a pivotal role in the development of this material. This team has challenged and improved our thinking in countless ways.

You would not be reading this book without the unceasing effort, intelligence, and conscientiousness of Lauren Buckalew, who managed all primary research field work and served as lead interviewer, project manager, and quality assurance czar for the book. Andy said it best when he pronounced, "I am in awe of Lauren." Bravo Lauren, and thank you.

To our children, parents, friends, and other relatives, we can't say thanks enough for the love, support, and forbearance you have shown us while we worked on this project. And to our wives, Susan, Jenn, Karen, and Heidi, we can now finally say to you the words you have longed to hear: "We finished the book." Thank you very, very much.

Appendix A: Digital Vortex Methodology

Survey Detail

During April 2015, the DBT Center conducted a blind online survey of 941 business leaders globally to understand the state of digital disruption. The characteristics of the survey respondents and their organizations are described in Table A1 on the following page.

Industry Ranking Methodology

The DBT Center industry ranking methodology is based on a combination of third-party and survey data. In order to assess the relative potential for digital disruption by industry, the following methodology was employed.

Step 1: Identify Indicators of Digital Disruption Potential

The analysis of digital disruption potential by industry began with the identification of key indicators of the potential for digital disruption described in Table A2.

The DBT Center believes these are meaningful indicators of the relative potential for digital disruption by industry because they address the following questions:

- Where are investors and the market placing their bets?
- How many companies are working to disrupt industries using digital technologies?
- When, and at what rate, is digital disruption likely to occur in an industry?
- With which business models are digital disruptors likely to attack industries, and what are their chances of success?
- What level of disruption are these digital disruptors likely to drive within an industry?

Respondent Company, by Location of Headquarters	United States. . . . . 41% China. . . . . .9% United Kingdom . . . . . . .9% India . . . . .8% Brazil. . . . . .6% Canada . . . . .6% Italy . . . . .6% Germany . . . . .5% France . . . . .4% Mexico . . . . .2% Russia . . . . .2% Australia . . . . .1% Japan 1%
Respondent Company, by Industry	CPG (Consumer Packaged Goods) & Manufacturing . . . 23% Financial Services . . . . . . 18% Retail. . . . . 12% Technology Products/Services . 10% Healthcare. . . . . .6% Telecommunications . . . . . .6% Education . . . . .5% Hospitality & Travel . . . . .5% Pharmaceuticals . . . . . . .5% Media & Entertainment . . . . .4% Oil & Gas . . . . .3% Utilities 3%
Respondent Company, by Annual Revenue	Less than $50 mil . . . . . . .4% $50 mil < $100 mil. . . . . . .9% $100 mil < $500 mil . . . . . 20% $500 mil < $1 bil . . . . . . 20% $1 bil < $5 bil. . . . . 22% $5 bil < $10 bil . . . . 11% $10 bil or more 14%
Respondent Roles and Functions	Company Executive (e.g., CEO, CIO). . . . . . . 33% Senior Vice President, VP . . . 29% Director . . . . 38% Information Technology (IT) . . 24% General Management . . . . 19% Finance . . . . 16% Manufacture, Supply, Logistics . . 7% Sales . . . . .6% Marketing . . . . .5% Customer Service . . . . . . .4% Human Resources. . . . . . .4% Legal, Risk Mngt, Compliance . . 4% Research & Development . . . . .4% Other . . . . .4% Procurement 2%

Table A1: Survey Detail
Source: Global Center for Digital Business Transformation, 2015

Investment	The level of investment in companies that are focused on using digital technologies to disrupt industries. This is an indicator of where investors are placing their bets and where they see the most opportunity for digital disruption to drive economic value.
Timing	The length of time until digital disruption has a meaningful impact on an industry and the rate of change that digital disruption will drive in the industry.
Means	The level of barriers to entry that digital disruptors face in an industry, and the means of disruption (such as the number of disruptive business models) they can use to surmount these barriers.
Impact	The extent of disruption (such as impact on market share of incumbents) and the level of existential threat that digital disruptors represent to an industry.

Table A2: Indicators of Potential for Digital Disruption
Source: Global Center for Digital Business Transformation, 2015

Step 2: Quantify Indicators of Digital Disruption Potential

After defining indicators of the potential for digital disruption, the next step was to identify the specific metrics used to quantify these indicators. Based on examination of dozens of potential metrics, we selected those listed below. Because these metrics were from different sources and in different units, they were translated to standardized z-scores. For indicators with more than one input metric, the z-scores for the metrics were averaged. The final step was to calculate a cumulative z-score for each indicator of disruption potential (see Table A3 next page).

Metric	Indicator	Definition
Venture capital in digital disruption	Investment	Number of venture-backed private companies valued at $1 billion or more by industry as of April 2015.[1]
Number of years to digital disruption	Timing	Mean number of expected years until an industry experiences an impact from digital disruption as predicted by industry.[2]
Extent of exponential rate of digital disruption	Timing	Percentage of industry executives that expect digital disruption in their industry over the next five years to be exponential (i.e., an increasingly rapid rate of change).[2]
Number of likely digital disruption models	Means	Out of five distinct disruptive digital business models tested in the survey, the mean number that executives believe are likely to have a disruptive impact on their industry within the next five years.[2]
Barriers to entry for digital disruptors	Means	Percentage of executives from each industry who believe barriers to entry for digital disruptors are nonexistent, very low, or low.[2]
Displacement of top market incumbents	Impact	Mean number of top 10 incumbents by market share that executives expect to be displaced by digital disruptors within the next five years.[2]
Risk of being put out of business	Impact	Percentage of respondents by industry that believe there will be a somewhat or significantly increased risk of being put out of business over the next five years due to digital disruption.[2]
Sources: 1) The Wall Street Journal, April 2015; 2) DBT Center survey, April 2015		

Table A3: Metrics Used to Quantify Potential for
Digital Disruption by Industry

Step 3: Calculate Industry Ranking for Digital Disruption Potential

For each industry, the cumulative z-scores for each indicator were summed to arrive at a cumulative z-score by industry. These scores were then used to arrive at the industry ranking, shown in Table A4.

Technology Products & Services	#1
Media & Entertainment	#2
Retail	#3
Financial Services	#4
Telecommunications	#5
Education	#6
Hospitality & Travel	#7
CPG & Manufacturing	#8
Healthcare	#9
Utilities	#10
Oil & Gas	#11
Pharmaceuticals	#12

Table A4: Industries Ranked by Potential for Digital Disruption
Source: Global Center for Digital Business Transformation, 2015

Step 4: Analyze Patterns

The scores calculated in Step 3 are illuminating beyond the level of individual industries. The order and groupings of industries highlight some key patterns about how digital disruption is likely to occur both within and across industries. The DBT Center used the scoring and underlying data to inform both the in-depth analysis of the patterns of digital disruption across industries and the Digital Vortex analysis that are the focus of this report.

Appendix B: Digital Disruption Diagnostic

On the next page you will find our Digital Disruption Diagnostic worksheet. (This is also available for free in a larger PDF format at digitalvortex.com). Complete the worksheet for your organization:

1. Specify the forms of value that support your current competitive positon. Provide examples.
2. Go through the 15 business models and assess the current threat level of each on a 0-10 scale, where 10 represents a "severe and imminent threat." Provide examples.
3. Think forward. Given the top business model threats you have identified, what forms of value will you need to compete in 4-5 years? Provide examples.
4. Identify the defensive and offensive strategies that you need to follow to achieve your desired future state. Provide examples.
5. Share your worksheet with colleagues in small groups.

You may need to repeat the process for different lines of business.

	Your Value Drivers		Which business models threaten you today?			Your Strategic Response
	Examples					
	Now	4-5 yrs		0-10 Scale	Examples	Examples
Cost Value $			Free / Ultra-low Cost			Harvest
			Buyer Aggregation			
			Price Transparency			
			Reverse Auctions			
			Consumption-based Pricing			
Experience Value 🕐			Customer Empowerment			Retreat
			Customization			
			Instant Gratification			Disrupt
			Reduced Friction			
			Automation			
Platform Value			Ecosystem			Occupy
			Crowdsourcing			
			Communities			
			Digital Marketplace			
			Data Orchestrator			

Worksheet: Digital Disruption Diagnostic   Source: Global Center for Digital Business Transformation, 2016

Appendix C:
Digital Business Agility Diagnostic

On the next page you will find our Digital Business Agility Diagnostic worksheet. (This is also available for free in larger PDF format at digitalvortex.com). Complete the worksheet for your organization:

1. Assess your current capabilities on a 0-10 scale, where 10 represents "very strong."
2. Identify opportunities to improve and enable each capability. Provide examples.
3. Identify digital technologies, tools, or applications that can support the enablement of each capability, based on what you've learned in *Digital Vortex*.

You may need to repeat the process for different lines of business.

	DBA-specific Capability	Focus Area	Current Capabilities (0-10)	Opportunities for Enablement	Digital Enablers
Hyperawareness	Behavioral Awareness	Workers			
		Customers			
	Situational Awareness	Operating Environment			
		Business Environment			
Informed Decision-making	Inclusive Decision-making	Diverse Perspectives			
		Inclusive Environment			
	Augmented Decision-making	Ubiquitous Analytics			
		Automated / Fast Decisions			
Fast Execution	Dynamic Resources	Agile Talent			
		Agile Technology			
	Dynamic Processes	Rapid Enablement			
		Rapid Intervention			

Source: Global Center for Digital Business Transformation, 2016

Worksheet: Digital Business Agility Diagnostic

Endnotes

Introduction

[1] "The Internet of Everything – a $19 Trillion Opportunity," Cisco Consulting Services, 2014, cisco.com/c/dam/en_us/services/portfolio/consulting-services/documents/consulting-services-capturing-ioe-value-aag.pdf

Chapter 1

[1] "Short Messaging Services versus Instant Messaging: Value versus Volume," *Deloitte*, 2014, deloitte.com/content/dam/Deloitte/au/Documents/technology-media-telecommunicatir thons/deloitte-au-tmt-short-messaging-services-versus-instant-messaging-011014.pdf

[2] Sarah Frier, "Facebook's $22 Billion WhatsApp Deal Buys $10 Million in Sales," *Bloomberg*, updated October 29, 2014, bloomberg.com/news/articles/2014-10-28/facebook-s-22-billion-whatsapp-deal-buys-10-million-in-sales

[3] Erik Heinrich, "Telecom Firms Face $386 Billion in Lost Revenue to Skype, WhatsApp," *Fortune*, June 23, 2014, fortune.com/2014/06/23/telecom-companies-count-386-billion-in-lost-revenue-to-skype-whatsapp-others/

[4] Liyan Chen, Ryan Mac, and Brian Solomon, "Alibaba Claims Title for Largest Global IPO Ever with Extra Share Sales," *Forbes*, September 22, 2014, forbes.com/sites/ryanmac/2014/09/22/alibaba-claims-title-for-largest-global-ipo-ever-with-extra-share-sales/#450bb5f97c26

[5] "The Unicorn List: Current Private Companies Valued at $1B And Above," *CB Insights*, accessed March 31, 2016, cbinsights.com/research-unicorn-companies

[6] Ibid.

[7] John Greenbough, "10 Million Self-driving Cars Will Be on the Road by 2020," *Business Insider*, July 29, 2015, businessinsider.com/report-10-million-self-driving-cars-will-be-on-the-road-by-2020-2015-5-6

[8] Paul Gao et al., "Disruptive Trends that will Transform the Auto Industry," *McKinsey & Company*, January 2016, mckinsey.com/industries/high-tech/our-insights/disruptive-trends-that-will-transform-the-auto-industry

[9] Michele Bertoncello and Dominik Wee, "Ten Ways Autonomous Driving Could Redefine the Automotive World," *McKinsey & Company*, June 2015, mckinsey.com/industries/automotive-and-assembly/our-insights/ten-ways-autonomous-driving-could-redefine-the-automotive-world

[10] Jenny Stanton, "Drone Delivery is Here! China's Largest Mail Firm to Deliver More than 1,000 Packages a Day to Remote Areas Using Fleet of Aircraft," *Daily Mail*, March 24, 2015, dailymail.co.uk/news/peoplesdaily/article-3009593/Drone-delivery-China-s-largest-mail-firm-deliver-1-000-packages-DAY-remote-areas-using-fleet-aircraft.html

[11] Nick Bilton, "Disruptions: How Driverless Cars Could Reshape Cities," *New York Times*, July 7, 2013, bits.blogs.nytimes.com/2013/07/07/disruptions-how-driverless-cars-could-reshape-cities/?_r=0

[12] Wendy Koch, "Self-Driving 'Robocabs' Could Help Curb Global Warming," *National Geographic*, July 6, 2015, news.nationalgeographic.com/energy/2015/07/150706-driverless-robot-taxis-could-curb-global-warming/

[13] Bob Morris, "Clayton M. Christensen: An Interview by Bob Morris," *Blogging on Business* (blog), June 9, 2011, bobmorris.biz/clayton-b-christensen-a-book-review-by-bob-morris

[14] Ainsley O'Connell, "Pluralsight Continues Its Acquisition Spree, Dropping $36 Million On Code School," *Fast Company*, January 27, 2015, fastcompany.com/3041515/fast-feed/pluralsight-continues-its-acquisition-spree-dropping-36-million-on-code-school

[15] "Interbrand Releases 2015 Best Global Brands Report," *Interbrand*, October 4, 2015, interbrand.com/newsroom/interbrand-releases-2015-best-global-brands-report/

[16] Trefis Team, "Q2 2015 U.S. Banking Review: Total Deposits," *Forbes*, September 1, 2015, forbes.com/sites/greatspeculations/2015/09/01/q2-2015-u-s-banking-review-total-deposits/#7282b2081e7d

[17] Charles Riggs, "15 Years Online!" *Wells Fargo Guided by History* (blog), May 17, 2010, blogs.wf.com/guidedbyhistory/2010/05/15-years-online/

[18] Charles Riggs, "Wells Fargo: 20 Years of Internet Banking," *Wells Fargo Guided by History* (blog), May 18, 2015, blogs.wf.com/guidedbyhistory/2015/05/internet-20-years/

[19] Greg Edwards, "Big Banks Report Steady Increases in Mobile Banking," *St. Louis Business Journal*, January 27, 2015, bizjournals.com/stlouis/blog/2015/01/big-banks-report-steady-increases-in-mobile.html

[20] Parmy Olson, "Under Armour Buys Health-Tracking App MyFitnessPal for $475 Million," *Forbes*, February 4, 2015, forbes.com/sites/parmyolson/2015/02/04/myfitnesspal-acquisition-under-armour/#65f8fce04db6

[21] Alyson Shontell, "Snapchat is a Lot Bigger than People Realize and It Could Be Nearing 200 Million Active Users," *Business Insider*, January 3, 2015, businessinsider.com/snapchats-monthly-active-users-may-be-nearing-200-million-2014-12

[22] Jerin Mathew, "Snapchat Raises $537.6m via Common Stock Sale at $16bn Valuation," *International Business Times*, May 30, 2015, ibtimes.co.uk/snapchat-raises-537-6m-via-common-stock-sale-16bn-valuation-1503598

[23] Geoffrey Moore, *Crossing the Chasm, Marketing and Selling High-Tech Products to Mainstream Customers* (New York: HarperBusiness, 1991)

[24] Weixin Zha and Stefan Nicola, "German Solar Records May Keep Traders Busy on Weekends," *Bloomberg*, April 15, 2015, bloomberg.com/news/articles/2015-04-15/german-power-grid-expects-a-season-of-record-solar-output

[25] Scott McCullough, "Report: Renewables Met 57% of Scotland's Electricity Demand in 2015," *Daily Record*, March 31, 2016, heraldscotland.com/news/14395942.Half_of_Scotland_s_energy_consumption_came_from_renewables_last_year/

[26] Alex Davies, "Elon Musk's Grand Plan to Power the World with Batteries," *Wired*, May 1, 2015, wired.com/2015/05/tesla-batteries/

[27] Ray Kurzweil, "The Law of Accelerating Returns," *Kurzweil Accelerating Intelligence* (blog), March 7, 2001, kurzweilai.net/the-law-of-accelerating-returns

[28] Matthew S. Olson and Derek van Bever, *Stall Points: Most Companies Stop Growing – Yours Doesn't Have To* (New Haven: Yale University Press, 2008)

[29] "The Problem with Profits," *Economist*, March 26, 2016, economist.com/news/leaders/21695392-big-firms-united-states-have-never-had-it-so-good-time-more-competition-problem

[30] "World Economic Outlook: A Survey by the Staff of the International Monetary Fund," *International Monetary Fund*, October 2015, imf.org/external/pubs/ft/weo/2015/02/pdf/text.pdf

[31] Richard Dobbs et al., "The New Global Competition for Corporate Profits," McKinsey Global Institute, September 2015, mckinsey.com/business-functions/strategy-and-corporate-finance/our-insights/the-new-global-competition-for-corporate-profits
[32] Ibid.

Chapter 2

[1] Alexander Osterwalder and Yves Pigneur, *Business Model Generation*, 2010, p. 14

[2] Howard Lock and James Macaulay, "Hospitality Business Models Confront the Future of Meetings," *Cornell Hospitality Industry Perspectives* 4 (2010): 6-15. June 1, 2010, scholarship.sha.cornell.edu/chrindper/4/

[3] Christopher Heine, "In a World of Constantly Deleted Apps, This Mobile Player Uses Cash to Keep Folks Coming Back," *AdWeek*, February 19, 2015, adweek.com/news/technology/world-constantly-deleted-apps-mobile-player-uses-cash-keep-folks-coming-back-163025

[4] Konrad Putzier, "Who Will Be the Airbnb of Office Space?" *The Real Deal,* July 2, 2015, therealdeal.com/2015/07/02/who-will-be-the-airbnb-of-office-space/

[5] J.B. Wood, Todd Hewlin, and Thomas Lah, *B4B: How Technology and Big Data Are Reinventing the Customer-Supplier Relationship* (n.p.: Point B Incorporated, 2013), pp. 70-71

[6] Alex Derber, "No Afterthought: Rolls-Royce and the Aftermarket," *MRO Network*, July 19, 2013, mro-network.com/analysis/2013/07/no-afterthought-rolls-royce-and-aftermarket/1345

[7] "Disrupting Banking: The FinTech Startups That Are Unbundling Wells Fargo, Citi and Bank of America," *CB Insights*, November 18, 2015, cbinsights.com/blog/disrupting-banking-FinTech-startups/

[8] Joseph M. Bradley et al., "The Advice Advantage: How Banks Can Close the 'Value Gap' and Regain Customer Trust," *Cisco Systems*, February, 2015, connectedfuturesmag.com/Research_Analysis/docs/ioe-financial-services-white-paper.pdf

[9] Joseph Bradley et al., "Winning the New Digital Consumer with Hyper-Relevance," *Cisco Systems*, January, 2015, cisco.com/c/dam/en/us/solutions/collateral/executive-perspectives/ioe-retail-whitepaper.pdf

[10] Hannah Yankelevich, "Big Data: Nordstrom's Innovation and Investment for the Future," Center for Digital Strategies at the Tuck School of Business (blog), February 4, 2013, digitalstrategies.tuck.dartmouth.edu/about/blog/detail/big-data-nordstroms-innovation-and-investment-for-the-future

[11] Meredith Bauer, "The Hottest Trend in 3D Printing: Shoes on Demand." *Sydney Morning Herald*, February 5, 2016, http://www.smh.com.au/technology/innovation/the-hottest-trend-in-3d-printing-could-change-the-way-you-buy-running-shoes-20160204-gmlbzp.html

[12] Yan Deng, "How Instacart's Pricing Changes Impact Retailers," *Viewpoints* (blog), February 9, 2016, supermarketnews.com/blog/how-instacarts-pricing-changes-impact-retailers

[13] Sara Ashley O'Brien, "Thousands Are Bypassing the Post Office with This App," *CNNMoney*, May 5, 2015, money.cnn.com/2015/04/21/technology/shyp-series-b/

[14] Seth Fiegerman, "Google Becomes a Rival to Amazon to Deliver Your Fresh Fruits and Veggies," *Mashable*, September 8, 2015, mashable.com/2015/09/08/google-express-fresh-groceries/#uL8CdTlHoSqN

[15] Adrian Gonzalez, "Amazon's 3D Printing Patent: The Quixotic Quest for Instant Delivery?" *LinkedIn Pulse* (blog), March 5, 2015, linkedin.com/pulse/amazons-3d-printing-patent-quixotic-quest-instant-adrian-gonzalez

[16] "Ask Alexa," Amazon, accessed April 11, 2016, amazon.com/gp/help/customer/display.html?nodeId=201549800

[17] "Grocery Click+Collect," Tesco, accessed April 1, 2016, tesco.com/collect/

[18] liquidnet.com, accessed May 20, 2016

[19] Ibid.

[20] Mike Gault, "Forget Bitcoin – What Is the Blockchain and Why Should You Care?" *Recode*, July 5, 2015, recode.net/2015/07/05/forget-bitcoin-what-is-the-blockchain-and-why-should-you-care/

[21] Laura Shin, "Bitcoin Technology Tested in Trial by 40 Big Banks," *Forbes*, March 3, 2016, forbes.com/sites/laurashin/2016/03/03/bitcoin-technology-tested-in-trial-by-40-big-banks/#5760b2c3d97a

[22] Thomas R. Eisenmann et al., "Strategies for Two-Sided Markets," *Harvard Business Review* 84 (October 2006), hbr.org/2006/10/strategies-for-two-sided-markets/ar/1

[23] Alexa Ray Corriea, "Debate Over Making Money off of Minecraft Leads to Player Outcry, Notch Dismay," *Polygon*, June 17, 2014, polygon.com/2014/6/17/5817194/debate-over-making-money-off-of-minecraft-leads-to-player-outcry

[24] John Biggs, "A Tiny Computer Attracts a Million Tinkerers," *New York Times*, January 30, 2013, nytimes.com/2013/01/31/technology/personaltech/raspberry-pi-a-computer-tinkerers-dream.html?_r=0

[25] "Join 2,940,000 Engineers with Over 1,260,000 Free CAD Files," GrabCAD Community, accessed April 5, 2016, grabcad.com/library

[26] Paul Rubens, "What Are Containers and Why Do You Need Them?," *CIO*, May 20, 2015, cio.com/article/2924995/enterprise-software/what-are-containers-and-why-do-you-need-them.html

[27] Charles Babcock, "Docker: Less Controversy, More Container Adoption In 2015," *InformationWeek*, January 26, 2015, informationweek.com/cloud/platform-as-a-service/docker-less-controversy-more-container-adoption-in-2015/d/d-id/1318771

[28] Ericka Chickowski, "8 Signs of Docker Ecosystem Empire-Building," *DevOps.com*, March 30, 2015, devops.com/2015/03/30/8-signs-of-docker-ecosystem-empire-building/

[29] Amy Larocca, "Etsy Wants to Crochet Its Cake and Eat It Too," *New York*, April 4, 2016, nymag.com/thecut/2016/04/etsy-capitalism-c-v-r.html

[30] Harrison Weber, "Etsy Now Has 54M Members. They Drove $1.93B in Sales Last Year," *VentureBeat*, March 4, 2015, venturebeat.com/2015/03/04/etsys-54m-members-drove-1-93b-in-sales-last-year/

[31] "The Appy Trucker," *Economist*, March 5, 2016, economist.com/news/business/21693946-digital-help-hand-fragmented-and-often-inefficient-industry-appy-trucker

[32] "Internet of Things in Logistics," *DHL Trend Research*, 2015, dpdhl.com/content/dam/dpdhl/presse/pdf/2015/DHLTrendReport_Internet_of_things.pdf

[33] Bernard Marr, "From Farming To Big Data: The Amazing Story of John Deere," *Data Science Central* (blog), May 7, 2015, datasciencecentral.com/profiles/blogs/from-farming-to-big-data-the-amazing-story-of-john-deere

[34] Hal Varian et al., *The Economics of Information Technology: An Introduction* (Cambridge: Cambridge University Press, 2004), p. 4

[35] Wikipedia contributors, "Adyen," *Wikipedia, The Free Encyclopedia*, accessed April 1, 2016, en.wikipedia.org/wiki/Adyen

[36] Jason Del Rey, "Adyen Is the $2 Billion Payments Startup You've Never Heard Of (Unless You're a Payments Nerd)," *Recode*, January 14, 2016, recode.net/2016/01/14/adyen-is-the-2-billion-payments-startup-youve-never-heard-of-unless-youre-a-payments-nerd/

[37] Sramana Mitra, "Billion Dollar Unicorns: Adyen is on a Roll," *One Million by One Million* (blog), October 7, 2015, sramanamitra.com/2015/10/07/billion-dollar-unicorns-adyen-is-on-a-roll/

[38] "Accept Apple Pay Online and In-Store," Adyen, accessed April 1, 2016, adyen.com/home/payment-network/apple-pay

[39] Lucy England, "Here's Why the Company that Takes Payments for Facebook, AirBnB and Spotify is Worth $1.5 billion," *Business Insider*, July 10, 2015, businessinsider.com/adyen-FinTech-unicorn-payments-facebook-airbnb-spotify-wired-money-2015-7?r=UK&IR=T

[40] Wikipedia contributors, "LinkedIn," *Wikipedia, The Free Encyclopedia*, accessed April 5, 2016, en.wikipedia.org/w/index.php?title=LinkedIn&oldid=713724958

[41] "Free LinkedIn Account Usage Among Members as of May 2015," *Statista*, accessed April 1, 2016, statista.com/statistics/264074/percentage-of-paying-linkedin-users/

[42] Siya Raj Purohit, "How LinkedIn Knows What Jobs You Are Interested In," *Udacity.com* (blog), May 21, 2014, blog.udacity.com/2014/05/how-linkedin-knows-what-jobs-you-are.html

[43] "LinkedIn Announces Fourth Quarter and Full Year 2015 Results," LinkedIn, February 4, 2016, press.linkedin.com/site-resources/news-releases/2016/linkedin-announces-fourth-quarter-and-full-year-2015-results

[44] "2 Million LinkedIn Groups," *Slideshare* (infographic), August 20, 2013, slideshare.net/linkedin/linked-in-groups-2013-infographic

[45] John Nemo, "LinkedIn Just Made a Savvy Business Move and Nobody Noticed," *Inc.*, April 26, 2016, inc.com/john-nemo/linkedin-just-made-a-savvy-business-move-and-nobody-noticed.html?cid=cp01002fastco

Chapter 3

[1] Dorian Lynskey, "How the Compact Disc Lost its Shine," *The Guardian*, May 28, 2015, theguardian.com/music/2015/may/28/how-the-compact-disc-lost-its-shine

[2] Neil Strauss, "Pennies that Add Up to $16.98: Why CDs Cost So Much," *New York Times*, July 5, 1995, nytimes.com/1995/07/05/arts/pennies-that-add-up-to-16.98-why-cd-s-cost-so-much.html

[3] Lynskey, "How the Compact Disc."

[4] "Why does the RIAA Hate Torrent Sites So Much?" *Music Business Worldwide*, December 6, 2014, musicbusinessworldwide.com/why-does-the-riaa-hate-torrent-sites-so-much/

[5] "IFPI Digital Music Report 2015," IFPI, 2015, ifpi.org/downloads/Digital-Music-Report-2015.pdf

[6] Don Dodge, "Napster – The Inside Story and Lessons for Entrepreneurs," *Don Dodge on The Next Big Thing* (blog), October 3, 2005, dondodge.typepad.com/the_next_big_thing/2005/10/napster_the_ins.html

[7] "Internet Growth Statistics," *Internet World Statistics*, accessed April 5, 2016, internetworldstats.com/emarketing.htm

[8] Maya Kosoff, "ClassPass, a Startup That Gym Rats and Investors Love, Is Now a $400 Million Company," *Business Insider*, May 6, 2015, businessinsider.com/classpass-400-million-valuation-2015-5

[9] Antonia Farzan, "Here's How Often You Have to Work Out to Make a ClassPass Membership Worth It," *Business Insider*, July 6, 2015, businessinsider.com/classpass-worth-it-2015-6

[10] Jenna Wortham, "ClassPass and the Joy and Guilt of the Digital Middleman Economy," *New York Times Magazine*, March 9, 2015, nytimes.com/2015/03/05/magazine/classpass-and-the-joy-and-guilt-of-the-digital-middleman-economy.html?_r=0

[11] Nathan McAlone, "Hot New York startup ClassPass is Generating $100 Million in Revenue, and It Just Poached a VP from Amazon to Be Its New CTO," *Business Insider*, March 17, 2016, businessinsider.com/classpass-hires-amazons-sam-hall-to-be-new-cto-and-cpo-2016-3

[12] Maya Kosoff, "Some Gym Owners Have Grown Wary of $400 Million Startup ClassPass: 'It's the Groupon of Exercise Studios'," *Business Insider*, May 19, 2015, businessinsider.com/how-classpass-wants-to-help-studio-owners-2015-5

[13] Brad Tuttle, "Everything You Need To Know About Amazon's New Rival Jet.com," *Money*, July 20, 2015, time.com/money/3964742/jet-com-compare-amazon-costco/

[14] Leena Rao, "Jet.com, the Online Shopping Upstart, Drops Membership Fee," *Fortune*, October 7, 2015, fortune.com/2015/10/07/online-shopping-jet-com/

[15] Rolfe Winkler, "Frenzy Around Shopping Site Jet.com Harks Back to Dot-Com Boom," *Wall Street Journal*, July 19, 2015, wsj.com/articles/frenzy-around-shopping-site-jet-com-harks-back-to-dot-com-boom-1437359430

[16] "How Jet Works: How to Get JetCash," Jet, accessed April 5, 2016, jet.com/how-jet-works/how-to-get-jetcash

[17] Michael E. Porter, *Competitive Strategy: Techniques for Analyzing Industries and Competitors* (New York: The Free Press, 1998), pp. 35-38.

[18] Teresa Novellino, "To Catch Amazon, Jet.com Needs to Fuel Up, Find Niches," *New York Business Journal*, July 30, 2015 bizjournals.com/newyork/news/2015/07/30/to-catch-amazon-jet-com-needs-to-fuel-up-find.html

[19] John Kell, "This Amazon Killer Is in Talks for a $3 Billion Valuation," *Fortune*, July 20, 2015, fortune.com/2015/07/20/amazon-killer-3billion-valuation-jet/

[20] Paula Rosenblum, "Jet.com: The Top Ten Things You Should Know," *Forbes*, August 5, 2015, forbes.com/sites/paularosenblum/2015/08/05/jet-com-the-top-ten-things-you-should-know/3/#5667b0ac6a3d

[21] Nick Huang, "Global Logistics Industry Outlook," January 28, 2014, *BusinessVibes*, businessvibes.com/blog/report-global-logistics-industry-outlook

[22] Erica E. Phillips, "Startups Compete for Freight Forwarding as They Wade Into Global Shipping," *Wall Street Journal*, July 17, 2015, wsj.com/articles/startups-compete-for-travel-agents-for-cargo-mantle-as-they-wade-into-freight-forwarding-1437167723

[23] Sam Whelan, "Hi-tech Newcomer Shakes Up the Adhoc Freight Sector by Cutting 30% Off Logistics Costs," *The Loadstar*, March 3, 2016, theloadstar.co.uk/high-tech-newcomer-shakes-adhoc-freight-sector-cutting-30-off-logistics-costs/

[24] Mark W. Johnson, *Seizing the White Space: Business Model Innovation for Growth and Renewal* (Boston: Harvard Business Review Press, 2010)

[25] Rita Gunther McGrath, *The End of Competitive Advantage: How to Keep Your Strategy Moving As Fast As Your Business* (Boston: Harvard Business Review Press, 2013) p. xvi

[26] W. Chan Kim and Renée Mauborgne, *Blue Ocean Strategy: How to Create Uncontested Market Space and Make the Competition Irrelevant* (Boston: Harvard Business Review Press, 2005, p. 49

[27] Ibid, p. 204

[28] Brandon Griggs and Todd Leopold, "How iTunes Changed Music, and the World," *CNN*, April 26, 2013, cnn.com/2013/04/26/tech/web/itunes-10th-anniversary/

[29] Steven Tweedie, "Apple Announces Apple Music, Its New Music Streaming App," *Business Insider*, June 8, 2015, businessinsider.com/apple-announces-new-apple-music-streaming-app-2015-6

[30] Christina Rogers, Mike Ramsey and Daisuke Wakabayashi, "Apple Hires Auto Industry Veterans," *Wall Street Journal*, July 20, 2015, wsj.com/articles/apple-hires-auto-industry-manufacturing-veteran-1437430826

[31] Bruce Brown and Scott Anthony, "How P&G Tripled Its Innovation Success Rate," *Harvard Business Review*, June 2011, hbr.org/2011/06/how-pg-tripled-its-innovation-success-rate

[32] Drew Harwell, "Gillette's Lawsuit Could Tilt the Battle for America's Beards," *Washington Post*, December 18, 2015, washingtonpost.com/news/business/wp/2015/12/18/gillettes-lawsuit-could-tilt-the-battle-for-americas-beards/

[33] "Blades," Dollar Shave Club, accessed April 6, 2016, dollarshaveclub.com/blades

[34] Rolf Winkler, "Dollar Shave Club Is Valued at $615 Million," *Wall Street Journal*, June 21, 2015, blogs.wsj.com/digits/2015/06/21/dollar-shave-club-valued-at-615-million/

[35] Jack Neff, "Dollar Shave Club Claims to Top Schick as No. 2 Razor Cartridge," *Advertising Age*, September 8, 2015, adage.com/article/cmo-strategy/dollar-shave-club-claims-top-schick-2-men-s-razor/300247/

[36] Serena Ng and Paul Ziobro, "Razor Sales Move Online, Away From Gillette," *Wall Street Journal*, June 23, 2015, wsj.com/articles/SB12147335600370333763904581058081668712042

[37] Ari Levy, "Shaving Wars Pit Tech Start-ups against Gillette," *CNBC*, April 8, 2015, cnbc.com/2015/04/08/s-pit-tech-start-ups-against-gillette.html

[38] Matthew Barry, "A Changing Environment for Online Shaving Clubs in the US," *Euromonitor International* (blog), February 21, 2016, blog.euromonitor.com/2016/02/a-changing-environment-for-online-shaving-clubs-in-the-us.html

[39] Steve Millward, "WeChat Still Unstoppable, Grows to 697m Active Users," *Tech in Asia*, March 17, 2016, techinasia.com/wechat-697-million-monthly-active-users

[40] Juro Osawa, "Tencent's WeChat App to Offer Personal Loans in Minutes," *Wall Street Journal*, September 11, 2015, wsj.com/articles/tencent-to-add-personal-loan-feature-to-wechat-app-1441952556?mod=e2tw

[41] Devin Leonard and Rick Clough, "How GE Exorcised the Ghost of Jack Welch to Become a 124-Year-Old Startup," *Bloomberg Businessweek*, March 17, 2016, bloomberg.com/news/articles/2016-03-17/how-ge-exorcised-the-ghost-of-jack-welch-to-become-a-124-year-old-startup

[42] Reuters, "GE Has Been Busy Selling Off Its Non-core Assets," *Fortune*, March 30, 2016. fortune.com/2016/03/30/general-electric-selling-assets/

[43] Ted Mann and Laurie Burkitt, "GE Deal Gives China's Haier Long-Sought Overseas Foothold," *Wall Street Journal*, January 15, 2016, wsj.com/articles/ge-deal-gives-chinas-haier-long-sought-overseas-foothold-1452904339

[44] "Form 10-K 2015," GE, 2015, ge.com/ar2015/assets/pdf/GE_2015_Form_10K.pdf

[45] Ed Crooks, "General Electric: Post-Industrial Revolution," *Financial Times*, January 12, 2016, ft.com/intl/cms/s/0/81bec2c0-b847-11e5-b151-8e15c9a029fb.html#axzz3yGmPePd5

[46] Kristin Kloberdanz, "GE's Got a Ticket to Ride: How the Cloud Will Take Trains into a New Era," *manufacturing.net* (advertisement), accessed April 6, 2016, manufacturing.net/news/2016/04/ges-got-ticket-ride-how-cloud-will-take-trains-new-era

[47] Ibid.

[48] Tomas Kellner, "The Power Of Predix: An Inside Look at How Pitney Bowes Is Using the Industrial Internet Platform," *GE Reports*, February 24, 2016, gereports.com/the-power-of-predix-an-inside-look-at-how-pitney-bowes-has-been-using-the-industrial-internet-platform/

[49] Crooks, "General Electric."

Chapter 4

[1] "Q4 15 Letter to Shareholders," Netflix, January 19, 2016, files.shareholder.com/downloads/NFLX/1837473908x0x870685/C6213FF9-5498-4084-A0FF-74363CEE35A1/Q4_15_Letter_to_Shareholders_-_COMBINED.pdf

[2] Emily Steel, "Netflix Refines Its DVD Business, Even as Streaming Unit Booms," *New York Times*, July 26, 2015, nytimes.com/2015/07/27/business/while-its-streaming-service-booms-netflix-streamlines-old-business.html?_r=1

[3] James Macaulay et al., "The Digital Manufacturer: Resolving the Service Dilemma," Cisco, November 2015, cisco.com/c/dam/en_us/solutions/industries/manufacturing/thought-leadership-wp.pdf

[4] Ethan Wolf-Mann, "Vinyl Record Revenues Have Surpassed Free Streaming Services Like Spotify," *Money*, October 1, 2015, time.com/money/4056464/vinyl-records-sales-streaming-revenues/

[5] Jen Wieczner, "Last Big Chunk of GE Capital Sold to Wells Fargo," *Fortune*, October 13, 2015, fortune.com/2015/10/13/ge-capital-wells-fargo/

[6] "KONE Joins Forces with IBM for IoT Cloud Services and Advanced Analytics Technologies," KONE Corporation, February 19, 2016, kone.com/en/press/press/kone-joins-forces-with-ibm-for-iot-cloud-services-and-advanced-analytics-technologies-2016-02-19.aspx

[7] Gary Shub et al., "Global Asset Management 2015: Sparking Growth with Go-to-Market Excellence," *BCG Perspectives*, July 7, 2015, bcgperspectives.com/content/articles/financial-institutions-global-asset-management-2015-sparking-growth-through-go-to-market-strategy/

[8] Julia Greenberg, "Financial Robo-Advisers Go into Overdrive as Market Rumbles," *Wired*, August 27, 2015, wired.com/2015/08/FinTechs-robo-advisers-go-overdrive-market-rumbles/

[9] Sarah O'Brien, "Will You Trust a Robot to Manage Your Money – When You're 64?" *CNBC*, June 2, 2015, cnbc.com/2015/06/02/will-you-trust-a-robot-to-manage-your-money-when-youre-64.html

[10] "Schwab Intelligent Portfolios", Charles Schwab, accessed April 6, 2016, intelligent.schwab.com

[11] "Schwab Posts First Robo Results; Q2 Earnings Beat Estimates," *ThinkAdvisor*, July 16, 2015, thinkadvisor.com/2015/07/16/schwab-posts-first-robo-results-q2-earnings-beat-e

[12] Lisa Schidler, "Schwab's Robo Spikes Suddenly To Nearer $5 Billion as 500 RIAs Sign On," *RIABiz*, October 27, 2015, riabiz.com/a/4957939840319488/schwabs-robo-spikes-suddenly-to-nearer-5-billion-as-500-rias-sign-on

[13] Alessandra Malito, "Schwab Launches Adviser-facing Robo Service," *Investment News*, June 23, 2015 investmentnews.com/article/20150623/FREE/150629976/schwab-launches-adviser-facing-robo-service

[14] Joe Morris, "Schwab Storms into 'Robo-Advisor' Sector," *Financial Times*, October 30, 2014, on.ft.com/1UuMKQE

[15] "Who We Are," BlackRock, accessed April 6, 2016, blackrock.com/corporate/en-us/about-us

[16] Leena Rao, "Blackrock Buys a Robo Advisor," *Fortune*, August 26, 2015, fortune.com/2015/08/26/blackrock-robo-advisor-acquisition/

[17] Alessandra Malito, "In the Wake of Blackrock's FutureAdvisor Deal, which Independent Robo-Adviser Will Be Bought Next?" *Investment News*, August 27, 2015 investmentnews.com/article/20150827/FREE/150829915/in-the-wake-of-blackrocks-futureadvisor-deal-which-independent-robo

[18] Brooke Southall, "Why BlackRock's Purchase of FutureAdvisor for $152 Million Could Be a Deal of Destiny," *RIABiz*, September 2, 2015, riabiz.com/a/4949175858888704/why-blackrocks-purchase-of-futureadvisor-for-152-million-could-be-a-deal-of-destiny

[19] "BlackRock to Acquire FutureAdvisor," BlackRock, August 26, 2015, blackrock.com/corporate/en-at/literature/press-release/future-advisor-press-release.pdf

[20] Michael Kitces, "BlackRock Acquires FutureAdvisor for $150M as Yet Another Robo-Advisor Pivots to Become an Advisor," *Nerd's Eye View* (blog), August 27, 2015, kitces.com/blog/blackrock-acquires-futureadvisor-for-150m-as-yet-another-robo-advisor-pivots-to-become-an-advisor-FinTech-solution/

[21] "BlackRock Solutions," BlackRock, accessed April 6, 2016, blackrock.com/institutions/en-axj/investment-capabilities-and-solutions/blackrock-solutions

[22] Kitces, "BlackRock Acquires FutureAdvisor."

[23] "Fidelity by the Numbers: Corporate Statistics," Fidelity, accessed April 6, 2016, fidelity.com/about-fidelity/fidelity-by-numbers/corporate-statistics

[24] Suleman Din, "Raising $100M, Betterment Sets Itself Apart in Robo Space," *Employee Benefit News*, March 29, 2016, benefitnews.com/news/raising-100m-betterment-sets-itself-apart-in-robo-space

[25] James J. Green, "Betterment Allies with Fidelity to Launch Betterment Institutional for Advisors," *ThinkAdvisor*, October 15, 2014, thinkadvisor.com/2014/10/15/betterment-allies-with-fidelity-to-launch-betterme

[26] "Fidelity Institutional Announces New Collaboration with LearnVest," Fidelity, accessed April 6, 2016, fidelity.com/about-fidelity/institutional-investment-management/collaboration-with-learnvest

[27] Liz Moyer, "Northwestern Mutual Is Buying Online Advice Provider LearnVest," *Wall Street Journal*, March 25, 2015, on.wsj.com/1xh64lh

[28] Lawrence Delevingne, "Robo Advisor Betterment Works with Fidelity in RIA Push," *CNBC*, October 15, 2014, cnbc.com/2014/10/15/robo-advisor-betterment-works-with-fidelity-in-ria-push.html

[29] Liz Skinner, "Fidelity Institutional Weighs Own Robo Offering," *Investment News*, December 2, 2014, investmentnews.com/article/20141202/FREE/141209982/fidelity-institutional-weighs-own-robo-offering

[30] Ron Lieber, "Fidelity Joins Growing Field of Automated Financial Advice," *New York Times*, November 20, 2015, nytimes.com/2015/11/21/your-money/fidelity-joins-growing-field-of-automated-financial-advice.html?_r=0

[31] Sarah Perez, "Nielsen: Music Streams Doubled In 2015, Digital Sales Continue To Fall," *TechCrunch*, January 7, 2016, techcrunch.com/2016/01/07/nielsen-music-streams-doubled-in-2015-digital-sales-continue-to-fall/

[32] Paul Resnikoff, "$9.99 Is 'Way Too Expensive' for Streaming Music, Study Finds," *Digital Music News*, January 7, 2016, digitalmusicnews.com/2016/01/07/9-99-is-way-too-expensive-for-streaming-music-study-finds/

[33] Jeremy Rifkin, *The Zero Marginal Cost Society* (New York: Palgrave Macmillan, 2014)

[34] Glenn Peoples, "PwC's Music Biz Forecast for the Next Four Years? More of the Same, Despite Looming Changes," *Billboard*, June 2, 2015, billboard.com/articles/business/6583239/pwcs-music-biz-forecast-for-the-next-four-years-more-of-the-same-despite

[35] Chris Taylor, "Apple's Business Model Is Backwards – And It Works Like Crazy," *Mashable*, October 23, 2013, mashable.com/2013/10/23/apple-free-software-expensive-hardware/#8mVXX0gECsqg

[36] Ibid.

[37] Matt Asay, "Thinking about the iPod as a Razor, Not a Blade," *CNET*, August 4, 2007, cnet.com/news/thinking-about-the-ipod-as-a-razor-not-a-blade/

[38] Andrew Tonner, "Apple's Services Segment: It's Bigger Than You Might Think," *Motley Fool*, September 7, 2015, fool.com/investing/general/2015/09/07/apples-services-segment-its-bigger-than-you-might.aspx

[39] Christine Moorman, "Why Apple Is a Great Marketer," *Forbes*, July 10, 2012, forbes.com/sites/christinemoorman/2012/07/10/why-apple-is-a-great-marketer/#404bb9be6cb0

[40] "Introducing Apple Music – All The Ways You Love Music. All in One Place." Apple, June 8, 2015, apple.com/pr/library/2015/06/08Introducing-Apple-Music-All-The-Ways-You-Love-Music-All-in-One-Place-.html?sr=hotnews.rss

[41] Micah Singleton, "Spotify Hits 30 Million Subscribers," *The Verge*, March 21, 2916, theverge.com/2016/3/21/11220398/spotify-hits-30-million-subscribers

[42] Corey Fedde, "Apple Music Hits 11 Million Subscribers: Why Spotify Isn't Worried," *Christian Science Monitor*, February 13, 2016, csmonitor.com/Business/2016/0213/Apple-Music-hits-11-million-subscribers-Why-Spotify-isn-t-worried

[43] Mark Hogan, "The 50 Best Playlists on Apple Music," *Vulture*, October 1, 2015, vulture.com/2015/10/50-best-playlists-on-apple-music.html

[44] Ethan Wolf-Mann, "Apple Music Is the 'PC' of the Music Streaming World," *Money*, October 19, 2015, time.com/money/4077990/apple-music-not-popular-with-young/

[45] Yoni Heisler, "Apple Music Beats Spotify to the Punch, Will be the First Streaming Service to Feature DJ Mixes," *BGR*, March 15, 2016,bgr.com/2016/03/15/apple-music-mashups-dj-remixes-streaming/

[46] Julia Greenberg, "Apple Tiptoes Into Original TV with Vice Show on Apple Music," *Wired*, March 23, 2016, wired.com/2016/03/apple-tiptoes-original-tv-vice-show-apple-music/

[47] Roland Banks, "Smartphones Are Changing TV Viewing Habits, Especially among the Younger Generation," *Mobile Industry Review*, October 26, 2015, mobileindustryreview.com/2015/10/smartphones-are-changing-tv-viewing-habits.html

[48] Jennifer Booton, "Pandora's Answer to Spotify and Apple Music Might Be Too Late," *MarketWatch*, November 18, 2015, marketwatch.com/story/pandoras-apple-music-rival-might-be-too-late-to-make-a-difference-2015-11-17

Chapter 5

[1] Roger L. Martin, "The Big Lie of Strategic Planning," *Harvard Business Review*, January 2014, hbr.org/2014/01/the-big-lie-of-strategic-planning

[2] Aileen Ionescu-Somers and Albrecht Enders, "How Nestlé Dealt with a Social Media Campaign against It," *Financial Times*, December 3, 2012, ft.com/cms/s/0/90dbff8a-3aea-11e2-b3f0-00144feabdc0.html#axzz41OkAJtML

[3] James Murray, "Greenpeace Lauds Nestlé and Ferrero Palm Oil Pledges, Slams Others," *GreenBiz*, March 7, 2016, greenbiz.com/article/greenpeace-slams-lack-business-progress-palm-oil-deforestation

[4] Nestlé and the Digital Acceleration Team Take Social to the Next Level with Socialbakers," Socialbakers, accessed April 6, 2016, socialbakers.com/resources/client-stories/nestle/

[5] Abbey Klaassen, "Nestlé's Global Program Produces Its Digital Disciple," *Advertising Age*, October 13, 2014, adage.com/article/digital/nestle-s-global-program-produces-digital-disciples/295359/

[6] "Nestlé and the Digital Acceleration Team," Socialbakers, accessed April 6, 2016, socialbakers.com/resources/client-stories/nestle/

[7] Shilpi Choudhury, "How Nestlé Uses Data Visualization for Social Media Monitoring and Engagement," *FusionBrew*, last updated September 13, 2015, fusioncharts.com/blog/2014/08/how-nestle-uses-data-visualization-for-social-media-monitoring-and-engagement/

[8] Evelyn L. Kent, "Cognitive Computing: An Evolution in Computing," *KMWorld* 24, no. 10 (November/December 2015), kmworld.com/Articles/News/News-Analysis/Cognitive-computing-An-evolution-in-computing-107027.aspx

[9] Judith Lamont, PhD, "Text Analytics Broadens Its Reach," *KMWorld* 24, no. 7 (July/August 2015), kmworld.com/Articles/Editorial/Features/Text-analytics-broadens-its-reach-104747.aspx

[10] "At a Glance," Deutsche Post DHL Group, accessed April 6, 2016, dpdhl.com/en/about_us/at_a_glance.html

[11] "DHL Invests $108 Million in Its Americas Hub," DHL, May 29, 2015, dhl.com/en/press/releases/releases_2015/group/dhl_invests_108_million_in_its_americas_hub.html

[12] "DHL Successfully Tests Augmented Reality Application in Warehouse," DHL, January 26, 2015, dhl.com/en/press/releases/releases_2015/logistics/dhl_successfully_tests_augmented_reality_application_in_warehouse.html

[13] Ibid.

[14] Charles Mitchell, Rebecca L. Ray, and Bart van Ark, "CEO Challenge 2014," The Conference Board, 2014, conference-board.org/retrievefile.cfm?filename=TCB_R-1537-14-RR1.pdf&type=subsite

[15] Brad Power, "How GE Applies Lean Startup Practices," *Harvard Business Review*, April 23, 2014, hbr.org/2014/04/how-ge-applies-lean-startup-practices/

[16] Will Knight, "Inside Amazon's Warehouse, Human-Robot Symbiosis" *MIT Technology Review*, July 7, 2015, technologyreview.com/s/538601/inside-amazons-warehouse-human-robot-symbiosis/

[17] "Coffee House Chains Ranked by Number of Stores Worldwide in 2014," Statista, accessed April 6, 2016, statista.com/statistics/272900/coffee-house-chains-ranked-by-number-of-stores-worldwide/

[18] Mark Wilson, "Mobile Orders Will Make Starbucks Coffee More Addictive than Ever," *Fast Company*, December 3, 2014, fastcodesign.com/3039308/mobile-orders-will-make-starbucks-coffee-more-addictive-than-ever

[19] Taylor Soper, "Mobile Payments Account For 21% of Transactions at Starbucks as Coffee Giant Rolls Out New Technology," *GeekWire*, October 30, 2015, geekwire.com/2015/mobile-payments-account-for-21-of-sales-at-starbucks-as-coffee-giant-rolls-out-new-technology/

[20] Natasha Lomas, "Starbucks' Mobile Pre-Ordering Goes International with London Launch," *TechCrunch*, October 1, 2015, techcrunch.com/2015/10/01/starbucks-takes-mop-to-london/

[21] Sarah Perez, "Starbucks' Mobile Order & Pay Now Live Nationwide, Delivery Service in Testing by Year-End," *TechCrunch*, September 22, 2015, techcrunch.com/2015/09/22/starbucks-mobile-order-pay-now-live-nationwide-delivery-service-in-testing-by-year-end/

[22] "Available in More Than 7,400 Stores and Customers Using the Starbucks App on iOS or Android Devices; International Expansion Coming in October," Starbucks, September 22, 2015, news.starbucks.com/news/starbucks-mobile-order-pay-now-available-to-customers-nationwide

[23] Julia Kowelle, "Starbucks Sales Set to Break $20bn – A Latte for Everyone on Earth," *The Guardian*, October 30, 2015, theguardian.com/business/2015/oct/30/starbucks-coffee-sales-set-to-break-20bn-a-latte-for-everyone

[24] Tricia Duryee, "Q&A: Starbucks Digital Chief Adam Brotman on Mobile Ordering, Delivery and International Availability," *GeekWire*, December 4, 2014, geekwire.com/2014/qa-starbucks-digital-chief-adam-brotman-mobile-ordering-delivery-international-availability/

[25] Amy Danise, "The Largest Auto Insurance Companies by Market Share," Insure.com, last updated December 3, 2015, insure.com/car-insurance/largest-auto-insurance-companies-by-market-share.html

[26] "Insurance Customers Would Consider Buying Insurance from Internet Giants, According to Accenture's Global Research," Accenture, February 6, 2014, newsroom.accenture.com/subjects/research-surveys/insurance-customers-would-consider-buying-insurance-from-internet-giants-according-to-accentures-global-research.htm

[27] Ibid.

[28] "Insurance-Tech Startups Are Invading The Multi-Trillion-Dollar Insurance Industry," *CB Insights*, June 5, 2015, cbinsights.com/blog/insurance-tech-startups-investment-growth/

[29] Steven Kauderer, Sean O'Neill and David Whelan, "Why It Pays for P&C insurers to Earn their Customers' Intense Loyalty," *Bain Insights*, August 28, 2013, bain.com/publications/articles/why-it-pays-for-pc-insurers-to-earn-their-customers-intense-loyalty-brief.aspx

Chapter 6

[1] Charles Coy, "Spotlight on Technology: Let Employees Voice Their Feedback," *Cornerstone on Demand*, January 22, 2014, cornerstoneondemand.com/rework/spotlight-technology-let-employees-voice-their-feedback

[2] Greg Petro, "The Future of Fashion Retailing: The Zara Approach (Part 2 of 3)," *Forbes*, October 25, 2012, forbes.com/sites/gregpetro/2012/10/25/the-future-of-fashion-retailing-the-zara-approach-part-2-of-3/#153e9aaa39a0

[3] Chris DeRose and Noel Tichy, "Here's How to Actually Empower Customer Service Employees," *Harvard Business Review*, July 1, 2013, hbr.org/2013/07/heres-how-to-actually-empower-customer

[4] "Overview," Officevibe, accessed April 6, 2016, officevibe.com/employee-engagement-solution

[5] Lisa He, "Google's Secrets of Innovation: Empowering Its Employees," *Forbes*, March 29, 2013, forbes.com/sites/laurahe/2013/03/29/googles-secrets-of-innovation-empowering-its-employees/#74d93ae7eb39

[6] "Enterprise Collaboration: Insights from the Cisco IBSG Horizons Study," Cisco, March 2012

[7] Edgar H. Schein, *Humble Inquiry: The Gentle Art of Asking Instead of Telling* (San Francisco: Berrett-Koehler Publishers, 2013), p. 2

[8] Rawn, "Measuring the Performance of Knowledge Workers," *IBM developerWorks* (blog), April 1, 2006, ibm.com/developerworks/community/blogs/rawn/entry/measuring_the_performance_of_knowledge?lang=en

[9] Dave Evans, "The Internet of Things: How the Next Evolution of the Internet is Changing Everything," Cisco, April 2011, cisco.com/c/dam/en_us/about/ac79/docs/innov/IoT_IBSG_0411FINAL.pdf

[10] Olivia Solon, "Why Your Boss Wants to Track Your Heart Rate at Work," *Bloomberg*, August 12, 2015, bloomberg.com/news/articles/2015-08-12/wearable-biosensors-bring-tracking-tech-into-the-workplace

[11] Hannah Kuchler, "Data Pioneers Watching Us Work," *Financial Times*, February 17, 2014, ft.com/intl/cms/s/2/d56004b0-9581-11e3-9fd6-00144feab7de.html

[12] Rachel Emma Silverman, "Tracking Sensors Invade the Workplace," *Wall Street Journal*, March 7, 2013, wsj.com/articles/SB10001424127887324034804578344303429080678

[13] Sue Shellenbarger, "Stop Wasting Everyone's Time," *Wall Street Journal*, December 2, 2014, wsj.com/articles/how-to-stop-wasting-colleagues-time-1417562658

[14] David Nield, "Do You Really Know Everything Your Phone Is Tracking on You?" *TechRadar*, July 25, 2015, techradar.com/news/phone-and-communications/mobile-phones/sensory-overload-how-your-smartphone-is-becoming-part-of-you-1210244

[15] Duncan Graham-Rowe, "A Smartphone that Knows You're Angry," *MIT Technology Review*, January 9, 2012, technologyreview.com/s/426560/a-smart-phone-that-knows-youre-angry/

[16] Elizabeth Dwoskin, "Lending Startups Look at Borrowers' Phone Usage to Assess Creditworthiness," *Wall Street Journal*, November 30, 2015, wsj.com/articles/lending-startups-look-at-borrowers-phone-usage-to-assess-creditworthiness-1448933308

[17] Tanaya Macheel, "Average Time to Close Mortgages Fell in February: Ellie Mae," *National Mortgage News*, March 16, 2016, nationalmortgagenews.com/news/origination/average-time-to-close-mortgages-fell-in-february-ellie-mae-1073931-1.html

[18] Sydney Ember, "See That Billboard? It May See You, Too," *New York Times*, February 28, 2016, nytimes.com/2016/02/29/business/media/see-that-billboard-it-may-see-you-too.html?ref=technology

[19] Ibid.

[20] David Bolton, "Wearables: Triple-Digit Growth in 2015 Signals Increased Interest," *ARC*, February 26, 2016, arc.applause.com/2016/02/26/wearables-shipments-2015-idc/

[21] Cliff Kuang, "Disney's $1 Billion Bet on a Magical Wristband," *Wired*, March 10, 2015, wired.com/2015/03/disney-magicband/

[22] Christopher Palmeri, "Why Disney Won't Be Taking Magic Wristbands to Its Chinese Park," *Bloomberg*, January 10, 2016, bloomberg.com/news/articles/2016-01-10/why-disney-won-t-be-taking-magic-wristbands-to-its-chinese-park

[23] Affectiva, accessed April 6, 2016, affectiva.com/

[24] Oliver Nieburg, "Smile for Candy: Hershey Eyes In-Store Excitement with Facial Recognition Sampler," *ConfectionaryNews.com*, July 31, 2015, confectionerynews.com/Manufacturers/Hershey-Smile-Sample-Facial-recognition-to-dispense-chocolate

[25] Ibid.

[26] Rob Matheson, "Watch Your Tone: Voice Analytics Software Helps Customer Service Reps Build Better Rapport with Customers," *MIT News*, January 20, 2016, news.mit.edu/2016/startup-cogito-voice-analytics-call-centers-ptsd-0120

[27] David Cohen, "How Facebook Manages a 300-Petabyte Data Warehouse, 600 Terabytes per Day," *SocialTimes* (blog), April 11, 2014, adweek.com/socialtimes/orcfile/434041?red=af

[28] Jason Del Rey, "How Amazon Tricks You into Thinking It Always Has the Lowest Prices," *Recode*, January 15, 2015, recode.net/2015/01/13/how-amazon-tricks-you-into-thinking-it-always-has-the-lowest-prices/

[29] Erik Kain, "Amazon Price Check May Be Evil, But It's the Future," *Forbes*, December 14, 2011, forbes.com/sites/erikkain/2011/12/14/amazon-price-check-may-be-evil-but-its-the-future/#3fa5861a6839

[30] Gregory T. Huang, "Diving Deeper Into Cybersecurity, Recorded Future Reels In $12M," *Xconomy*, April 16, 2015, xconomy.com/boston/2015/04/16/diving-deeper-into-cybersecurity-recorded-future-reels-in-12m/#

[31] Alicia Boler-Davis, "How GM Uses Social Media to Improve Cars and Customer Service," *Harvard Business Review*, February 12, 2016, hbr.org/2016/02/how-gm-uses-social-media-to-improve-cars-and-customer-service

[32] Rob Preston, "GM's Social Media Plan: It's Not About Likes," *Forbes*, August 18, 2015, forbes.com/sites/oracle/2015/08/18/gms-social-media-plan-its-not-about-likes/#55a26e4c2eae

[33] Dan Primack, "This Software Startup Is Battling Slavery," *Fortune*, December 21, 2015, fortune.com/2015/12/21/software-startup-battling-slavery/

[34] Ibid.

[35] "FedEx Company Statistics," Statistics Brain, accessed April 6, 2016, statisticbrain.com/fedex-company-statistics/

[36] "BP at a Glance," BP, accessed April 6, 2016, bp.com/en/global/corporate/about-bp/bp-at-a-glance.html

[37] Julie Bort, "Cisco Teams Up with Robot Company So It Can Watch Hundreds of Robots on Factory Floors," *Business Insider*, October 5, 2015, businessinsider.com/cisco-fanac-for-iot

[38] "Mining Firm Quadruples Production, with Internet of Everything," Cisco, 2014, cisco.com/c/dam/en_us/solutions/industries/docs/manufacturing/c36-730784-01-dundee.pdf

[39] Ibid.

Chapter 7

[1] Justin Worland, "Google's Former CEO: Amazon Is Biggest Rival," *Time*, October 14, 2014, time.com/3505713/google-amazon-rivals/

[2] Adam M. Kleinbaum, Toby E. Stuart and Michael L. Tushman, "Communication (and Coordination?) in a Modern, Complex Organization," Working Paper 09-004 (Harvard Business School, 2008), hbs.edu/faculty/Publication%20Files/09-004.pdf

[3] Sarah Jane Gilbert, "The Silo Lives! Analyzing Coordination and Communication in Multiunit Companies," *Working Knowledge*, September 22, 2008, hbswk.hbs.edu/item/the-silo-lives-analyzing-coordination-and-communication-in-multiunit-companies

[4] Ranktab, accessed April 7, 2016, ranktab.com/explore/

[5] Shana Lebowitz, "Three Unconscious Biases That Affect Whether You Get Hired," *Business Insider*, July 17,2015, businessinsider.com/unconscious-biases-in-hiring-decisions-2015-7

[6] Jane Porter, "You're More Biased than You Think," *Fast Company*, October 6, 2014, fastcompany.com/3036627/strong-female-lead/youre-more-biased-than-you-think

[7] Sara Ashley O'Brien, "Biased Job Ads: This Startup Has a Fix," *CNN*, May 5, 2015, money.cnn.com/2015/03/20/technology/unitive-diversity/

[8] "Premium Appliance Producer Innovates with Internet of Everything," Cisco, 2014, cisco.com/c/dam/en_us/solutions/industries/docs/manufacturing/appliance_producer_innovates_with_ioe.pdf

[9] Ibid.

[10] Scott A. Christofferson, Robert S. McNish, and Diane L. Sias, "Where Mergers Go Wrong," *McKinsey Quarterly*, May 2004, mckinsey.com/business-functions/strategy-and-corporate-finance/our-insights/where-mergers-go-wrong

[11] Sujeeb Indap, "IBM Bets on Mergers and Algorithms for Growth," *Financial Times*, January 12, 2016, ft.com/cms/s/0/11010eea-ae5f-11e5-993b-c425a3d2b65a.html#ixzz3x2lpWTb9

[12] Steve Dunning, "Why IBM is in Decline," *Forbes*, May 30, 2014, forbes.com/sites/stevedenning/2014/05/30/why-ibm-is-in-decline/#752439814c53

[13] Barb Darrow, "Why IBM Is Dropping $2.6 Billion on Truven Health," *Fortune*, February 18, 2016, fortune.com/2016/02/18/ibm-truven-health-acquisition/

[14] Sujeeb Indap, "IBM Bets on Mergers and Algorithms for Growth," *Financial Times*, January 12, 2016, ft.com/cms/s/0/11010eea-ae5f-11e5-993b-c425a3d2b65a.html#ixzz3x2lpWTb9

[15] "M&A Accelerator," IBM, accessed April 7, 2016, ibm.com/services/us/gbs/strategy/mna/

[16] "Where We Operate," P&G, n.d., pg.com/en_US/downloads/media/Fact_Sheets_Operate.pdf

[17] Tom Davenport, "How P&G Presents Data to Decision-Makers," *Harvard Business Review*, April 4, 2013, hbr.org/2013/04/how-p-and-g-presents-data

[18] Doug Henschen, "P&G's CIO Details Business-Savvy Predictive Decision Cockpit," *InformationWeek*, September 11, 2012, informationweek.com/it-leadership/pandgs-cio-details-business-savvy-predictive-decision-cockpit/d/d-id/1106234?

[19] "Latest Innovations: Business Sphere," P&G, n.d., pg.com/en_US/downloads/innovation/factsheet_BusinessSphere.pdf

[20] "Data Analytics Allows P&G to Turn on a Dime." *CIO Insight*, May 3, 2013, cioinsight.com/it-strategy/big-data/data-analytics-allows-pg-to-turn-on-a-dime?utm_source=datafloq&utm_medium=ref&utm_campaign=datafloq

[21] "Tom Davenport, "How P&G Presents Data."

[22] Sue Hildreth, "Data+ Awards: Procter & Gamble Puts Worldwide BI Data in Executives' Hands," *Computerworld*, August 26, 2013, computerworld.com/article/2483948/enterprise-applications/data--awards--procter---gamble-puts-worldwide-bi-data-in-executives--hands.html

[23] "Tom Davenport, "How P&G Presents Data."

[24] "Senior Managers View the Workplace More Positively than Front-Line Workers,"American Psychological Association, May 12, 2015, apa.org/news/press/releases/2015/05/senior-managers.aspx

[25] Amy Adkins, "Employee Engagement in U.S. Stagnant in 2015," *Gallup*, Jan 13, 2016, gallup.com/poll/188144/employee-engagement-stagnant-2015.aspx

[26] Susan Sorenson and Keri Garman, "How to Tackle U.S. Employees' Stagnating Engagement," *Gallup*, June 11, 2013, com/businessjournal/162953/tackle-employees-stagnating-engagement.aspx

[27] Steven Rosenbush and Laura Stevens, "At UPS, the Algorithm Is the Driver," *Wall Street Journal*, February 16,2015, wsj.com/articles/at-ups-the-algorithm-is-the-driver-1424136536

[28] Ibid.

[29] Ibid.

[30] "The Decentralized Control Room" (case study), DAQRI, accessed April 7, 2016, daqri.com/home/case-studies/case-ksp/

[31] "Gartner Says Customer Relationship Management Software Market Grew 13.3 Percent," *Gartner*, May 19, 2015, gartner.com/newsroom/id/3056118

[32] Shira Ovide and Elizabeth Dwoskin, "The Data-Driven Rebirth of a Salesman," *Wall Street Journal*, September 17, 2015, http://www.wsj.com/articles/the-data-driven-rebirth-of-a-salesman-1442534375

[33] Ibid.

[34] Tim Bradshaw, "CES 2016: L'Oréal Gets a Makeover with Move into Wearable Tech," *Financial Times*, January 6, 2016, ft.com/intl/cms/s/0/c61c4bd4-b45c-11e5-8358-9a82b43f6b2f.html

[35] Steve Bertoni, "Oscar Health Using Misfit Wearables To Reward Fit Customers," *Forbes*, December 8, 2014, forbes.com/sites/stevenbertoni/2014/12/08/oscar-health-using-misfit-wearables-to-reward-fit-customers/#3bbc88b92574

[36] Jonah Comstock, "With $400M Injection, Tech-savvy Health Insurer Oscar Eyes 1M Member Mark," *MobiHealthNews*, February 23, 2016, mobihealthnews.com/content/400m-injection-tech-savvy-health-insurer-oscar-eyes-1m-member-mark

Chapter 8

[1] Jared Lindzon, "The State of the American Freelancer in 2015," *Fast Company*, June 26, 2015, fastcompany.com/3047848/the-future-of-work/the-state-of-the-american-freelancer-in-2015

[2] Guy Gilliland, Raj Varadarajan, and Devesh Raj, "Code Wars: The All-Industry Competition for Software Talent," *BCG Perspectives*, May 27, 2014, bcgperspectives.com/content/articles/hardware_software_human_resources_code_wars_all_industry_competition_software_talent/

[3] Drafted, accessed April 7, 2016, drafted.us/

[4] Lauren Weber, "Your Résumé vs. Oblivion," *Wall Street Journal*, January 24, 2012, wsj.com/articles/SB10001424052970204624204577178941034941330

[5] James Manyika et al., "Connecting Talent with Opportunity in the Digital Age," *McKinsey Global Institute*, June 2015, mckinsey.com/insights/employment_and_growth/connecting_talent_with_opportunity_in_the_digital_age

[6] Jacqueline Smith, "Why Companies Are Using 'Blind Auditions' to Hire Top Talent," *Business Insider*, May 31, 2015.

businessinsider.com/companies-are-using-blind-auditions-to-hire-top-talent-2015-5

[7] "Pam Baker, "Visier's New Release Offers Real-Time Workforce Analytics," *Fierce Big Data*, December 3, 2014, fiercebigdata.com/story/visiers-new-release-offers-real-time-workforce-analytics/2014-12-03

[8] Melissa E. Mitchell and Christopher D. Zatzick, "Skill Underutilization and Collective Turnover in a Professional Service Firm," *Journal of Management Development* 34, no. 7 (July 2015): 787-802, DOI: 10.1108 /JMD-09-2013-0112

[9] Phil Wainewright, "Workday Analytics Recommends Your Next Career Move," *Diginomica*, November 4, 2014, diginomica.com/2014/11/04/workday-analytics-recommends-next-career-movve-predictive-future/#.VnHX4t-rQqI

[10] Ben Kepes, "Moving IT Beyond the 'Department of No'," *Forbes*, September 27, 2013, forbes.com/sites/benkepes/2013/09/27/moving-it-beyond-the-department-of-no/

[11] Joseph Bradley et al., "Fast IT: Accelerating Innovation in the Internet of Everything Era," Cisco, 2014, cisco.com/c/dam/en/us/solutions/collateral/executive-perspectives/fastit_findings.pdf

[12] Ibid.

[13] Ibid.

[14] "IT as a Strategic Business Resource," *Forbes Insights*, 2015, cisco.com/c/dam/en/us/solutions/collateral/data-center-virtualization/application-centric-infrastructure/strategic-business-resource.pdf

[15] "Executive Guidance for 2016: Accelerated Corporate Clock Speed," Corporate Executive Board, 2015, cebglobal.com/content/dam/cebglobal/us/EN/top-insights/executive-guidance/pdfs/eg2016ann-accelerating-corporate-clock-speed.pdf

[16] Joseph Bradley et al., "The Impact of Cloud on IT Consumption Models," Cisco, 2013, cisco.com/c/dam/en_us/about/ac79/docs/re/Impact-of-Cloud-IT_Consumption-Models_Study-Report.pdf

[17] Global Oil & Gas Capital Expenditure Over $1 Trillion," *Energy Digital*, August 23, 2012, energydigital.com/utilities/2434/Global-Oil-Gas-Capital-Expenditure-Over-1-Trillion

[18] Dan Verel, "Can Cohealo Bring the Sharing Economy to Hospitals?" *MedCityNews*, October 20, 2014, medcitynews.com/2014/10/cohealo-uber-ride-sharing-medical-equipment-sharing/?rf=1

[19] Dazhong Wu et al., "Cloud Manufacturing: Drivers, Current Status, and Future Trends," in *ASME 2013 International Manufacturing Science and Engineering Conference collocated with the 41st North American Manufacturing Research Conference, Volume 2: Systems; Micro and Nano Technologies; Sustainable Manufacturing*, proceedings.asmedigitalcollection.asme.org/proceeding.aspx?articleid=1787092, doi:10.1115/MSEC2013-1106

[20] Wikipedia contributors, "3D Hubs," *Wikipedia, The Free Encyclopedia*, accessed April 7, 2016, en.wikipedia.org/w/index.php?title=3D_Hubs&oldid=704069571

[21] Michael E. Porter, *Competitive Advantage: Creating and Sustaining Superior Performance*, (New York: The Free Press, 1985) p.37

[22] Steve Bertoni, "Meet Adyen: The Little-Known Unicorn Collecting Cash for Netflix, Uber, Spotify and Facebook," *Forbes*, January 20, 2016, forbes.com/sites/stevenbertoni/2016/01/20/meet-adyen-the-little-known-unicorn-collecting-cash-for-nextflix-uber-spotify-and-facebook/#5f28ffbc2dd6

[23] "Why Customers Leave – And How to Keep Them," Nomi, accessed April 7, 2016, 3ez6hf6v2zy5uytw2a9dvi13.wpengine.netdna-cdn.com/wp-content/uploads/2014/01/Why-Customers-Leave-Whitepaper.pdf

[24] "Real Time In-store Analytics with RetailNext," RetailNext, January 2014, retailnext.net/wp-content/uploads/2014/01/RetailNext-Data-Sheet-Real-Time-In-Store-Analytics.pdf

[25] Dorinda Elliott, "Tencent: The Secretive, Chinese Tech Giant That Can Rival Facebook and Amazon," *Fast Company*, April 17, 2014, fastcompany.com/3029119/most-innovative-companies/tencent-the-secretive-chinese-tech-giant-that-can-rival-facebook-a

[26] Peter J. Williamson and Eden Yen, "Accelerated Innovation: The New Challenge from China," *MIT Sloan Management Review*, April 23, 2014, sloanreview.mit.edu/article/accelerated-innovation-the-new-challenge-from-china/

[27] Michael Wade, Y. Fang and W. Kang, "Tencent: Copying to Success," case study 3-2274, *IMD Business School*, 2011

[28] James Macaulay et al., "The Digital Manufacturer: Resolving the Service Dilemma," Cisco, November 2015, cisco.com/c/dam/en_us/solutions/industries/manufacturing/thought-leadership-wp.pdf

[29] Chris Lo, "Digital Wind Farms and the New Industrial Revolution," *Power Technology*, December 10, 2015, power-technology.com/features/featuredigital-wind-farms-and-the-new-industrial-revolution-4644602/

[30] Daniel Gross, "Siemens CEO Joe Kaeser on the Next Industrial Revolution," *strategy+business*, February 9, 2016, strategy-business.com/article/Siemens-CEO-Joe-Kaeser-on-the-Next-Industrial-Revolution?gko=efd41

[31] "From Virtual Space to Outer Space," *Pictures of the Future* (digital magazine), April 13, 2015, siemens.com/innovation/en/home/pictures-of-the-future/industry-and-automation/digital-factory-plm.html

[32] Stephanie Neil, "Has PTC 'Ubered' the Automation Industry?" *Automation World*, December 29, 2015, automationworld.com/all/has-ptc-ubered-automation-industry

[33] Sarah Scoles, "A Digital Twin of Your Body Could Become a Critical Part of Your Health Care," *Slate*, February 10, 2016, slate.com/articles/technology/future_tense/2016/02/dassault_s_living_heart_project_and_the_future_of_digital_twins_in_health.html

[34] Greg Bensinger, "Amazon Wants to Ship Your Package Before You Buy It," *Wall Street Journal*, January 17, 2014, blogs.wsj.com/digits/2014/01/17/amazon-wants-to-ship-your-package-before-you-buy-it/

[35] Joel Barbier et al., "Cybersecurity as a Growth Advantage," Cisco, April 2016, https://www.cisco.com/c/dam/m/en_us/offers/pdf/cybersecurity-growth-advantage.pdf

[36] Steve Blank, "Lean Innovation Management – Making Corporate Innovation Work," *Steve Blank* (blog), June 26, 2015, steveblank.com/2015/06/26/lean-innovation-management-making-corporate-innovation-work/

Conclusion

[1] Wikipedia contributors, "Holacracy," *Wikipedia, The Free Encyclopedia*, accessed April 7, 2016, en.wikipedia.org/w/index.php?title=Holacracy&oldid=713630893

[2] Alison Griswold, "Zappos Stopped Managing Its Employees. They Don't Seem Too Happy About It." *Slate*, May 8, 2015, slate.com/blogs/moneybox/2015/05/08/zappos_holacracy_many_employees_choose_to_leave_instead_of_work_with_no.html

[3] Laura Reston, "Tony Hsieh's Workplace Dream: Is Holacracy a Big Failure?" *Forbes*, July 17, 2015, forbes.com/sites/laurareston/2015/07/17/tony-hsiehs-workplace-dream-is-holacracy-a-big-failure/#314f90735ccd

[4] Benjamin Snyder, "Holacracy and 3 of the Most Unusual Management Practices Around," *Fortune*, June 2, 2015, fortune.com/2015/06/02/management-holacracy/

[5] R. H. Coase, "The Nature of the Firm," *Economica* 4 No. 16 (November 1937), pp. 386-405, DOI: 10.2307/2626876

[6] Elliot Maras, "Are Smart Contracts the Future of Blockchain?" *CryptoCoinsNews*, January 13, 2016, cryptocoinsnews.com/smart-contracts-future-blockchain/

[7] Nathaniel Popper, "Ethereum, a Virtual Currency, Enables Transactions That Rival Bitcoin's," *New York Times*, March 27, 2016, nytimes.com/2016/03/28/business/dealbook/ethereum-a-virtual-currency-enables-transactions-that-rival-bitcoins.html

[8] Gian Volpicelli, "Smart Contracts Sound Boring, But They're More Disruptive Than Bitcoin," *Motherboard*, February 16, 2015, motherboard.vice.com/read/smart-contracts-sound-boring-but-theyre-more-disruptive-than-bitcoin

[9] DJ Pangburn, "The Humans Who Dream of Companies that Won't Need Us," *Fast Company*, June 19, 2015, fastcompany.com/3047462/the-humans-who-dream-of-companies-that-wont-need-them

[10] Gavin Wood, "Bazaar Services," *Ethereum Blog* (blog), April 5, 2015, blog.ethereum.org/2015/04/05/bazaar-services/

[11] Joe Fassler, "Can the Computers at Narrative Science Replace Paid Writers?" *The Atlantic*, April 12, 2012, theatlantic.com/entertainment/archive/2012/04/can-the-computers-at-narrative-science-replace-paid-writers/255631/

[12] Michelle Starr, "World's First 3D-printed Apartment Building Constructed in China," *CNET*, January 19, 2015, cnet.com/news/worlds-first-3d-printed-apartment-building-constructed-in-china/

[13] Paul Krugman, "Robber Baron Recessions," *New York Times*, April 18, 2016, nytimes.com/2016/04/18/opinion/robber-baron-recessions.html?_r=0

[14] Edward Teach, "A Fortress Balance Sheet," *CFO*, June 18, 2009, cfo.com/banking-capital-markets/2009/06/a-fortress-balance-sheet/

[15] Paul Krugman, "The Big Meh," *New York Times*, May 25, 2015, nytimes.com/2015/05/25/opinion/paul-krugman-the-big-meh.html

[16] Joseph Schumpeter, *Capitalism, Socialism and Democracy* (London: Routledge, 1942)

[17] Khan Academy, accessed April 7, 2016, khanacademy.org/

[18] "Press Room", Khan Academy, accessed April 7, 2016, khanacademy.zendesk.com/hc/en-us/articles/202483630-Press-room

Index

229

About the Authors

Jeff Loucks is a director with the Cisco Digitization Office and a visiting scholar at the Global Center for Digital Business Transformation, an IMD and Cisco initiative. Jeff works with Global 500 firms and innovative startups to explore the strategies and concrete steps companies must take to thrive in an era of digitization. Through fifteen years of research, writing, and consulting, Jeff has helped companies capitalize on technological change by transforming their business models. Jeff is especially interested in the strategies organizations use to adapt to accelerating change. An extensive academic background complements his technology expertise. He wrote his PhD dissertation on Machiavelli (one of the world's great strategists) and draws upon philosophy, psychology, and political science to understand both institutional and human responses to today's escalating challenges. Jeff has a BA in political science from The Ohio State University, and an MA and PhD in political science from the University of Toronto. He resides in Ohio with his wife and two sons.

James Macaulay is a director with the Cisco Digitization Office and a visiting scholar at the Global Center for Digital Business Transformation, an IMD and Cisco initiative. With nearly two decades of high tech experience, and an extensive body of published research, he has been at the forefront of Cisco's thought leadership to define digital market transitions and their implications. He is a professional researcher and works with companies around the world to design their digital change roadmap. Prior to Cisco, he spent seven years as an entrepreneur, running a consulting startup focused on high tech market research and strategy. He has managed technology research portfolios in both the private and public sectors, having served as an analyst with Gartner in Silicon Valley and the Canadian Department of Foreign Affairs and International Trade in Brussels. James holds a BA (with honors) from Dalhousie University and an MA from the University of Toronto, both in political science. He currently lives in British Columbia with his wife and two children.

Andy Noronha is a director in the Cisco Digitization Office, where he works to develop research and insights that will help guide the future of digitization for the company, and its customers. He is also a visiting scholar at the Global Center for Digital Business Transformation, an IMD and Cisco initiative, where he conducts research and works with executives from companies seeking to remain competitive in an era of digital disruption. With 20 years of experience in the technology industry, he possesses a strong background in helping companies remain competitive in the world of business where technology is constantly evolving. He started his career as an analyst at Gartner, where he led the energy practice and delivered consulting engagements for global technology companies. He later went on to co-found a market research and consulting firm that helped technology vendors to improve their sales and marketing efforts in vertical markets. He is very interested in understanding how technology will transform the lives of future generations. Andy holds a BS in bioengineering from the University of California, Berkeley. He currently lives in Southern California with his wife and two children.

Michael Wade is the Cisco Chair in Digital Business Transformation and Professor of Innovation and Strategy at IMD, a Swiss-based business school focusing on executive education. He is the Director of the Global Center for Digital Business Transformation, an IMD and Cisco initiative. Michael has more than 50 articles and presentations to his credit in leading academic journals and conferences and has written seven books and more than 20 case studies based on his experience working with organizations. He co-directs IMD's Leading Digital Business Transformation executive program, and has designed several customized programs for companies such as Credit Suisse, Vodafone, Maersk, Zurich Financial, PSA Peugeot Citroën, and Cartier. He has provided consulting services, executive education, and expert evaluations to public and private sector organizations, including IBM, LVMH, Nestlé, Google, and Novartis. Michael obtained Honors BA, MBA and PhD degrees from the Richard Ivey School of Business, University of Western Ontario, Canada. He has lived and worked in seven countries and currently resides with his family in Switzerland.

GLOBAL CENTER FOR DIGITAL
BUSINESS TRANSFORMATION
An IMD and Cisco Initiative

About the Global Center for Digital Business Transformation

The Global Center for Digital Business Transformation (DBT Center) is a joint initiative of the International Institute for Management Development (IMD) and Cisco that brings together innovation and learning for the digital era. The DBT Center is a global research hub at the forefront of digital business transformation, where executives engage to solve the challenges created by massive market transitions. The DBT Center seeks out diverse viewpoints from a wide range of organizations – startups and incumbents – to bring new ideas, best practices, and disruptive thinking into the process. The collaboration combines Cisco's technology leadership with IMD's expertise in applied research and developing global leaders, focusing on the organizational change required for digital transformation. The DBT Center is physically located on IMD's campus in Lausanne, Switzerland.

Learn more:
imd.org/dbtcenter
dbtcenter@imd.org
linkedin.com/groups/8341644
@DBT_Center

About IMD

imd.org

IMD is a top-ranked business school, recognized as the expert in developing global leaders through high-impact executive education. The school is 100% focused on real-world executive development; offers Swiss excellence with a global perspective; and has a flexible, customized, and effective approach IMD is ranked first in open programs worldwide and in the top 3 in executive education worldwide - 5 years in a row (Financial Times 2012-2016). IMD is based in Lausanne (Switzerland) and has an Executive Learning Center in Singapore.

CISCO.

About Cisco

cisco.com

Cisco (NASDAQ: CSCO) is a worldwide leader in IT that helps companies seize the opportunities of tomorrow by proving that amazing things can happen when you connect the previously unconnected. Cisco is headquartered in San Jose, California, and has over 70,000 employees and more than 400 offices globally.

Lightning Source UK Ltd.
Milton Keynes UK
UKOW01n1312230916

283666UK00001B/4/P